WRITING THE NATURAL WAY

ALSO BY
GABRIELE RICO

Western Literature: Themes and Writers (with G. Robert Carlsen)

Living Literature: Beginnings (with Hans P. Guth)

Discovering Fiction (with Hans P. Guth)

Discovering Literature: Stories, Poems, Plays (with Hans P. Guth)

Discovering Poetry (with Hans P. Guth)

*Balancing the Hemispheres: Brain Research and
the Teaching of Writing* (with Mary Frances Claggett)

Pain and Possibility: Writing Your Way Through Personal Crisis

Designing Essays (with Kate Evans and Janelle Melvin)

To Write Is to Know (audiotape)

Garantiert Schreiben Lernen Von der Seele Schreiben

WRITING THE NATURAL WAY

Using Right-Brain Techniques to Release Your Expressive Powers

GABRIELE RICO

Jeremy P. Tarcher/Putnam
a member of
Penguin Putnam Inc.
New York

When I knew whose work it was, I made every attempt to locate those students and workshop participants whose writing is reproduced in this book. When I did not, I used "Student."

Most Tarcher/Putnam books are available at special quantity discounts for bulk purchase for sales promotions, premiums, fund-raising, and educational needs. Special books or book excerpts also can be created to fit specific needs. For details, write Putnam Special Markets, 375 Hudson Street, New York, NY 10014.

Jeremy P. Tarcher/Putnam
a member of
Penguin Putnam Inc.
375 Hudson Street
New York, NY 10014
www.penguinputnam.com

Library of Congress Cataloging-in-Publication Data

Rico, Gabriele L.
    Writing the natural way : using right-brain techniques
to release your expressive powers / Gabriele Rico.—Rev. ed.
      p. cm.
    Includes bibliographical references and index.
    ISBN 0-87477-961-8
     1. English language—Rhetoric.   2. Left and right (Psychology).
3. Creative writing. 4. Expression.   I. Title.
PE1408.R566   2000   99-049296 CIP
808'.042—dc21

Printed in the United States of America

20 19 18 17 16 15

This book is printed on acid-free paper. ∞

Book design by Mauna Eichner

ACKNOWLEDGMENTS

Since no work grows in isolation, I want to honor the following people who continue to be part of my life:

Neurosurgeon Joseph Bogen, who is a source of unending knowledge on the split-brain; Professor Elliot Eisner of Stanford, under whose mentorship these ideas flourished; Hans Guth, my boon companion, who introduced me to the world of publishing; Renee Fuller and James Conner, for believing in my work; Kate Evans and Janelle Melvin, former students, poets, and now co-authors with me on *Designing Essays*; Tyler Volk, writer of the Foreword, who builds amazing bridges between disciplines in search of the meta-patterns that guide us; Joan Baez, who never stops growing into new creative modes of expression; Danny Smith, my conscientious assistant.

Publisher Jeremy Tarcher saw the possibilities in this book in 1980, and Joel Fotinos has shepherded this second edition through with tact and grace. Laura Bellotti's sensitive editing and sure-footedness in the world of words saved the day, and David Groff, my editor, tackled this project with equanimity.

Finally, I wish to acknowledge the gifted poets in these pages whose work inspires us, my Writing-Intensive participants every-where (especially those at the Omega Institute, Esalen, New York Open Center, and Interface), and, most of all, the thousands of students and former students who experimented with me all these years and whose natural writing forms the heart of this book.

The author would like to thank the following for permission to reprint.

"Mi calle," by Jesus Alarcon, Jr., is reprinted from Naomi Shihab Nye's essay "Dia de dulce/Sweet Day" in *Luna, Luna: Creative Writing Ideas from Spanish, Latin American, and Latino Literature,* edited by Julio Marzan by permission of Teachers and Writers Collaborative, 5 Union Square West, NY, NY 10003.

Margaret Atwood, "Last year I devoured..." is an exerpt from "Circe/Mud Poems" from *Selected Poems.* New York: Houghton Mifflin, 1974. Reprinted by permission of Houghton Mifflin Publishers.

Joan Baez, "Abstinence." Courtesy of Joan Baez.

Joan Baez, "Colleen." Courtesy of Joan Baez.

Joan Baez, "Kindergarten." Courtesy of Joan Baez.

Joan Baez, "Maybe." Courtesy of Joan Baez.

Joan Baez, "Red." Courtesy of Joan Baez.

"Pain Penetrates," by Mary Barnard, from *Sappho: A New Translation.* Reprinted by permission of University of California Press.

"Improvisation," from *Les Barricades Mysterieuses,* by Jared Carter, was reprinted by permission of the Cleveland State University Poetry Center.

"Refugee Ship," by Lorna Dee Cervantes, is reprinted with permission from the publisher of *A Decade of Hispanic Literature: An Anniversary Anthology* (Houston: Arte Publico Press-University of Houston, 1982).

Raymond Chandler, from *The Little Sister.* Copyright renewed 1976 by Helga Greene. Reprinted by permission of Houghton Mifflin Company.

e. e. cummings, "Buffalo Bill's," is reprinted from *Tulips and Chimneys* with permission of Liveright Publishing Corporation. Copyright 1923, 1925 and renewed 1951 by e. e. cummings. Copyright 1973, 1976 by trustees for the e. e. cummings Trust. Copyright 1973, 1976 by George James Firmage.

Tiffany Darrough, "Family History," is reprinted by permission of the author.

William Faulkner, *The Hamlet.* Copyright 1964 by William Faulkner. Reprinted by permission of Random House.

Jule Langerhorst Fichter, "Working." Courtesy of the artist.

F. Scott Fitzgerald, *The Great Gatsby.* Copyright 1925 by Charles Scribner's Sons. Reprinted by their permission.

Giacometti, used by permission of Hans Grether Trust.

"Reflection on the Vietnam War Memorial" and "Three Brothers in the Snow" from *The Singing Underneath* by Jeffrey Harrison (New York: E. P. Dutton) were reprinted by permission of the author.

Robert Hass, "Song." Reprinted by permission of the author.

John Hawkes, *Second Skin.* Copyright 1964 by New Directions. Reprinted by their permission.

Ernest Hemingway, *For Whom the Bell Tolls.* Copyright 1940 by Ernest Hemingway. Reprinted by permission of Charles Scribner's Sons.

Walter Hilke for untitled ink drawing, courtesy of the artist. Celle, Germany.

Hiroshige, *Evening Snow at Kambara.* By permission of Heibonsha, Ltd., Tokyo.

"The Pear Tree," by Paula Jones Gardiner from *Bus Poems: Telling Our Stories,* King County Public Art Program of Seattle, reprinted by permission of the author, from *Believed to Cause Night,* Barbarian Press, Missiai, B.C.

James Joyce, *Ulysses.* Copyright 1946 by Nora Joseph Joyce. Reprinted by permission of Random House, Inc.

For my husband, Richard, with whom, YES

For my daughters, Stephanie, Susanne, and Simone,
who are so much a part of my work

*Knowing anything in its deepest sense
means knowing how to be creative with it.*
ELLIOT EISNER, STANFORD U.

Lesson #1: Everything in the cerebrum is double.
Is it duplicate, like the runners of a sleigh?
Or is it like a team of horses pulling the sleigh?
Take one runner off the sleigh, and it won't go.
Take one horse away, and the other horse
can still pull the sleigh.
Not as fast, not as far, but adequately.

Lesson #2: The function of the brain is double—
Like a team of horses, not like the runners on a sleigh.

JOSEPH E. BOGEN, M.D., 1998

*The Human
Mind is the design
that designs itself—
and continually
redesigns itself.*

D. N. PERKINS

CONTENTS

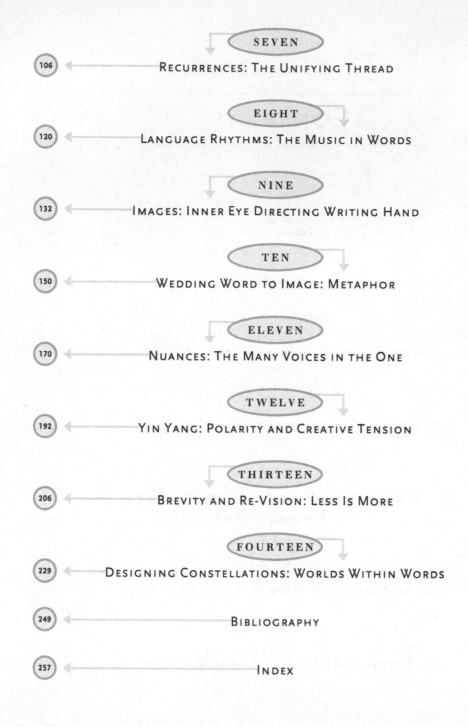

FOREWORD

In recalling my reading of the original edition of *Writing the Natural Way*, two core experiences come to mind. The first was the surprise of encountering a book on words that made visual patterns its very foundation. Visual patterns in a book about writing? Is Gabriele Rico teaching us how to write or how to draw? How can visual clusters of ideas help us create fresh, articulate prose?

Pattern-making is, in fact, the key step in Gabriele's powerful program. Visual patterns tap directly into the thinking mode of the brain's right hemisphere, a mode she terms the Design mind. The Design mind thinks in systems, in structures, in pictures. This fact—that the right brain is relatively pictorial and holistic in contrast to the verbal, part-oriented left brain—has been discovered and confirmed by neurobiologists and psychologists. We do, of course, need both parts and wholes. Gabriele urges the harmonious integration of trees and forest along the writer's path. But before the writing begins we are asked to linger in the realm of the forest, and this is where clustering comes to play a formative role.

To my mind, the processes in this book supersede any traditional ways of engaging the writing process. In Gabriele's process of "clustering," the core theme appears as the literal, palpable, visual nucleus of a cluster. From this nucleus radiate ideas, feelings, and images, like beams from a star, each becoming in turn its own center for related radiations.

The resulting patterns are very much like nature—like swirls in water, like tree branches, like composite flowers. Although the final product—your poem, letter, essay, or chapter—necessarily manifests as linear, your right brain will nevertheless ensure that a pictorial logic suffuses with an integrity akin to the very heart-beat that sustains our bodies yet remains hidden to everyday awareness.

My second memorable surprise came in the particulars of Gabriele's process. Before encountering her book, I had worked out a number of universal principles of organization, which I called "meta-patterns." These meta-patterns apply to both nature and our minds, the latter exhibited in creations of culture from art and religion to politics and literature. To my surprise and delight, there is an almost one-to-one correspondence between my meta-patterns and Gabriele's right-brain techniques. For example, her "clusters" relate to what I call "centers." Her "creative tension" is the meta-pattern of "binary," the elemental whole consisting of two parts. Her technique of "recurrence" is a form of the meta-pattern of "cycle"—with one vital nuance that had not occurred to me: Recurrence, Gabriele maintains, is a helpful pattern for writers only when the cycle is not quite perfect.

That brings us to "rhythm," which Gabriele employs to make the writing flow, to create what I had called the meta-pattern of the "arrow." As a final example, in her "trial-web shift"—what I had called "break"—Gabriele teaches us how to utilize the brain's ability to create moments of synthesis more consciously.

These similarities have made me think that Gabriele and I are on to something deeper than either of us had suspected. Are nature's patterns etched into our minds from millions of years of hominid evolution? If nature constellates, does the mind? If so, how do we tap this power for writing? This book is about constellating our thoughts, images, feelings into patterns to make our expressions resonate from the deep structures of our minds.

As it turns out, Gabriele and I are not alone in this venture. Big, universal patterns are also being elucidated by cognitive linguists. The "image schemas" of George Lakoff and Mark Johnson are tantalizingly similar to my meta-patterns and to Gabriele's mind tools. Thus the techniques you will learn in this book might just be much more than mere techniques—they might be THE mind tools.

Tyler Volk
Biology Department, New York University
Author of *Metapatterns Across Space, Time, and Mind*

PREFACE

Writing the Natural Way has been designed to inform and inspire all writers—beginning or advanced—to call on and enhance their own creative powers. We possess a designing mind. We live in a world of cultural designs. The most intimate facet of learning is self-design, giving us a sense of identity in time and space. We are designers, active agents of thought and language, not passive receivers. The act of writing is one of the most intensely creative acts we can engage in.

As I was redesigning and updating this book for its second edition, I wondered how I came to name the two sides of the brain "Sign" and "Design" mind; I realized that my fascination with the human brain as pattern-seeker and pattern-maker—as "designer"—has been with me for twenty-five years.

"Design" suggests pattern. A design is an expressed pattern of meaning. A design is not a part but a whole. Think of a painting in a frame; think of a poem on a page; think of a musical score. A design shows the "big picture." A design, although it may be only a preliminary sketch, a plan, an idea, already has scope and purpose, however tentative.

By contrast, "Sign" comes from the Latin *signare*, to mark with a sign. Sign has to do with recording, chronicling, with notation, with handwriting—all those things we do to leave tracks of our thoughts and ideas in time and space. Think of the first scratchings on bone to mark the passing of a lunar cycle; think of a signature; think of a word in a whole page of writing. Signs show little packets of information, things we can separate out and name, words we can look up in a dictionary.

The human mind is the design that designs itself—and continually redesigns itself. Other mammals are designs but do little self-designing. We humans are so taken with design that we not only design and redesign everything around us, but even ourselves. As a designer of yourself, you never know more than yourself.

DAVID PERKINS,
HARVARD UNIVERSITY

Sign and Design mind strategies working in tandem are essential to creative acts, giving us our stunning flexibility to imagine and record. Sign differentiates; Design synthesizes. Sign records features; Design infers the whole from a few features. Sign distinguishes; Design connects. Wrote William James in 1911, "A human being should not limit himself to either, any more than a pair of scissors can cut with a single one of its blades." The creative process, then, is the ongoing oscillation between the mind's ability to form a hazy big picture and then to sequence the details to clarify and "hold" it, then to redesign, and to clarify further. This collaboration of Sign and Design mind has led to stupendous human creative acts. Two brains are indeed better than one!

Between these two root strategies of mind, we construct our mental world—and we make marks on paper to hold our visions, feelings, thoughts, ideas in infinite patterns of meaning—as many as there are human beings willing to be expressive. And that's where you—holding this book—come in.

You are thinking about writing, or about getting better at it, or about finding ways to write more naturally, more readily. Historically, creative expression has been considered the domain of the most gifted, but now we know we all have the gift of language. What stops us is fear of failing, or a lack of inspiration, or feelings that we don't know how, we can't be very good at it, we don't know where to start. "Clustering," the associative brainstorming process at the heart of this book, jump-starts you so you don't have to wait for inspiration to strike as our ancestors had to wait for lightning to get fire. With clustering you can detect tentative designs of your mind's making, intuit a sense of direction through trial-web shifts, call up images and metaphors, and play with recurrences. This edition emphasizes the power of the circle, giving you deeper insights into the nature and workings of clustering, which self-organizes spontaneous associations. Clustering, I have come to see, allows us to see seemingly random backward and forward loops of an emerging pattern of meaning.

But there is more: I have added three new chapters: one on Voice, one on Improvisation (Re-Creations), and one on Brevity. In 1980, I believed a chapter on Voice to be superfluous because the entire book seemed to me to be about finding our voices. But the Voice chapter reminds us that there are many voices within us waiting to be released into language; we always are engaged in multilogues. This awareness of multilogic voice leads to self-reflective acts.

The Improvisation chapter adds an entirely new dimension to writing, engaging you in a powerful new technique of Re-Creation, which illustrates scientist Michael Polanyi's conclusion that our tacit knowings are enormous—but that we don't often enough access them because we don't know how to tap into them and improvise. The new technique of Re-Creation produces stunning writing in less than three minutes.

The Brevity chapter grew out of the original Less Is More chapter, but with major new insights into the brevity of expression by (1) honoring, thus experimenting with, brevities because they often reveal the essence of things we struggle to say, and (2) the playful process of paring an already improvised piece to unlock the surprises of mind.

In the final chapter, I explain the idea of Constellation, which is a new concept developed over the past two years. Until recently, I just didn't have a word for this last, most important, culminating idea. I didn't have language to describe the emergence of what *groups* together—like a magnet that attracts the filings around it. I hadn't been able to articulate how people naturally shape smaller vignettes into larger patterns, into constellations of meaning. Constellating recapitulates smaller wholes to form an organic, larger whole.

The creative process, elusive and deeply satisfying, is the ultimate frontier of the human mind. Learning to walk on this unsystematic, jagged, irregular, meandering path makes each of us a pioneer of our own in-built potential. When we activate this creative potential again and again, our mental flexibility grows, and we discover designs we didn't know were there.

My ongoing experiments with techniques of natural writing over the past twenty-five years in classrooms, workshops, and seminars have culminated in this second edition. I can say with even greater conviction that writing is a much more natural process if we learn to flow with, rather than fight, the cooperative rhythms of our Sign and Design minds. We all are works in progress, and

getting out of the way of our natural need to be creative is a life-
long process. Or, as writer Tobias Wolff so aptly says it:

> In the arms of language, children will join the human family. They will
> learn what has gone before, and they will learn what is left to be done.
> In language they will learn to laugh, and to grieve, and to be consoled
> in their grief and to console others. In language they will discover who
> they are.

ONE

OPENING: LETTING THE WRITER IN US OUT

If you can speak, form letters on the page, know the rudiments of sentence structure, take a telephone message, or write a thank-you note, you have sufficient language skills to learn to write the natural way. Formal knowledge of grammar is not a prerequisite. Just as a flawless piano-playing technique may not deliver a moving performance, a thorough training in the mechanics of writing does not necessarily produce good writing—and it rarely produces writing from within. Fortunately, the potential for natural writing is already within all of us; it is not too late for any of us to learn.

Central to natural writing is an attitude of wonder. If you recall wondering about things as a child, if you daydream occasionally, if you find yourself creating a story out of something that happened to you for the entertainment of your listener, you can develop—through the exercises in this book—the ability to generate written words more easily, to express your ideas more authentically, to develop your own "voice"—that manner of expression unique to you.

We all have heard the saying that so-and-so is a "born writer." This fallacy puts the born writer in a different category from most of us—or so we think—since *we* have to struggle so hard with writing. And we are so dissatisfied with the results. In truth, the innate human need that underlies all writing, the need to give shape to your experience, is a gift we all possess from

> *When we were little we had no difficulty sounding the way we felt; thus most little children speak and write with real voice.*
> PETER ELBOW, *Writing with Power*

earliest childhood. Yet only a few of us keep on expressing this need through a sustained relationship with language, our natural urge for self-expression inhibited by the weight of rules and prescriptions. This is sad because children's writing naturally has an expressive power, an authenticity that inherently captures the sound of an individual on the page, an ability we seem to lose the more we learn about writing.

Our loss begins in school, when the process of writing is taught to us in fragments: mechanics, grammar, and vocabulary. Writing becomes fearful and loathsome, a workbook activity. Students write as little as possible, and, once out of school, they tend to avoid the entire process whenever possible. As a result, few people turn to writing as a natural source of pleasure and gratification.

Let us begin with the whole, with the fundamental human desire for giving shape to experience, for expressiveness, for creating form and structure out of the confusion that constitutes both our inner and outer worlds. Natural writing is first of all an act of self-definition of what you know, what you discover, what you wonder about, what you feel, see, hear, touch, taste—all of which reflects the many-faceted crystal that you are. The result of expressing your experience is a unique voice: yours. Your voice is expressed in storytelling, in pictures, in sound, in feelings, and above all in the focus you discover each time you write. Each of these characteristics of natural writing forms one of the chapters of this book, ultimately enabling you to achieve connectedness and coherence, texture and rhythm, authenticity and emotional intensity in your striving toward expressive power.

If you have tried writing but found your products dull, or if you have found the process itself painful and all too often frustrating, this book is for you. *Writing the Natural Way* is designed to take you from wherever you are as a writer, be you beginner or professional, fluent or blocked, old or young, and to rekindle your creative expressive powers that began when you first learned to speak—in the uninhibited delight you had in using words long before formal rules and painful criticism blocked your natural drive for self-expression. Learning to write naturally does not de-

Writing itself is one of the great, free human activities. There is scope for individuality, and elation, and discovery. In writing, for the person who follows with trust and forgiveness what occurs to him, the world remains always ready and deep, an inexhaustible environment, with the combined vividness of an actuality and flexibility of a dream. Working back and forth between experience and thought, writers have more than space and time can offer. They have the whole unexplored realm of human vision.

WILLIAM STAFFORD,
Writing the Australian Crawl

pend on literary terminology and grammatical classifications. Instead, natural writing depends on gaining access to a part of your mind we normally do not associate with writing skills. Contacting that part of your mind enables you to discover your own unique and natural voice, which is your primary source of expressive power.

TWO MODES OF KNOWING: SIGN AND DESIGN

Just as two heads are better than one for solving problems, so two brains are better than one when it comes to writing naturally.

The first step toward gaining originality and freedom of expression is to become aware of the two-sided nature of your mental makeup: one thinks in terms of the connectedness of things and events, the other thinks in terms of parts and sequences. Once we become aware of these different ways of processing our thoughts, we can not only learn to channel each one appropriately toward different phases of the writing process, but we can also learn to ensure that they work cooperatively for the greatest possible creative interaction.

Most teachers of writing, certainly all investigators of the creative process, tend to agree that there are at least two distinctly different aspects of any creative act that sometimes come into conflict: the productive, generative, or "unconscious" phase; and the highly conscious, critical phase, which edits, refines, and revises what has been produced. Call it unconscious and conscious, artist and critic (I call it the Sign and Design minds, for reasons explained below), but whatever the nomenclature the task is to reserve these functions for their appropriate phases and to have them work harmoniously rather than conflict with one another.

In *On Becoming a Writer*, an insightful 1934 book, novelist Dorothea Brande recognized these two conflicting sides of the writer's personality and the necessity for cultivating what she called the unconscious.

I have adopted the terms Sign mind and Design mind for these two aspects of creative thought because they characterize

People often lack any voice at all in their writing because they stop so often in the act of writing a sentence and worry and change their minds about which words to use. They have none of the natural breath in their writing that they have in speaking. . . . We have so little practice in writing, but so much more time to stop and fiddle as we write each sentence.

PETER ELBOW, *Writing with Power*

What soul took thought and knew that adding "wo" to man would make a woman? The difference exactly. The wide w. The receptive o. Womb. . . . Seven years since I wed wide warm woman, white-thighed. Wooed and wed. Wife. A knife of a word that for all its final bite did not end the wooing. To my wonderment.

JOHN UPDIKE, *"Wife Wooing"*

one of the most fundamental distinctions between the workings of the left and right hemispheres of the brain. Recent discoveries in brain research have shown that the left hemisphere, or Sign mind, is largely occupied with the rational, logical representation of reality and with parts and logical sequences. It has the capacity of ordering thought into communicable syntactic form—the way words are put together to form sentences. It acts as critic, censor, and error corrector. It splits the world into clearly definable units and classifies them by giving them clear-cut definitions—such as "woman: a female human being"—composed of unambiguous words used to denote meaning. Words used as signs have a precise and narrow scope. "Woman," for example, is a linguistic sign de*sign*ating a particular kind of human being that none of us confuses with children or men.

By contrast, the right hemisphere, or Design mind, constantly thinks in complex images; it seeks patterns to make designs of whatever it encounters, including language, which, instead of clear-cut signs, become *designs* of nonliteral meaning. If the Sign mind defines woman as a female human being, the Design mind gives us a "feel" of womanness through patterning, as John Updike does in his story "Wife Wooing."

Although each is a distinct way of expressing the same idea, only one has richness, depth, and originality, the qualities that permit us to understand something profound: Updike's perception of "womanness."

These are the qualities achieved by natural writing—not the stark, conventional, dull expression of a familiar idea, but all the nuances of meaning implicit in the language design that evokes emotion through its sensory images. And these sensory, evocative, unconventional capacities for expression seem to reside in the right hemisphere of the brain.

In writing naturally, participation of both sides is crucial, the one to give you access to the explanatory sign qualities of clear and unambiguous language as well as the sequencing powers necessary to writing; the other to perceive and express the more evocative design qualities of language as word images, rhythm, recurring pattern, and metaphor, all of which charge a passage emotionally.

Most of the methods of training the conscious side of the writer—the craftsman and the critic in him—are actually hostile to the good of the artist's side; and the converse of this proposition is likewise true. But it is possible to train both sides of the character to work in harmony, and the first step in that education is to consider that you must teach yourself not as though you were one person, but two.

DOROTHEA BRANDE,
On Becoming a Writer

Moreover, the thought pattern characteristic of the right brain lends itself to the formation of original ideas, insights, discoveries. We might describe it as the kind of thought prevalent in early childhood, when everything is new and everything has meaning. If you have ever walked along a beach and suddenly stopped to pick up a piece of driftwood because it looked to you like a leaping impala or a troll, you know the feeling of pleasure that comes from the sudden recognition of a form. Your Design mind has perceived connections and has made a pattern of meaning. It takes the logical, rational acts and facts of the world you know, the snippets of your experience, the bits and pieces of your language capabilities, and perceives connections, patterns, and relationships in them. While the right brain does this naturally, it is often overpowered by the logical, critical processes of the left brain ("That's not a leaping impala, it's just a piece of driftwood!"). We are going to learn how to cultivate and gain easy access to the right brain's creative potential for expressive power.

Risking an analogy, I might say that your Design mind attends to the melody of life, whereas your Sign mind attends to the notes that compose the melodies. And here is the key to natural writing: The melodies must come first.

Unfortunately, most of us have learned to write not in a state of release but by rule, with the result generally being flat, dull, turgid—most certainly not original, natural, free. The most fundamental difference between writing by rule and natural writing is that the former is imposed from without, whereas natural writing emerges from within. Our almost exclusive exposure to Sign-mind skills in writing courses from elementary school through graduate school has all too often resulted in an intense dislike of writing, even fear. Such one-sidedness has blocked us from—or failed to make use of—our creative, image-seeking mode, sadly limiting our natural potential for satisfying creative expression.

For these reasons, this course focuses on awakening and developing our much neglected Design mind in writing. Our right brain has been a stepchild in education—and in our lives. Much of the excitement of tapping your inner writer comes from restoring it to full function.

The pure origins of poetry [are] the simple human need to record a pain or a joy and to know that one's own words are more than enough.
SANDFORD LYNE

The poetic works outward to prose, then to ordinary life. Poetry is the most direct and simple means of expressing oneself in words.
NORTHROP FRYE

INTERPLAY FOR CREATIVE POWER

For us, a mind without a story is a mind without meaning. And meaning is the essence of our consciousness. Our story-engrossed brain seems to believe that . . . we exist because we tell the story of our existence.
RENEE FULLER

Ultimately, a finished piece of writing or a painting or a sculpture—in short, any creative product—is the result of the collaboration between the talents of the two hemispheres, but in their proper sequence and in their proper interplay. During the generative phase of the writing process, while we are forming new ideas intuitively, we want to turn off the critical/logical/censoring Sign mind to be free of analytic reasoning. Once we begin to record and structure these ideas, the sequencing Sign mind comes into play with the envisioning Design mind. The continuous oscillation between a sense of the whole you have envisioned and the parts with which you sequence that vision into a more clearly delineated whole enables you to get your vision onto paper. Finally, when you reread what you have written and analyze it for structure, word choice, and appropriateness of detail, you are depending almost exclusively on your Sign mind's predilection for correctness. Working together in complementary fashion instead of tripping each other with inappropriate signals, your two minds can produce a whole symphony of talents.

HOW TO USE THIS BOOK

Throughout this book, "Directing Your Hand" is an invitation to develop your natural writing skills by writing brief vignettes—short, compressed, evocative pieces that are self-contained wholes. The book is structured in such a way that you will start with a Design-mind search for something to say, build on that newly acquired Design-mind skill by learning seven writing techniques developed to tap the creative abilities of your Design mind, and finally achieve the cooperation of both Sign and Design minds in producing vignette after vignette that will be written naturally, spontaneously, pleasurably.

In the beginning you will relearn the fresh, childlike attitude of wonder through clustering; later you will develop your inborn receptivity to pattern-making through the trial web, regain the playfulness of language rhythms and recurrences, draw on your natural imaging powers, reclaim the ability to think metaphorically, reconcile opposites to build creative tension, and balance original vision with revision. The culminating chapter leads you into a sustained piece of natural writing, combining all of the techniques presented throughout the book.

The techniques, each an aspect of natural writing, build on each other. Each helps you develop originality, authenticity, and expressive power. With the addition of each new technique, you will also be practicing what you have learned in the previous chapters. Do the chapters in sequence, but feel free to go back for more experience with any element that you found appealing or wanted to practice more. The techniques can be used with any subject of your choosing. Use your imagination and enjoy the results.

The Writer's Notebook: Your Track Record

In order to chart your own writing progress, keep your writing together in a spiral-bound notebook or loose-leaf binder, on lined or unlined paper, according to your preference. Should you elect to type or use a computer, keep your writing in a manila folder. Date each writing experience and begin a fresh page for each new assignment. Each chapter will suggest several writing experiences, so by the end of the course you will have compiled a thick folder recording your progress.

Reread whenever you wish. In the course of your writing you will become your own best critic if you allow yourself to be guided by the degree of satisfaction you feel each time you read over what you have written. Pleasure, satisfaction, even amazement at your products are not uncommon responses. You will become immersed in the creative process as you learn to write comfortably and naturally; it will enrich your perceptions of, and reactions to, many aspects of your life, for the creative attitude affects all you do and see.

Writing Tools

A writing tool is an extension of your hand that is in turn directed by your brain. Of necessity I have learned—since I do

I write entirely to find out what I'm thinking, what I'm looking at, what I see, and what it means.
JOAN DIDION

The deepening need for words to express our thoughts and feelings which, we are sure, are all the truth that we shall ever experience . . . makes us listen to words when we hear them, loving them and feeling them, makes us search the sound of them . . .
WALLACE STEVENS,
The Necessary Angel

much writing—to compose directly on a keyboard. For my purposes, it is far more efficient than longhand, just as computers are more efficient than typewriters. However, for exploratory stages or for trying to untangle a fuzzy thought, I have found that I invariably return to pen and writing pad. Experiment with various writing tools until you find the medium that helps your thoughts flow most freely. In the end, you must do what feels right for you. Some people are not at all intimidated by technology Others think even a typewriter is positively diabolical.

Time and Place: Creators as Creatures of Habit

Choose a time of day for writing and stick with it until it becomes a habit. If you are an early riser, get out of bed fifteen minutes before it is "officially" time to start your day and do an activity in your writer's notebook. If you are a night owl, reserve some time before you customarily go to bed to write every night, or at least every weeknight. Should you be so lucky as to have some time to yourself before or after lunch, take these moments to fill your notebook.

Then find your place: the warm kitchen at 5 A.M. when everyone else is asleep, an extra bedroom, your bed, a corner of the local library, even your car parked along the beach or at a lookout post above the city. Like jogging or brushing teeth, make it happen every day, and sooner or later you will look forward to this time for exploring your own creative potential. If fifteen minutes is not enough time—and soon it won't be because you'll want more time to write—you can extend it or pick up your writer's notebook at other, less predictable times.

Sound and Design: Reading Aloud

"Heard melodies are sweet," wrote Keats. Language is meant to be heard as well as read. Think about it: Research shows that infants respond powerfully to the sound of the human voice, so learning language begins with our ears. Our earliest childhood is filled with sounds of stories being read to us, with skipping rhymes and riddles. Our brains are attuned to the subtleties of

One doesn't learn how to do art, but one learns that it is possible by a certain adjustment of consciousness to participate in art—it's a natural activity for one not corrupted by mechanical ways.
WILLIAM STAFFORD

Finished persons are very common—people who are closed up, quite satisfied that there is little more to learn.
ROBERT HENRI

voice intonation and pauses. According to Joseph C. Pearce, a student of brain processes, sound—and particularly the sound of words—stimulates the brain into attention, as he explained in *The Bond of Power*.

Read your writing aloud—to yourself or to someone else, if you wish. Listening to the sound of your language will make you aware of its stylistic rhythms as well as the design of its content. The qualities of natural writing, such as wholeness, recurrences, language rhythms, image power, metaphoric connection, and creative tension, which were sadly overlooked during most of your schooling, come to the foreground when read or heard aloud.

Directing Your Hand

Let yourself know where you are as a writer right now, before going on to chapter 2. For many of you, a blank page generates feelings ranging from mild uneasiness to sheer terror. Don't expect to write a masterpiece yet. You simply want an indicator of your present level of skill to let you see how far you've come by the end of the course.

Try to write quickly and without censoring yourself or worrying about proper grammar or form. Don't worry about how you start or end. In chapter 2 you'll discover a liberating technique that will erase the anxiety of the blank page, give you focus, help you know where to start, and tell you what you want to say. But for now, it's important to have a point of reference to come back to.

Limit yourself to five minutes of writing for each of the four entries suggested below. If you cannot muster that much writing, don't worry. Your minimum should be a few sentences and your maximum a page, at most, for each entry. These parameters give you plenty of leeway.

> *Writing 1* Write something about yourself. Do so from any perspective you wish.

> *Writing 2* Describe a feeling, such as fear, love, sadness, or joy.

The brain is fluid, a constantly changing instrument of extreme subtlety. Just as no one can step into the same river twice, so too can no one think the same thought twice. For the act of thinking changes the thinker. Indeed, the thinker is the thought; the thought gives birth to the thinker who, in turn, creates the thought anew. . . . The unfolding of meaning in time produces the whole gesture of the mind's dance. Within this gesture, brain and consciousness are sustained just as the fountain lives by virtue of the water that flows through it.

DAVID PEAT

Writing 3 Write about someone you care for.

Writing 4 Write anything you can think of about the word "write."

Creation is inherently relational—there cannot be creation without interconnection. Similarly it is evolutionary— creation is quite specifically the story of how things change.
CHARLES JOHNSTON, M.D.

Improvisation, writing, painting, invention—all creative acts—are forms of play, the starting place of creativity in the human growth cycle, and one of the great primal life functions.
STEPHEN NACHMANOVITCH,
Free Play

After Writing

It is quite likely that for one entry or another you chewed the proverbial pencil for some moments, whereas another flowed relatively smoothly once you got started. It is also likely that writing about yourself gave you more trouble than writing about someone you care for, and that describing a feeling left you frustrated. Writing about "write" probably became a chronicle of the feelings you experienced while you were writing the other three entries. As you progress through the chapters, it will be interesting to see how your perceptions about writing will change.

Let's look at some typical responses to writing about writing:

ON WRITING

Writing is a painful processing. It is also one of the biggest sources of shame and fear. All my writing have [sic] been done with reluctance and the results have always been unsatisfying.

I understand the importance of writing and have a strong desire to write well. On the first day of my writing lab, I saw a sign that said, "people who cannot express themselves in writing are slaves." That sign pierced my heart. And again I felt shame.

Writing exposes my ignorance, my poor vocabulary, my inability of imagination, and my shallow knowledge which I desperately want to hide as much as my naked body. It is embarrassing to show others what I wrote because they know and I know it is junk!

COLLEGE FRESHMAN

Often we assume we are bad writers when we are not. The above student, an English as a Second Language writer, has considerable command of the language, shows passion for what he is saying, and isn't even aware of his own eloquence.

And the following student, a young woman, was already quite

articulate at the beginning, but very negative about her own writing. In four months she grew to realize that she had options to express herself differently for different purposes, in different voices, with different challenges:

WRITE

"Must"—a must that must flow and doesn't. W-R-I-T-E—a most arduous task that cannot be performed well by one who is unable to see what there is to say—i.e., what needs to be said, what asks to be said, what has to be said, what must. Mussed-up ideas are not a followed path. Yearning to be clear in words makes writing for her the most prized goal she can attain because it allows her to say what needs to be said, what cannot rest within until it is out, frowned upon though it might be by some, laughed at, loved, or lamented by others or herself. The reason for doing it reaches into her being like the hub of a great spinning wheel, able to turn daily doings into starry midnight places in the middle of the day.

CINDY LUBAR

WRITING

Writing can be
as simple as seeing
as basic as being
as natural as breathing
as filling as eating and
as vital as seeking.

CINDY LUBAR

The gift of insight—of making imaginative new connections—is there for anyone who persists, experiments, and explores. In most lives insight has been accidental. We wait for it as primitive man awaited lightning for a fire. But making mental connections is our most crucial learning tool, the essence of human intelligence: to forge links; to go beyond the given; to see patterns, relationships, context.

MARILYN FERGUSON

Different style, sense of ease, and fluidity. Different options. Different ways of seeing, of expressing. In the first piece, the writer focuses on the struggle to write; in the second, in a different moment in her life, on the pleasure of writing.

And here is what a Japanese student new to the United States wrote about writing. Although relatively unaccustomed to writing in English, she captures in very few, evocative words the essence of what many students feel when they think about the word "write": fear and promise.

WRITING

To start writing makes difference,
    but awkward.
Idea is larger than sail,
wide enough to be ocean.
To confess makes me fear
    like being in fire.
My ideas are branches of tree,
but sticky wind takes them away.

MACHIKO YOSHIDA

At the end of the semester Machiko wrote about an English teacher who had handed her back her essay, saying "This is not English—it is not organized at all . . ." and she recounts the effect of this comment: "My feeling of fear toward writing, speaking, and myself overwhelmed me even in my native language. . . . Today still, when I have to talk to a stranger, words cannot come out well." She quotes Steven Nachmanovitch on the necessity of play in writing: "There is a time to experiment without fear of consequences, to have a play space safe from fear of criticism."

A Last Word and Heading On

Expressive power in the form of storytelling is a basic human impulse rooted in our Design mind's desire to give form to our experience, to create meaning out of a world that all too often appears chaotic and fragmented. Although we tell stories long before we learn to print the simplest words on paper, the record of our self-definition takes on permanence only when we write it down, a potent tool in the process of growth, insight, and self-awareness. In so doing, we begin to express our own unique perception of our world.

As you read and work through the chapters to come, writing

will once more become a natural expressive form rather than drudgery, a source of enormous satisfaction rather than an irritant, a means of expansion rather than fearful contraction. The enormous potential of language is accessible to all of us.

The first step is to immerse yourself in the design-seeking process called *clustering*, the subject of chapter 2. By tapping into the right brain, clustering not only frees your expressive power but also helps you discover what you have to say, encouraging a flow instead of a mere trickle. Let's go on to experience this doorway into your Design mind.

CLUSTERING: THE DOORWAY TO YOUR DESIGN MIND

Nature operates by profusion. Think of the nearly infinite number of seeds that fall to earth, only a fraction of which take root to become trees; of those five thousand or so drones that exist solely to ensure the fertilization of one queen bee; of the millions of sperm competing so fiercely to fertilize one small egg.

Similarly, human beings engaged in the creative process explore an astronomical number of possible patterns before settling on an idea. Novelist John Gardner suggests that writers need some magic key for getting in touch with these secret reserves of imaginative power. What we lack is not ideas but a direct means of getting in touch with them.

Clustering is that magic key. In fact, it is a master key to natural writing. It is the crucial first step for bypassing our logical, orderly Sign-mind consciousness to touch the mental life of daydream, random thought, remembered incident, image, or sensation.

Clustering is a nonlinear brainstorming process akin to free association. It makes an invisible Design-mind process visible through a nonlinear spilling out of lightning associations that allows patterns to emerge. Through clustering we naturally come up with a multitude of choices from a part of our mind where the experiences of a lifetime mill and mingle. It is the writing tool that accepts wondering, not-knowing, seeming chaos, gradually mapping an interior landscape as ideas begin to emerge. It is an openness to the unknown, an attitude that says "I wonder where this is taking me?" Clustering acknowledges that it's okay to start writing not knowing exactly what, where, who, when, and how. Most writers acknowledge that this is how it inevitably is, anyway.

Too many of us get stuck because we *think* we should know where to start and which ideas to develop. When we find we don't, we become anxious and either force things or quit. We forget to wonder, leaving ourselves open to what might come. Wondering means it's acceptable not to know. It is the natural state at the beginning of all creative acts, as recent brain research shows.

Though we cannot force the birth of an idea, we can do the next best thing: We can cluster, thus calling on the pattern-seeking Design mind and bypassing the critical censorship of the Sign mind, which relieves the familiar anxiety about what to say and where to start and opens us to the freedom of expression we knew in childhood.

The Emergence of Design in Clustering

Clustering, as already suggested, is a Design-mind function. It marks the first step for all the techniques described in this book and for all the writing tasks you will engage in from now on. Just as many natural forms come in clusters—grapes, lilacs, spider eggs, cherries—so thoughts and images, given free rein, seem to come in clusters of associations.

I've been watching my own mind associate for years, and I have read much about creative process. Most studies attempt to methodize creativity. My gut feeling was always "No, that's not how it works." Some, like novelist Henry James, came at the question of creativity from an angle that appealed to my own sense of what happens when we associate. He wrote, "The whole of anything cannot be told; we can take only what groups together." And critic Northrop Frye observed that any word or phrase can become a "storm center of meanings, sounds, and associations, radiating out indefinitely like ripples in a pool."

Every nightmare hints at the secret reserves of imaginative power in the human mind. What the stalled or not-yet-started writer needs is some magic for getting in touch with himself, some key.

JOHN GARDNER, NOVELIST

Mental life is the result of the brain's serendipitous sidesteps, its knack for discovering new uses for old structures, in turn making leaps to develop new ways of seeing.

WILLIAM CALVIN

First, I do not sit down at my desk to put into verse something that is already clear in my mind. If it were clear in my mind, I should have no incentive or need to write about it. . . . We do not write in order to be understood; we write in order to understand.

C. DAY LEWIS, *The Poetic Image*

However, when, in the Stanford library, I came across a visual image of a creative search in Anton Ehrenzweig's *The Hidden Order of Art* (Figure 2-1), I knew then my gut feelings about "clusters" were somehow right. His image of the creative process supports the idea that creative work is done in interim stages involving interim decisions and that we must resist the desire for certainty, the need to visualize precisely the final product.

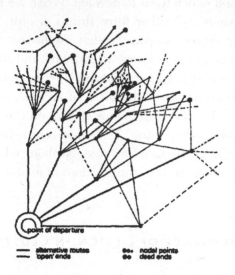

Figure 2-1

In describing his image, Ehrenzweig wrote about "points of departure," "open ends," "alternative routes," and "nodal points"— as well as "dead ends." "Open ends" will yield the as yet unpredictable—will yield only the as-yet-unknown, will yield to the incipient sense of pattern; they describe the human reaching for meaning, of meaning-ful-ness.

In a moment of insight, the word "clustering" popped into my head to describe this radiating phenomenon of nonlinear connection around a "storm center of meanings" which I call the "nucleus." And clustering it has been ever since, the term I use to express the primary technique of natural writing. A nucleus word or short phrase acts as the stimulus for recording all the associations that spring to mind in a very brief period of time.

Figure 2-2 shows you a student sample of clustering spilled onto paper around the nucleus phrase (LETTING GO). The cluster-

Figure 2-2

ing was accomplished in a minute or two, the resulting writing in about five minutes, as a direct result of the ideas that came to mind during the clustering process.

Letting go of one's children happens inch by inch over the years so that when it finally happens, that last quarter inch is not hard. Letting go of anger is a giant rebounding from the intensity of my anger, lifting me up with the air, weightless, rocking me softly as feathers sprung loose, rushing me along like blossoms in the spring wind, dropping me as gently as snowflakes falling. Letting go of past dreams and hopes requires more effort, but I can do it, and once I've taken that icy plunge, there's nothing like the invigoration of it, and nothing like pushing off from shore into the deeper waters, slowly rolling over on one's back and getting that sun-slanted view of mountains and arching sky. But letting go of pain is a mirror image of *me*. I look at pain, and I see me at three years old sitting in a closet hunched with knees drawn up, scowling, brows furrowed into an angry slash across the face. When I feel pain, I turn to hold

The eye is the first circle; the horizon which it forms is the second; and throughout nature this primary figure is repeated without end.
RALPH WALDO EMERSON

I thought you could beat, pummel, and thrash an idea into existence. Under such treatment of course any decent idea folds up its paws, fixes its eyes on eternity, and dies.
RAY BRADBURY

and comfort that child. But she is voracious, comfortless, and all my holding on does no good. She is the worm in the center of my universe.

SHEILA SAPIR

The thing that differentiates the human brain from the computer is the talent, or knack, or quirk, which the brain has established of logical and also illogical relationships. Emotion, humor, fear, hate—all these come from unlikely juxtapositions of seemingly random bits in the storage banks, or the cauldron. The contents of the cauldron are not readily accessible to me until two or more random bits clot together in some associational relationship and float to the surface. Then I take these items out, a coagulation, and turn the lump this way and that until I see a pattern that may or may not become a story.

JOHN D. MACDONALD

The establishment of a point in chaos lends this point a concentric character of the primordial. The order thus created radiates from it in all directions.

PAUL KLEE

The cluster around the nucleus "letting go" reflects this writer's emotional interests—of children, of anger, of the past, of pain. It also reflects her images of "letting go"—a "weightless floating in air," and the coolness of a mountain-lake swim. The vignette itself focuses on degrees of "letting go" with a progressive intensification of difficulty: children are the easiest because it is done "inch by inch," and pain the most difficult; when she feels pain, the writer tells us, she becomes a "comfortless child" who is the "worm in the center of my universe."

Note that not everything from the cluster is used: "balloons" and "holding onto the balloon" are left out. Other things are slightly changed. It is important to understand that clustering is the Design mind's shorthand and offers options, not all of which need find their way into the finished product.

Yet clustering is not merely the spilling of words and phrases at random, but something much more complex: For the Design mind, each association leads inexorably to the next with a logic of its own even though the Sign mind does not perceive the connection. Making connections has much more to do with the complexity of images and emotional qualities associated and held fast on paper until we suddenly—or gradually—perceive them as having a pattern or meaning. Even when we can't decipher the words of a cluster generated in another language, as in Figures 2-3 and 2-4, we have a visual sense of a mind at work, making nonlinear connections or associating images around a nucleus in search of meaning.

The Nucleus: Finding Your Voice

Clustering always unfolds from a center, like ripples generated by a rock thrown into a pond. That center can be a nucleus word or phrase, or it can be a dominant impression, as we shall see later.

Nucleus comes from the latin *nucula*, meaning "kernel" or "little nut"; it is the seed that contains all potential growth. If a

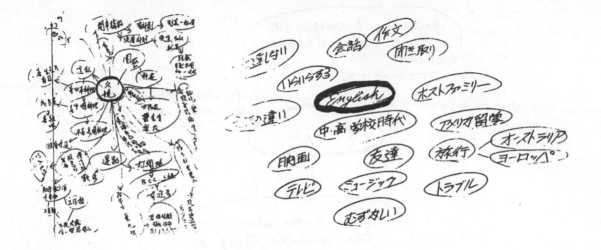

Figure 2-3   Figure 2-4

nucleus word is allowed to filter through your personal experiential sieve, it will always generate writing expressive of your unique consciousness. That is the essence of natural writing: expression that is unique and authentic to you, your own "voice" heard in words written on the page.

Any word or phrase has the potential for getting the attention of your Design mind. Although you may not know its precise Sign-mind dictionary definition, as the word echoes through your Design mind, it is like a magnet, picking up images, certain feelings and emotional nuances, lines of songs or poems, similar rhythms—whatever your pattern-seeking right brain perceives as related.

Figure 2-5, for example, is the first-time clustering experience of a professor of English, a published poet, and clearly a lover of literature. When confronted with the nucleus word (TIME), he complained that all he could think of to cluster were lines of poems having to do with time. But these reflect his rich reading background; one also gets the feeling that the sound of these lines were resonating in his Design mind just waiting to be tapped. Following the cluster is the vignette generated by these lines that helped him to discover a focus.

The sphere is the elementary division of inside and outside. If there were to be a symbol for the "thingness" of anything, I would guess we'd agree on the sphere, or, on the page, the circle. . . . Metapatterns are those key patterns that exemplify the sphericity of the deepest forms of knowledge, the interlinking of all things and ideas in the universe.

TYLER VOLK

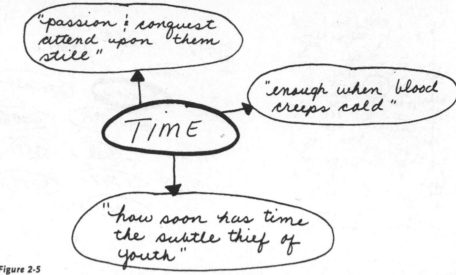

Figure 2-5

How deeply aware of time are the poets—the quickness of its passing, the fragility of the now, the terror of its going. Dylan Thomas sings: "Time enough when the blood creeps cold and I lie down but to sleep in bed," pissing in his pants with the terror of it. Yeats, sick now and having proposed to Maude Gonne for thirty years and been said no to and thinking that it's all over for him and looking at the swans wheeling up from the dark waters of Coole and seeing them fly away lover by lover, writes out of the barren sadness of his soul: "Passion and conquest attend upon them still." It's all over for him, he feels. And Milton, a mere boy to my middle-aged sight, writes: "How soon hath time, the subtle thief of youth, stolen in truth my three and twentieth year." I may have the figures wrong, but I know the feeling— for I am forty-eight, I am forty-eight, I am forty-eight.

NILS PETERSON

A nucleus word tends to evoke clusters of associations unique to each individual responding to it. For Nils Peterson, "time" became far more than the literal Sign-mind definition of "a nonspatial continuum in which events occur in apparently irreversible succession from the past through the present to the future," as the dictionary gives it. The word for him became emotionally charged through all his association with the emotional nuances expressed by other poets long dead.

As noted in chapter 1, the Sign mind's use of language is largely explanatory whereas the Design mind's use of language is largely evocative. The former pigeonholes, conceptualizes, discriminates, analyzes, defines, constricts, and specifies, whereas the latter, in complementary fashion, connects, associates, suggests, and evokes. Let me illustrate how a nucleus word can evoke Design-mind associations that are initially out of the range of awareness of the Sign mind. Figure 2-6 is the work of a freshman composition student who was clustering for the first time. This student's Design mind clustered the nucleus (NARROW) readily enough, as you can see. It triggered a number of associations primarily derived from images: "tubes," "channels," "openings," "bridges." But here is the interesting thing: as he began to write, this student's Sign mind was still insisting that "narrow" had no

Figure 2-6

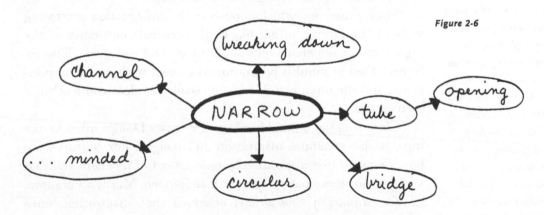

meaning for him at all. Then see what happened as he used the Design-mind images made accessible through clustering.

Narrow is a word that has no particular meaning to me. It's not that I don't want to write, it's just that, when I think of narrow, I associate it with narrow bridges, narrow channels, generally just narrow openings. For example, a narrow-minded person does not seem like a well-rounded person. Narrowing down to something is a tunneling down or reducing down. Narrowing the chances or narrowing down the competition is like breaking down the resistance, which is what this clustering exercise just did to me. I realize I was wrong about what I said in the first sentence. The word, narrow, does have meanings to me, after all.

[Clustering] is like fishing. But I do not wait very long, for there is always a nibble—and this is where receptivity comes in. To get started, I will accept anything that occurs to me. Something always occurs, of course, to any of us. We can't keep from thinking.

WILLIAM STAFFORD,
"A WAY OF WRITING"

In most lives insight has been accidental. We wait for it as primitive man awaited lightning for a fire. But making mental connections is our most crucial learning tool, the essence of human intelligence: to forge links; to go beyond the given; to see patterns, relationship, context.

MARILYN FERGUSON,
The Aquarian Conspiracy

Although far from deathless prose, this vignette illustrates the extent to which the Design mind can exercise its powers of associations without the direct awareness of the more logical Sign mind. In his writing, this student moved from insisting that "narrow" had no meaning for him to the realization that "I was wrong about what I said in the first sentence. The word, narrow, does have meanings to me, after all." He also brings us back to the beginning of his vignette, showing us where his thinking started. Interestingly, this technique of referring back to the beginning and thus coming full circle seems to develop naturally out of clustering and Design-mind thinking.

Since clustering, which appeals to the information-processing style of the Design mind, blocks the critical censorship of the Sign mind, it undercuts tension, anxiety, and resistance. The receptive Design mind is programmed to deal with novelty, ambiguity, and the unknown. If we are receptive, ideas come of their own accord.

Clustering not only unblocks and releases Design-mind knowings, it also generates inspiration and insight. For centuries we have assumed that inspiration leaps at us out of nowhere and that we have no choice but to wait for it to happen. Marilyn Ferguson, in *The Aquarian Conspiracy*, observes that inspiration, once thought to be the province of only a chosen few, is available to all of us if only we learn to develop our innate capacities.

Finally, clustering is a self-organizing process. As you spill out seemingly random words and phrases around a center, you will be surprised to see patterns forming until a moment comes—characterized by an "aha!" feeling—when you suddenly sense a focus for writing. This moment is similar to watching clouds, and seeing just clouds; then, in a sudden moment of recognition you see a horse or a duck or Lincoln's profile. It is a moment of pattern recognition. The emotional surge of good feeling that accompanies this moment allows you to begin writing. I have never seen it fail. (The emotionally charged "aha!" will be discussed in detail in chapter 5.)

GENERAL PRINCIPLES OF CLUSTERING

To create a cluster, you begin with a nucleus word, circled, on a fresh page. Now you simply let go and begin to flow with any current of connections that come into your head. Write these down rapidly, each in its own circle, radiating outward from the center in any direction they want to go. Connect each new word or phrase with a line to the preceding circle. When something new and different strikes you, begin again at the central nucleus and radiate outward until those associations are exhausted.

As you cluster, you may experience a sense of randomness, or, if you are somewhat skeptical, an uneasy sense that it isn't leading anywhere. That is your logical Sign mind wanting to get into the act to let you know how foolish you are being by not setting thoughts down in logical sequences. Trust this natural process. We all cluster mentally throughout our lives without knowing it; we have simply never made these clusterings visible on paper.

Since you are not responsible for any particular order of ideas or any special information, your initial anxiety will soon disappear, and in its place will come a certain playfulness. Continue to cluster, drawing lines and even arrows to associations that seem to go together, but don't dwell on what goes where. Let each association find its own place. If you momentarily run out of associations, doodle a bit by filling in arrows or making lines darker. This relaxed receptivity to ideas usually generates another spurt of associations until at some point you experience a sudden sense of what you are going to write about. At that point, simply stop clustering and begin writing. It's as easy as that.

There is no right or wrong way to cluster. It is your Design mind's shorthand and it knows where it is headed, even if you don't. Trust it. It has a wisdom of its own, shaping ends you can't

The straight line leads to the downfall of mankind. The straight line . . . does not exist in nature. . . . Any design undertaken with the straight line will be stillborn.
FREDENSREICH HUNDERTWASSER

really evaluate yet. This wisdom has nothing to do with logic; should you try to apply logic to what you have just clustered, this sense of knowing where you're headed will be destroyed. Simply begin to write. The words will come; the writing takes over and writes itself.

Directing Your Hand

Find a quiet place to write where you won't be interrupted. Plan on about ten minutes or so for both clustering and writing. In your writer's notebook, on the next blank page, write Vignette #1 and date it.

1. Write and circle the word (TURN) in the upper third of the page, leaving the lower section for writing. We'll start with this word because it is one of the easiest words I used in my experimental classes, and I still do. The movement the word suggests never fails to invite a vignette.

2. Let your unrestricted Design mind make connections, and cluster whatever comes to mind when you write the word "Turn." Avoid judging or editing yourself. Simply let go and write. Let the words or phrases that come to you radiate outward from the nucleus word—using lines and arrows if you wish—drawing a circle around each word or phrase that comes to you. Don't think too long or analyze. There is an "unthinking" quality to this process.

3. At first your Sign mind will try to interfere, as it is uncomfortable with the seeming silliness or randomness of clustering. Reassure yourself that this randomness is an important first stage of the creative process.

4. Allow clustering to continue naturally. If you reach a point where no further words or phrases come to mind, keep the flow coming by doodling a bit—drawing arrows on your existing cluster.

5. You will know when to stop clustering when you feel an urge to write. It may happen suddenly, like an "Aha!" or

Everything we name enters the circle of language, and therefore the circle of meaning. The world is a sphere of meanings, a language.

OCTAVIO PAZ

Human beings invent language and then use language to reinvent the world. We project our alphabetic minds through language as a prototype by which we reconnoiter, test, and discover.

TYLER VOLK

it may surface gradually, as though you were slowly un-
veiling a sculpture. Chapter 5 explains this urge or "mental shift" more thoroughly. For now, the shift is identified by a certain satisfying feeling that you have something
to write about.

6. Now write, either ignoring the cluster altogether or scan-
ning it for specifics. Through the process of clustering, your
Design mind has perceived a pattern of meaning—so trust
in the natural writing flow which that pattern will dictate.
Take about five minutes. As you write, your consciousness
will oscillate from Design-mind vision or pattern to Sign-
mind sequencing and parts. Don't feel that you must use
everything in your cluster. Ignore what doesn't fit.

7. Come full circle and complete your vignette by referring
to what started your thought process when you first began to write. You might repeat a word or phrase or refer
to a dominant thought or emotion; this will give your vignette a sense of wholeness. (We'll talk more about this in
chapter 6, on "recurrences.")

8. Read aloud what you have written. Make changes until
you have a strong sense that everything in your vignette
belongs.

After Writing

You have just accomplished your first cluster with full participation of your Design mind and the resulting vignette with full cooperation of both Sign and Design minds. You allowed yourself to
experience the temporary chaos without which natural writing
cannot occur. You may have felt awkward to begin with, making circles and scattering words about on the page, but very likely
the associations came anyway.

Let me share with you some very brief vignettes of first-time
clusterers who expressed surprise at what they produced.

Figure 2-7 is the cluster and vignette of a woman whose first
language is German. While visiting the United States from Ger-

many, she happened to participate in a workshop I was giving in Nevada. Notice some German words in her cluster. Clearly, her Design-mind cluster tapped into some profound, immediate questions in her life at the time. Her cluster contains both "Yes!" and "No!" The opening sentence of her vignette begins with "Yes, I will return." Her closing sentence is not quite as assured, ending, as it does, in a question. Throughout, the play on "turn" and "return" weaves the fabric of the piece. This "yes" to "returning home" must have been a major fork in this writer's life journey.

TURN, TURN, TURN

Yes, I will return. My face will be new.
There will be new faces. To return home
without fear, without anger, is a turning
point in life. Maybe I will turn my back on
all that happened in earlier years, lately, late,
last, lesson learned through the turn—and
the return. Who is it that I turn to, that I
return to?

G.L.

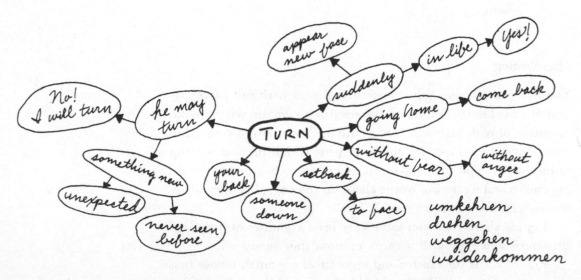

Figure 2-7

Figure 2-8 is the writing of a woman just returning to college who believed she couldn't write.

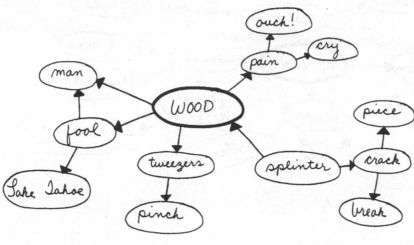

Figure 2-8

The technique of clustering gives you access to the patterns and associations of your Design mind. It provides you with essentially two things: *choices* from which to formulate and develop your thought, and a *focus* meaningful enough to impel you to write. Facts or words in isolation are meaningless until they are brought into relationship by a consciousness that can create relationships. A word, filtered through the sieve of your unique consciousness, allows you to create something from nothing through the medium of words, and here you have the beginning of reawakening your natural writing powers.

Here are some typical comments of first-time clusterers: "It was so easy!" and "I normally have a terrible time getting started, but after I clustered, I wrote without a moment's pause" and "I was so absorbed it was as though I was in another space" and "It's funny—when I circled that last cluster word, I knew exactly what I would write about." Perhaps one of these responses is similar to yours. First-time clusterers express amazement, delight, wonder, surprise at the discovery of their latent creative drive.

Clustering is effective because it seems to be a reflection of

Splinter is a terrible word. Its sound is synonymous with the sensation: jagged, sharp, piercing, like the nagging voice of a dissatisfied wife. I remember vacationing in Tahoe. The pier was old, worn, and wooden; the boards as rough as a face full of scabs. Running along it, my foot caught the attention of an angry spike of wood, injecting itself cleanly and deeply into the ball of my foot. If I screamed it was not from the pain initially felt, but from anticipated sensations. It's not the hole the shot makes but the length of the slim sword that brings pain.

LAURIE WELTE

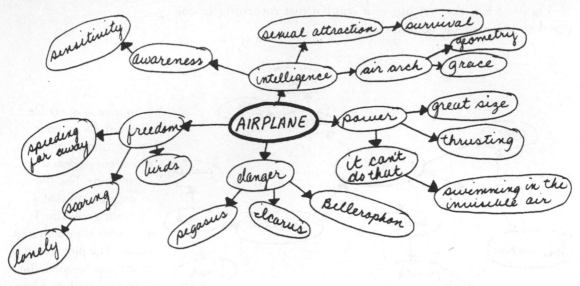

Figure 2-9

A huge silver jet airplane is making a graceful arch in the light blue morning sky, material evidence, to me, of the human mind. It is intelligence and courage thrusting above environment, at home with the impossible, powerful proof of the attraction of intellect in natural selection, as sensual as a strip tease.

LAVELLE LEAHEY

the way the Design mind naturally works—that is, it clusters for patterns meaningful to it all the time as it scans its universe. Thus, if you are one of the rare clusterers who experience some frustration, it is not your Design mind but your Sign mind that is likely to be the culprit. (See the quotation from Lavelle Leahy and the cluster in Figure 2-9.) In the beginning your Sign mind may try to take over because it likes to take command of anything to do with language (we'll see why this is true in chapter 3). But, since clustering is random and nonlinear, your Sign mind begins to retreat from the challenge. You may experience its resistance as "I can't do this" or "this is stupid" or "how childish."

Should you experience resistance to the novelty of clustering, go through the motions of drawing circles and lines around a stimulus word, as in Figure 2-10.

Simply relax and doodle, letting the circles and lines shape a pleasing pattern. That very nonlinear act will break down your resistance, and you will find yourself filling in those inviting empty circles with the associations that are inevitably triggered by the nucleus word.

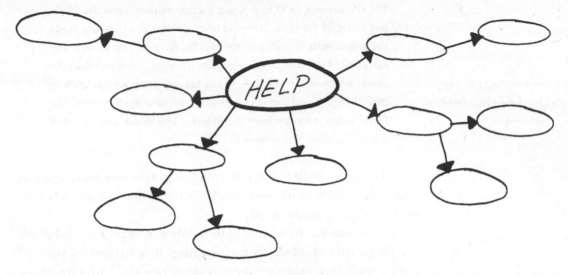

Figure 2-10

PLAYING WITH THE POWER OF THE CIRCLE

When I first developed the clustering process, I followed an impulse to circle the words as they spilled out onto paper, for each word and phrase seemed to be a complex, self-contained mini-whole in my mind. As I explored this impulse further, I recalled learning that the circle is primary in all human ritual, having its beginnings in human circles around fires, storytellers, dancers, or priests.

One of the archetypal strengths of clustering lies in what biologist Tyler Volk calls the "metapattern" of the circle: "We began life as simple, floating spheres. Our own spherical origin echoes the starting shape from which virtually all living things emerge. The sphere proclaims some original, functional, and perhaps even aesthetic truth." A Native American named Black Elk wrote this about circles:

> Everything an Indian does is in a circle, and that is because the Power of the World always works in circles, and everything tries to be round.

Why do we say "circle of friends" rather than "square"? Why do we admire those who are well rounded, not well triangulated? Why do we speak of spheres of influence, knowledge, and power? The sphere is the elementary division of inside and outside.

TYLER VOLK

To me a cluster is an expanding universe with each word a potential galaxy capable at each moment of throwing out universes of its own.

**A RENO TEACHER
AFTER A WORKSHOP**

The sky is round, and I have heard that the earth is round like a ball, and so are all the stars. The wind in its greatest power, whirls. Birds make their nests in circles, for theirs is the same religion as ours. The sun comes forth and goes down again in a circle. The moon does the same, and both are round. Even the seasons form a great circle in their changing, and always come back again to where they were. The life of a man is a circle from childhood to childhood, and so it is in everything where Power moves.

Clustering brings to my mind truths I may have lost sight of.
A STUDENT

The circle, unlike the man-made squares and rectangles of cribs and coffins, walls and windows that "box" us in, is a natural, flowing, organic shape.

Circles are the first intelligible shapes to appear in children's drawings. And children love clustering; it is natural to them. I tried it with first-graders—there was not one child who could not write after clustering, however briefly. The example below came from a second-grade group cluster, beginning with the nucleus ROUND, on the board, after which children clustered for themselves (Figure 2-11). This child had never even heard of personification—which didn't stop him at all!

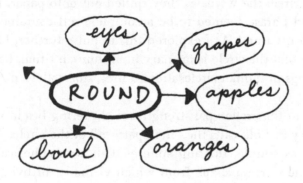

Figure 2-11

▶ ROUND

Once there was an apple and an orange that fell in love. But their fathers didn't let them get married. But they wanted to so badle that they threatened to jump into a bowl of fruit and get eaten by the hu-

mans. Then they threatened to lie down in the street and get run over
and that was the end of that and and the two fathers jumped into a
bowl of fruit and they got eaten and NOBODY lived happily ever after.

2ND-GRADER

By its very nature the circle centers, focuses. For this reason,
circling my mind-spills and connecting them to make webs
seemed a natural act. As the cluster expanded before my eyes,
each encircled mini-whole gradually became part of a larger
whole, a pattern of meaning that took shape when I began to
write.

Circle forms spilled on a page visually and physically—in
the movement of your arm, your hand, your pen on the page—
reinforce the nonlinearity of Design-mind thought. The circle
implicitly suggests bringing into being, activating, animating
the pattern-making forces of the creative process. A circle is beginning and birth, womb and egg. It is wholeness. You will see
how the cluster's circled words contain the seeds of a whole thought.

CLUSTERING AND VIGNETTES

Clustering virtually always generates writing that possesses the
quality of wholeness, of something completed, requiring neither
subtraction nor addition, like a finished sculpture or a painting.
The two prime characteristics of aesthetic experience are wholeness and a sense of pleasure.

To achieve wholeness, whether on a small scale or large, we
will concentrate on "vignette" writing. A vignette, unlike a paragraph, is a whole, a complete thought or statement on a subject,
a fully expressed idea, even a very short story with a fully developed plot. When you write a "paragraph" the unspoken assumption is that it is unfinished, that it won't be complete until something comes before or after it. A paragraph, we learned in school,
is a unit in a composition having a beginning, a middle, and an
end. Until we learned about paragraphs and topic sentences, we
had little trouble with natural expression.

Clustering and its resulting vignettes take us back to the

unfettered ability we had in childhood to express a complete thought naturally. A vignette leaves no unfinished business; it stands as an aesthetic whole, and it develops naturally from clustering. You won't have to work at it. Moreover, a vignette can be the length of one paragraph or several, or it can be a free-verse poem or a dialogue. In fact, the writing of longer pieces is actually a natural process of writing a series of self-contained vignettes, mini-wholes, which then become entwined into a larger, more comprehensive whole. (Most professional writers work this way.) We shall explore the how of this phenomenon in the final chapter of this book. The important point now is that a vignette is a self-contained whole, complete in itself.

Capturing this sense of wholeness is best achieved through brief writing experiences deliberately limited to time spans of five to ten minutes. This emphasis on the vignette not only propels the Design mind into action but gives the critical censor of the Sign mind no time to intrude with its "yes, but . . ." objections. And from these brief spurts you will experience almost immediate writing success and see dramatic improvement as you begin to incorporate further techniques of natural writing.

COMING FULL CIRCLE: CLOSURE

Just as clustering tends to beget wholeness of design without effort on your part, so does it influence your vignettes in such a way that your writing can't help but come full circle. The reasons for this phenomenon will be discussed in detail in chapter 4. For now, you should know that "closure," or coming full circle, is the result of active Design-mind participation that brings to the writing process an awareness of having grouped together, connected, and related relevant elements of an idea out of the infinite possibilities available to our brain. Through clustering we make a pattern around a given nucleus word, and, as we write, that clustered pattern exerts its power to such an extent that we are largely incapable of leaving the writing "hanging."

Such cohesiveness rarely happened before I developed the techniques of this book. Like many writing teachers, I required my students to do journal writing, ostensibly to stimulate the flow of ideas. The results were largely disappointing, often degenerating into mundane, diarylike entries without beginning or end, such as "I wish I were at the beach today instead of school. I'm hungry. After school is out I have to go to work, ugh . . ." and so on. Clustering, because it taps associations that generate patterns of ideas rather than such sequential thinking, does not produce this shallow, uninteresting rattling off of events. Instead, clustering naturally stimulates coming full circle, producing an inner unity out of a multiplicity of associations because the cluster itself is already a Design-mind pattern, an organic whole.

MODELING: LEARNING FROM THE MASTERS

Modeling, the use of a master's work for your own expressive purposes, also operates from our ongoing emphasis on wholeness. The culminating exercise for each chapter will be to model your own writing on that of a professional writer's, using your newly acquired tools for tapping your Design mind. Modeling uses a professional's writing for inspiration to do one's own. Its purpose is to give you a structure, an aesthetic pattern to follow, within which to treat your own discovered content. Modeling relieves you of the anxiety of having to think of everything at once, allowing your writing to flow more naturally. Artists learn their skills through modeling established works of art. Children learn language by imitating their parents' speech patterns. It makes sense that the qualities of good writing can be learned by taking cues from the masters.

Modeling appeals to your Design mind because it makes you aware of language rhythms and a spatial arrangement of words on which you will pattern your own writing. Modeling a professional piece of writing is simply one more way of contacting your inner writer to re-create your own unique inner world. It will also lead you to a better understanding of what a writer's "voice" is—his or her unique style and content of expression—which in turn will help you become more conscious of the shape of your own writing and, ultimately, of your own emerging voice.

In each chapter we will be modeling a brief selection of prose or poetry to reinforce the Design-mind techniques presented in the chapters: wholeness, recurrences, language rhythms, images, metaphors, and creative tension. I frequently use brief poems in these modeling exercises because poems are vignettes, total patterns to which we respond first and foremost as a whole. We tend to fear writing poems only because we have preconceived notions of their difficulty. Yet my students continually discover that poetry is a natural vehicle for their expressive purposes because of its compression and brevity.

Let's experience the process of expressing your own thoughts within a given shape.

Directing Your Hand

Model American poet Peter Meinke's untitled poem by writing a tribute to someone you deeply care for: a teacher, relative, friend, lover—you might even choose someone you don't know, such as an author who has had a significant impact on your outlook on life.

UNTITLED

this is a poem to my son Peter
whom I have hurt a thousand times
whose large and vulnerable eyes
have glazed in pain at my ragings
thin wrists and fingers hung
boneless in despair, pale freckled back
bent in defeat, pillow soaked
by my failure to understand.
I have scarred through weakness
and impatience your frail confidence forever
because when I needed to strike
you were there to be hurt and because
I thought you knew
you were beautiful and fair

your bright eyes and hair
but now I see that no one knows that
about himself, but must be told
and retold until it takes hold
because I think anything can be killed
after a while, especially beauty
so I write this for life, for love, for
you, my oldest son Peter, age 10, going on 11.

PETER MEINKE, AMERICAN POET

1. Read Peter Meinke's poem aloud, preferably more than once, so that your Design mind can absorb its rhythms and images.

2. In your writer's notebook write the name of the person who is the subject of your tribute in the center of a page and circle it. This is your nucleus. Cluster anything that comes to mind about that person: feelings, personality, idiosyncrasies, failings, strengths, attitudes, associations with objects or places, physical attributes, whatever surfaces.

3. Continue to cluster for two to three minutes or until you experience a shift from randomness to a sense that you have something to write about.

4. Now begin your vignette with "This is a poem to _____, _____." Glance at the Meinke poem from time to time for a sense of its phrasing and rhythm and, as you write, draw on your cluster for details.

5. Spend five to ten minutes writing improvisationally. Don't labor over your vignette. Remember that this is only a draft; you can always go back and make changes later. The less time you spend on your piece at this stage, the less you're likely to lose the free-flowing associations of your Design mind.

6. When you finish, read your vignette aloud. Make as many changes as you wish by adding or subtracting words and phrases. Notice that, although your piece is unique, it will

reflect patterns found in Meinke's poem. This similarity is the result of your Design mind's sensitivity to established patterns.

Note that Meinke's poem momentarily moves beyond the intensely personal to the universal when he suggests that we must articulate praise because ". . . no one knows that/about himself, but must be told/and retold until it takes hold." See if you were able to reach for a truth that is both particular and universal. The Meinke poem comes full circle with "so I write this for life, for love, for/you, my oldest son Peter," hooking it back to its beginning. Bring your tribute full circle, too.

After Writing

Now that you have written a poem using clustering, go back to your earlier writing in your writer's notebook, the before-instruction writing in which you described someone you cared for. Reread it and reread the vignette you just completed. The clustered, modeled version is probably richer in detail, more concise, more evocative, more polished, more rhythmic. Your words seem to have woven a noticeable pattern. And chances are, too, that you felt greater satisfaction when you were finished than you usually do after writing.

However great or small your sense of pattern or your feeling of satisfaction, your inner writer is beginning to surface. Gradually you will become aware of certain feelings that characterize a surge of creative activity: a sense of ease, increased confidence, pleasure, exhilaration, sometimes amazement that what flows from your pen seems so effortless.

To illustrate the fact that each response to modeling is unique and personal, I include a poem that grew out of this activity in a workshop I gave in Colorado. After clustering and writing, this participant held the paper toward me and said, "I don't think I can read it, but I'd like to share it. Would you read it?" I did. There was a stunned silence. Her vignette reads as follows:

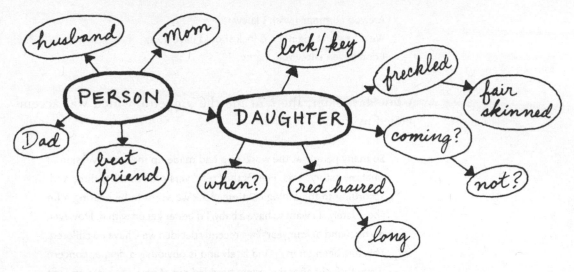

Figure 2-12

This is a poem
to my daughter.
I do not know you; I may never know you.
What am I saying?
I've always known you.
You were born, deep inside me, a child myself
as I mothered, powdered, cuddled baby dolls.
I never doubted you'd come along someday.
Funny, I used to think of you more often when I was younger,
juggling an up-and-down relationship with my mother.
And comparing.
Now she's my best friend and I miss you,
I need you now.

    I've pictured you often:
    long, lanky limbs, tumbling over rocks
    at our cabin. Hair, long and flowing,
    probably red. A splattering of freckles
    across your fair-skinned face,
    random, like raindrops.

Are you coming? I wish I knew.
We'd be great together. A lock should have a key.
I don't even know your name.

A few days later, she sent me the vignette, which was accompanied by a note. It read:

So many people at the workshop had made up their own version of what my "story" was. Here's the "real" version: I'm thirty-three and, according to the biological time clock we seem to be hearing a lot about lately, if I want to have a baby, I'd better get on with it. However, my husband of four years has recently decided we'll have *no* children. This has been on my mind lately and is obviously a deeper concern than I thought after this poem tumbled out of my right brain and left me shaking.

Open to the Design mind, we allow images, ideas, and experiences to enter our consciousness that reflect powerful archetypal concerns of all human beings but all too often remain unacknowledged and unexpressed.

A Last Word and Heading On

Clustering, the basic technique of natural writing, can be used to generate ideas for writing of any form: essays, poems, short stories, business reports, song lyrics, even novels. I have used it with students in a business-communication course to ease the inhibitions common to letter writing and the fear of writing reports. Students have used clustering to write songs, to generate insights for their essay exams, to prepare for a verbal confrontation with a friend; one student showed me clusters that had generated ideas for a piece of ad copy for his journalism class. Clustering, with its access to the pattern-making Design mind, is a powerful inspirational/organizational tool; it always reassures us that we have something to say. Best of all, we don't have to worry about the sequence or syntax of ideas; we simply create connections and relationships as the cluster unfolds effortlessly.

Although it is human nature to resist the unfamiliar, the unconventional, give clustering a chance. Don't prematurely bring down the curtain on a process that is certain to produce enormous changes in your writing, your attitude toward writing, and your assessment of your own creative powers. In making the invisible process of your Design mind visible through clustering, you avail yourself of the rich array of choices on which natural writing thrives.

Surprisingly, this storehouse of choices is much more accessible to young children than it is to adults, for reasons we will explore briefly in the following chapter on the childhood origins of natural writing. An understanding of your untutored childhood creative powers, in turn illuminated by an understanding of the development of the two sides of your brain in chapter 4, will afford you new insights for tapping your own creative potential in general and for enhancing your natural expressive powers in particular.

THREE

THE RECEPTIVE "I":
THE CHILDHOOD ORIGINS
OF NATURAL WRITING

PATTERN

Without play, learning and evolution are impossible. Play is the taproot from which original art springs; it is the raw stuff the artist channels and organizes. Technique itself springs from play, by testing the limits and resistances of our tools.

STEPHEN NACHMANOVITCH

Learning is discovering pattern in the "blooming buzzing confusion" of a child's earliest impressions. Perhaps the first pattern we become aware of is the eye as the first circle; we look at our mother's eyes, all the while internalizing the good feelings it produces. This is the beginning of aesthetic experience, when the patternings of our internal world achieve congruence with some aspect of the outside world. The word "aesthetic" comes from the Greek root *aisthethis,* meaning both sensation (world without) and feeling (world within). Two components of aesthetic activity are consciousness of a unified whole and pleasure when the patterns of our inner world mesh with some aspect of the outer world. Infants ceaselessly structure their world, venturing always into uncharted spaces. Their increasing awareness of patterns, such as the circle shape, brings pleasure and helps them create personal meaning. According to psychologist Anton Ehrenzweig:

> The very young child's vision is still global and takes in the entire whole, which remains undifferentiated according to its component details. This gives the child artist the freedom to distort color and

shapes . . . But to him—owing to his global unanalytic view—his work is realistic . . . the early work is better in its aesthetic achievement than the timid art of the older child.

Between the ages of two and three, children have the urge to make marks in the sand or on paper. The first shape all children in all cultures draw is a circle pattern. The second thing they do is to put something inside this circle shape—two dots for eyes, or a cross. My youngest daughter Simone was no exception. But her predilection for overall shape patterns was pronounced. Here are four "drawings" (Figure 3-1) she made between 2½ and 3¾ years old. It's almost as if she had "birdness," "horseness," "catness" in mind as she struggled with the felt-tip pen, drawing large and whole, unaware of, or uninterested in, detail—yet expressing a sense of pattern that has nothing to do with skill. A poem by Lisel Mueller highlights some of the characteristics of children's drawing.

When someone asks, "When did you start to write?" there is no way to respond adequately and briefly: for the question starts with a wrong assumption. Poetry, for instance, is not something that one takes up and begins to do; it is something everyone is caught up in, early, and a few keep on doing.

WILLIAM STAFFORD

"*Birdie*" *Simone, 2½*   "*Birdie*" *Simone, 3½*   *Simone, 3½*   *Simone, 3¾*

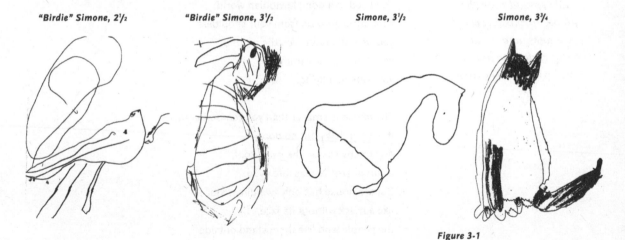

Figure 3-1

DRAWINGS BY CHILDREN

1. The sun may be visible or not
   (it may be behind you,
   the viewer of these pictures)
   but the sky is always blue
   if it is day. If not,

the stars come almost within your grasp;
crooked, they reach out to you,
on the verge of falling.
It is never sunrise or sunset,
there is no bloody eye
spying on you across the horizon.
It is clearly day or night,
it is bright or totally dark,
it is here and never there.

2. In the beginning, you only needed
your head, a moon swimming in space,
and four bare branches;
and when your body was added,
it was light and thin at first,
not yet the dark chapel
from which, later, you tried to escape.
You lived in a non-Newtonian world,
your arms grew up from your shoulders,
your feet did not touch the ground,
your hair was streaming,
you were still flying.

3. The house is smaller than you remembered,
it has windows but no door.
A chimeny sits on the gable roof,
a curl of smoke reassures you.
But the house has only two dimensions,
like a mask without its face;
the people who live there stand outside
as though time were always summer—
there is nothing behind the wall
except a space where the wind whistles,
but you cannot see that.

LISEL MUELLER

When language begins, the first words to appear are the naming words—nouns—naming what matters most to the child:

"Mama," "Baba," "birdie," "moon." As soon as the naming words are connected to a DO-ing word, children create a pattern of perceived action: "Birdie fly!" "Moon go." A child's earliest verbal pattern is the connecting of a noun that is *identified* and a verb that *acts*. When they put them together, they have the beginnings of a story, as in "Baba come."

By age three or so children have sufficient motor skills to scribble patterns meaningful to them into the sand or onto paper. The first pattern drawn by children in all cultures is a circle shape, however lopsided. And the first embellishment is almost always two circles within the circle, the eyes, creating the illusion of the human face.

At a later stage comes a new awareness of pattern-making—the dawning that those black squiggles in books *mean* something, that they make a story pattern when their parents turn the pages of a book. For me, at four, one of my strongest memories is of my first glimmerings that print somehow held mysterious meanings. I had three older sisters who read and who themselves made black marks on paper that carried messages. I would watch them at their homework, making patterns on the page, would beg for a piece of paper, and—a leftie—would take my pencil in my hand and scribble angles and curves across the page, line after line. Then I would run to one of them, holding out my sheet of mysterious marks, begging, "What does it say," certain of some magic meaning in my scribbles. Of course, it said nothing, and they would let me know it! But I would soon learn that the meaning discovered in early verbalizing gives rise to the discernment of patterns in letters strung together in particular ways on a page, the beginning of literacy.

Play

As children, we discover patterns of meaning through play. The great German student of play, Huizinga, argued that "civilization arises and unfolds in, and as, play." Perhaps we play because it is a way of discovering meaning and because play is pleasureable. Huizinga tells us that play has a quality of action that differs

To invite intuition to do its thing once the brain is bearing the heavy weight of accumulated data is something akin to balancing a boulder on the head of a bird and then urging it to fly.

DAVID J. SCHLAFER

The child in the human is its growing tip, alive throughout our lifespan . . . One of the labors of adulthood is to befriend in ourselves those handicapped and underdeveloped parts of our nature we have set aside.

M. C. RICHARDS

from ordinary life. It produces intensity, absorption. As the direct opposite of seriousness its positive qualities are many, among them, that it

- is a voluntary act—a free act

- is not "real" life

- has a temporal limit: a beginning and an end

- can be repeated for its pleasurable effect

- has a spatial limit—creates its own order

Above all, play, contrary to some notions, is not just wasting time; it is a profound learning experience; we associate it with story, absorption, spontaneity, joy, and wonder, all descriptors of a small child's stunning learning curve. The deepest, most lasting, learning is grounded in play.

WONDER

Wonder is so central to creative behavior that D. H. Lawrence elevated it to the status of a sixth sense. Philosopher Sam Keen writes, "To wonder is to live in the world of novelty rather than law (or habit), of delight rather than obligation, and of the present rather than the future." Wonder requires receptivity, curiosity, participation, openness, and an intuitive sense, all characteristics of Design-mind thought and the sine qua non of natural writing. Children come with these qualities. As we mature we tend to lose them, to suppress them, to forget them. To relearn the creative attitude of wonder, we need to reintegrate it into our worldview principally because wonder is the other side of control.

Children create their own realities in response to wonder. The child from two to five, according to Russian linguist Kornei Chukovsky, is the most inquisitive creature on earth in the service of comprehending its world. He cites five-year-old Volik's conversation with his mother:

Language is our meeting place, the sea we all live in. When I watched my children learning to talk I had the sense that they were not so much learning language as being claimed by it, taken into its arms as if it were another parent, and so it is. In the arms of language children will join the human family. They will learn what has gone before, and they will learn what is left to be done. In language they will learn to laugh, and to grieve, to be consoled in their grief, and to console others. In language they will discover who they are.
TOBIAS WOLFF, NOVELIST

After swallowing each bite, Volik would stop and listen to what was happening inside of him. Then he would smile and say: "It just ran down the little ladder to the stomach."

"What do you mean—down the little ladder?"

"I have a little ladder there (and he pointed from neck to stomach); everything I eat runs down this ladder . . . and there are other little ladders in my arms and legs . . . all over what I eat runs down little ladders to my body. . . ."

"Did someone tell you all this?"

"No, I saw it myself."

"Where?"

"Oh, when I was in your tummy, I saw the kind of ladders you had there and that means that I, too, have the same kind. . . ."

Wondering, as you can see from Volik's virtuoso performance, leads naturally to a second fundamental act of early childhood: the child's propensity to struggle toward patterns of meaning.

STORYING AND CHILDHOOD

Storying occurs in all cultures and with all children. As soon as children learn the noun/naming function, they can point to objects and people. As soon as they learn verb/actions, they can describe what happens: "Mommy, look . . . birdie, fly!" Our predisposition for language, according to Noam Chomsky, is innate—syntax seems to be built into our Sign mind. We don't *teach* our children to speak; they seem to learn it by osmosis. For this reason, Chukovsky calls every two-year-old a "linguistic genius":

Every child becomes for a short period of time a linguistic genius. . . . There is no trace left in the eight-year-old of this creativity with words, since the need for it has passed; by this age the child already has fully mastered the basic principles of his native language. If his former talent for word invention and construction had not abandoned him, he would, even by the age of ten, eclipse any of us with his suppleness and brilliance of speech.

According to psychobiologist Renée Fuller, the story functions as our cognitive organizer. Story comprehension, appearing surprisingly early in child development, allows a two-year-old to follow a simple story. A toddler's two-word sentences are already a miniature story, and story increasingly becomes meaning.

Before story comprehension, a child's vocabulary consists of four or five isolated words. Fuller reminds us, "almost overnight his vocabulary explodes and he starts to make sentences," and, as vocabulary makes a sudden spurt, a child's image of his world expands exponentially as he daily transcends his previous understanding and reorganizes it into an ever-expanding world picture.

The brain does not learn or remember as though it were a central library of information. Rather it learns through a variety of expanding maps.

I. ROSENFIELD

THE MAGIC OF THE WRITTEN WORD

At some point in our development—as early as age two and certainly by five—we realized that those black curvy lines on pages in books made up the stories we loved to hear. Once we learned to identify letters with sounds, whole new worlds opened up to us. The words read to us or that we began to read ourselves fired our imaginations with images that allowed us to step out of our daily world to be surrounded by ghosts and princes and monsters. In the next shift of understanding—learning to print those lines ourselves—we gained the power to put stubby crayon to paper to make our earliest storying efforts a little more permanent. Our story on the page became a silent testimonial of the patterns our mind liked to construct because they carried meaning for us. In the example below, six-year-old Sam, just beginning to untangle the mysteries of the alphabet focused on the sacred "NO," the most obvious "rool" and the easiest to spell. Implicit in this first attempt to construct a pattern is a much longer story, too complex for a six-year-old to be able to put into language, much less write down. By using a simple "no" followed by a verb, Sam means much more: No wearing shoes because they track in dirt. You can't be mean to others because it makes them feel bad. You can't call someone else names because it has no social merit. In our earliest attempts at making symbols on paper, we are reduced to the simplest of all patterns since we do not as yet have the fine motor skills or the knowledge to produce a more sophisticated version. What children know at this stage and what they can express in writing are radically different. What they feel and know about calling names or exploding bullets can only be captured in word-patterns as simple as the circle of the mother's eye. For Sam, writing "No" . . . and following it by what is taboo, is an amazing leap of expanding awareness, as is Reid's "nevr."

ROOLS BY SAM KINGSBURY, 6

NO wearing shoos.
NO being meen.
NO kolling nams.

Similar to Sam's pattern of NO is six-year-old Reid's "Nevr" pattern: Reid's story shows an embryonic awareness of cause and effect: never do *this* . . . because it will lead to *that*.

NEVER

Nver bit a bulet. Ther dangrris,
they can ixplod in your fas
and herrt you badle.

REID KINGSBURY, 6

The limited skills of a six-year-old's writing make the written expansion of "story" still difficult, but the elements of the story's plot are very much in evidence. Let me illustrate with another six-year-old's writing.

THE BUTTER FLY

Once a pona time there was a little butter fly. He saw a garden full of luvly flowors. Then it was night so the butter fly went to bed. The nexst morning was the first of May. So the little buttur fly went to the garden and saw that a little flowor was dead. So the little buttefly went to the onewer of the garden. But she sead oh so the oner went and watered her plants so the little flowor spowted up. The end.

By filling in the omitted details from the child's cues, the story might be rounded out something like this:

THE BUTTERFLY

Once a pona time there was a little butter fly. [As he was flying around in the world] he saw a garden full of luvly flowors. [He was so happy, he just flew around all day and settled on many of the flowers because he loved their bright colors, but] Then it was night so the butter fly went to bed. The nexst morning was the first of May [significant day—the writer's birthday] so the little buttur fly went to the garden and saw that a little flowor was dead. [He sat down and cried because he didn't want the pretty flowers to die. Then he had an idea for saving the flower.] So the little butter fly went to the onewer of the garden. [to tell her the flower was dead, and he began to cry] But she sead oh. [don't cry, I can do something that will make everything ok again] So the oner went and watered her plants [and as she did, the flower thirstily drank the water] and the little flowor spowted up. ['sprouted' up once more, and the butterfly was very happy]. The end

Three things characterize this six-year-old's story: a sense of both global happiness and global sadness, a recognizable closure, and not enough detail to fill obvious gaps. There is a kind of idiomatic logic into whose spaces the reader pours the missing details. Yet, this six-year-old has created a pattern in which the sense of the whole is more critical to her than the missing parts. And, as we read her story, we have little trouble gleaning the meaning of the story's pattern.

Directing Your Hand

Turn to your Writer's Notebook, date and number your entry. Look at Figure 3-2. It is a child's drawing of herself, including three things she liked about herself. Take a minute or so to play a little: Draw an image of yourself with your nondominant hand. This should put you in the mode of a child just learning to draw. Include in your drawing three things you like about yourself.

Move from drawing to clustering (ME/MYSELF/I) (with your dominant hand), then write quickly for two or three minutes in response to the drawing/cluster. Be curious to see how your vignette will turn out.

Figure 3-2

look look aren't I lovely—
I look Just as-
Beautiful as
God wan'ted
me to. My tite
are Just right
MY Brane Jwork
I like my face-
it is so pretty.

Figure 3-3

🔊 MY LOOKS

Look, look, aren't I lovely!
I look just as lovely as God
wan'ted [sic] me to.
My tits are just right
My brane [sic] works
I like my face
    it is so pretty

6-YEAR-OLD, RENO, NV

This young poet knew what was good about herself, and she didn't hesitate to tell it like it is—with shockingly adult language, to boot!

Directing Your Hand

In your Writer's Notebook, date and number a new page. Cluster the word (HIGH) and see what associations you come up with. As soon as you experience a sense of direction, write quickly for five or so minutes. Only when you've come full circle do you want to reread and make additions and subtractions.

After Writing

As you cluster your way through the activities in this book, you will be suprised again and again that any word or phrase, when filtered through your experiential sieve, will yield associations—and therefore thoughts and images. In this natural way, the writing will come.

OUR NEED TO CREATE MEANING

In the second grade, my daughter Simone already loved words. One day I found a piece of paper in her room, her handwriting on it almost indecipherable (Figure 3-4). Here's what was on the paper:

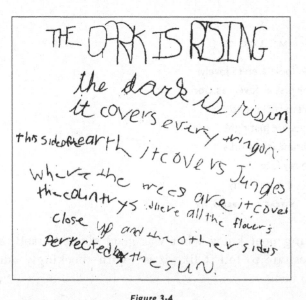

Figure 3-4

THE DARK IS RISING

The dark is rising.
It covers everything on this side of the earth
it covers jungles where the trees are
it covers the countrys [sic] where all the flowers close up
and the other side is pertected [sic] by the sun.

SIMONE RICO, AGE 7

I was puzzled. Yes, it was her leftie handwriting. Yet, I couldn't imagine how she could come up with such a title at her age; it didn't sound like something she would say. Later that day, I found a novel for adolescents, checked out by one of her older sisters, entitled *The Dark Is Rising*, by Susan Cooper. There it was! Mystery solved! Something about the phrase on that book cover had evoked images in Simone's mind that were so strong that she was emotionally nudged to express what this phrase meant to *her*, incorporating all she understood about the darkness of the world at that time in her little life. She needed to create meaning out of something that was both mysterious and intriguing: the phrase "the dark is rising." I suddenly remembered back to when my father used to listen to Schubert's Symphony #8, *Die Unvollendete*, "The Unfinished." In German the article *die* is feminine, so, in my five-year-old mind I imagined an incomplete, "unfinished" woman, in retrospect, the headless, armless Venus of Cyrene (Figure 3-5), which I had apparently seen in an art book on our shelves. So, for me, the music of Schubert always evoked the image of a woman without arms who could not reach out to hug or hold, a woman without a head who could not speak, a woman without a brain who could not think. I felt such childish sorrow when I heard the music, only I did not know why.

Years later, I understood that the word "unfinished," tied to the feminine article in the German of "that which is incomplete," evoked a sense of loss that I could never have put into words then. But, like Simone and the mysterious book title, I created meanings by connecting in my mind the word "unfinished," the way the Schubert music sounded, and the image of the headless, armless Venus. We create such patterns of meaning every day and later transcend them to incorporate new "bumps" of understanding. Thus, patterns of meaning are always subject to revision at another point in our lives.

Figure 3-5

Directing Your Hand

We are all moved to create meaning, to transcend our current patterns of understanding. A simple example: When we hear a particular song, we may associate it with a pivotal event from our past, and this memory or "story from the past" gives the song a heightened emotional charge. In your Writer's Notebook, number and date a new page. Cluster a short phrase from a song you heard in your childhood. Go with the image that phrase evokes—the one that has a visceral or emotional charge. It will lead you to what wants to be written. Give your vignette a title and write for four to five minutes. Only then go back and cut or add or correct.

After Writing

You probably noticed in your writing that a particular phrase and the image it evoked carried a distinct emotional meaning. Very often such an image marks something whose import can be verbalized only after considerable time has passed. Given words, the significance of this image is illuminated in a new way.

STAGES OF CREATIVE DEVELOPMENT

Art educator Harry Broudy classified three stages of creative development that have a remarkable correspondence with brain development (to be discussed in chapter 4): innocent, conventional, and cultivated.

The Innocent Eye, Ear, and Hand

Innocent creative expression lasts from about age two to age seven. In this stage, children have few preconceived notions about what the world *ought* to be like, about how they *should* feel, about what they *must* do by prescription. Every day is improvisational.

Writing in this stage is compressed and metaphoric and vivid—and largely unselfconscious. First-grader Jesús Alarcon does not worry about which of his two languages is more appropriate, so he improvises with both.

 MI CALLE

bright and shiny   straight and cracked
y clean sidewalks y picturas de animales
y people
trees beside the sidewalks
hills 7 mountains
and the most importante
is myself
great things around mi calle
street that leads to the city
tiendas y buildings
bonito gatitos around
mi calle

y casas y perros y barkingful wonder
buildings
and houses
roosters around mi casa   su casa
who
do you think I
am am am

JESUS ALARCON, FIRST-GRADER

Often, when children enter school, the intuitive learning strategies they bring with them are not useful in a setting where many children formally come together and order, conformity, and correctness are valued. One of my students wrote about how her initial enthusiasm for writing was squelched in the first grade:

I wrote my first short story when I was six. Miss Butterfield told us we could write anything we liked. I can still feel the surge of excitement and power I felt at her words. She sat at her desk in front, and we were allowed to go up one at a time to get help with difficult words. My mind fluttered with the glitter and glow of fairy tales, but my first word was "once" and I had to go up to my teacher to find out it didn't start with a "w." Writing was hard. The pencil was a slippery yellow pole in my hand, and the paper skidded on the surface of my desk. "Once there was a . . ." I couldn't spell "fairy." I got back in line and waited until Miss Butterfield could help me again. The classroom was full of labored breathing and the scratching of pencil on paper. I can no longer remember what my second sentence was going to be, but I remember the feel of its brilliance fading and finally dying as the bell rang and Miss Butterfield collected our stories.

MAUREEN SLADEN

Although we've learned a lot in the past forty years about putting ideas first, correctness second, it is something we have to remember again and again, because the fragility of the innocent stage is so easily swallowed up by the next stage: the conventional eye, ear, and hand.

The Conventional Eye, Ear, and Hand

From about ages eight through sixteen, our manual dexterity has strengthened through continually improving eye-hand coordination. There is considerable improvement in handwriting skills. We gain mastery over the mechanics of language. We also gradually eliminate the logical gaps in our stories—characteristic of our earlier stage of perception—as intense preoccupation with the whole vision gives way to preoccupation with correctness. As a result, our writing and oral storying become increasingly conventional and literal, with an accompanying loss of the spontaneity and originality that characterized our earlier efforts.

At this stage our vocabulary is firmly grounded. We use words everyone else uses. We have little need to invent metaphors to communicate. By now we know that a star is "a hot gaseous mass floating in space" in contrast to our innocent stage, when we noticed, "Look that star is like a flower without a stem!"

This is our reassuring stage; it feels good to have familiar labels to classify the world around us; it feels good to be grounded in a consensual reality (I know! As an eleven-year-old German stranger in a land whose language was Greek to me, it was painful not to be part of the "in-group" of language which my classmates drew on as naturally as breath. It felt awkward at best, humiliating at worst, to be a gangly eleven-year-old sitting in the tiny chairs of a second-grade classroom, feeling like Gulliver in the land of the Lilliputians, with *all* those other kids, four years younger, speaking fluently.) This stage finds the growing child aspiring to an exaggerated conformity. Our writing becomes more anxious, less spontaneous—and very generalized.

Although we learn to speak freely and naturally through listening and trial and error, when we learn to write we're constricted by rules, corrections, and often artificial—thus hard to follow—prescriptions having little to do with natural expressiveness. Imagine how children would fare if they had to learn to speak by a process equivalent to the way they are usually taught to write. Because our increasing store of words grounds us in the security of clear and unambiguous references. We happily learn to classify the world around us. We also begin to label our perceptions uniformly so that our language mimics that of our peers: "She's so cool." "He's so lame." At this stage, we become so conventional that many of our expressions are clichés and slang terms, dictated by the particular generation that spawns them.

Our writing tends to be insistently literal and riddled with overused and trite language or observation. Most of us at this stage slide into a negative attitude about writing; we write only when required: book reports, perfunctory thank-you notes, and tests, endless tests. Writing is now perceived as a chore, becoming tedious, anxiety-provoking, and pleasureless—thoroughly Sign mind. Our childish, free-wheeling expressive powers, grounded in a sense of wonder, and our own developing pattern-seeking skills, become mired in the ruts of convention.

The conventional stage is where many of us get stuck. Our creative potential narrows, and our trust in spontaneity begins to ebb into the river of the commonplace.

Moving into the state of the cultivated eye, ear, and hand can be achieved only by simultaneously transcending the stage of the conventional eye, ear, and hand and recapturing the stage of the innocent eye, ear, and hand to move into the next state: the cultivated eye, ear, and hand. "It takes a long time to grow young again," observed Pablo Picasso.

The Cultivated Eye, Ear, and Hand

In this stage, we consciously reintegrate the spontaneity of the innocent eye, ear, and hand and cultivate it for a mature expression of our creative impulses. Paradoxically, the very way to move beyond the conventional is not to try harder but to take a seeming step backward to re-cultivate wonder, improvisation, playfulness—and then to join it to our learning, experience, interests, values, skills, and willingness to grow.

In moving beyond the stage of the conventional, we can not only become creatively playful again but we can also learn to transcend the blocks to natural expressiveness. By developing the natural writing skills that are highlighted in the forthcoming chapters of this book, we can merge the intuitiveness of childhood with the insight of adulthood. What surfaces is a childhood act recontextualized into an adult viewpoint. The writing serves as a testament to transformation:

📼 TOY

> Somehow the thing was alive, walking, or a little miracle, flying. Next, the urge to aim at the feathery fluff took over. Then, the shiny wooden stock and blue trigger and tiny copper ball shocked a bird—a small one. The thud on the packed dirt echoed inside the blue enamel silo across the barnyard. Funny film over a dead bird's eye proves it was never alive. My brain's just a sparrow, too.

Toy triggered "beebee gun," leading to the memory of the thoughtless taking of a life. The "cultivated" transformation, coming in the writing of this vignette, lies in the adult insight "My brain's just a sparrow, too."

Directing Your Hand

Experience a return to the innocent eye, ear, and hand that characterized your early interaction with the world. Practice a few moments of *active quiescence* by closing your eyes, simply becoming aware of your breath as it moves in and out.

1. When you are ready, number and date a new page in your Writer's Notebook. Let the word TOY pass before your mind's eye, clustering as many of your childhood toys as will appear until a particular want says, "Here I am—write about me!" Circle the toy twice and cluster from it for details you might otherwise forget, letting associations flow, knowing that one will trigger the next; this is the nature of your Design mind.

2. Write quickly for no more than five minutes from the point of view of your adult self looking back. Begin your vignette with "I only wanted . . ." and stay in the past tense.

3. Only when finished, read what you have written, making any changes you wish, adding, subtracting, shaping.

4. Now number and date a new page for an about-face: Retell the same story, but this time write as if you *were* that child *in* that particular experience, in the present tense as though it were happening to you right this moment. How does this want in connection with the toy feel? Quote conversations if you wish. Go back to your cluster, but don't refer back to the first version. Write quickly for no more than five minutes.

5. When you have come full circle, reread what you have written and add and subtract until you are satisfied.

After Writing

Read both versions aloud and notice the differences: in intensity, in language, in attitude, in voice. The first version is likely to be one step removed from a feeling of direct emotional involvement; it is the adult looking back at how it felt. The second version probably feels more authentic. Re-entering your childhood imagination probably brought you closer to a sense of receptivity and innocence of vision than did the recollection from the adult's point of view.

You can play with multiple versions of a particular story from your life, thereby exploring the story's different dimensions. Your stories change shape as you tell them from the vantage point of a different period of your life. How you saw your father at six is not how you saw him at sixteen, or at twenty-six. Memory, like history, is in an ongoing state of revision.

Here is a present-tense re-telling by a woman who is a legend in her own time. What makes her particularly interesting in the context of this book is that she believed she didn't have writing skills.

One day the telephone rang. She told me that she was using *Writing the Natural Way* and asked if I could "tutor" her. "I can't," I said, but suggested she attend a one-day "Writing the Natural Way" workshop at UC Berkeley. There was a moment's hesitation: Then, "I'm not very suited to academic stuff," she said. I said, "Don't worry, it's all experimental, playful, improvisational; we build on what all human beings already know how to do." All I recall is her exclamation, "There would have to be a—a—death before I would miss it!" She came. She wrote. There was no fanfare. She tapped into a deep need for expression through writing, perhaps as a way of moving beyond a stuck place. Joan Baez is her name, and she has given me permission to feature a few of her pieces written in the last few years. Here she clustered "I remember . . ." from the first edition of WTNW. Written in the present tense, her memory reads as follows:

KINDERGARDEN

It's quiet out here except for the mockingbird, and some kids playing at the other end of the schoolyard, and the thumping of my heart. Sourgrass and miner's lettuc grow where I sit at the foot of the redwoods. After school the kids like to climb the huge oak trees and scare their parents to death. I do not climb. I am a coward who stays close to the ground.

I'm dressed in my overalls because the boys will pull my skirt up in kindergarden and the teachers will only say "Stand up for yourself" but I cannot, and they don't protect me for a minute. I think they should. They are so big. My mind wanders off. It's nice to be dreamy and sleepy where I squat here brushing away gnats and listening to the voices of the little kids on the jungle gym.

I feel sad for the she-she boy who's like a girl because everyone hates him and they push him. I'm the only one who'll play with him, and he isn't much fun. He's very white and sad and has pretty eyes. He is scared of the Saint Bernard who lives on the grounds, who is as big as a truck and always wants to play. Yesterday he came running toward us wagging his tail and I screamed and toppled over and rolled down the slope and wet my pants.

I love the older boys and want to feel their arms. I'm so little they won't even notice if I get near and reach out and touch them while they stand in the dirt on the big diamond trading things.

The shady patch where I'm sitting is damp and mossy with a few sun mottles.

Inside my heart thumps away and I gaze through my sleepy eyes at the long grasses and buttercups and weeds with the tiny orange flower and I know we are different and separate from everything, my heart and I, and being this way makes us very very tired. I'm sure there is another me with a thumping heart somewhere, lonely and leaning, just like this, against a tree.

JOAN BAEZ

The "cultivated" eye not only remembers but is also able to articulate the feelings of loneliness and "cowardice" and alienation associated with that memory.

A Last Word and Heading On

As we grow into adulthood we continuously move into the safety of the habitual, the known. Our writing can also become safer, more guarded, more joyless. To reach our cultivated potential, we need to learn the flexibility of creative thinking again and again and again. The primary way to achieve it is to draw, or paint, or sing, or write, or consciously engage in other creative acts. With writing, we need to re-involve ourselves with the richness of language that, once upon a time—when we were children—came to us naturally. Elements of the spontaneity and sense of wonder that permeate children's speech and writing are accessible to all of us. The strategies in this book will involve your Design mind so fully that writing will once more become a natural, expressive, and joyful experience.

Chapter 4 clarifies the unique workings of your Design mind and its cooperation with your Sign mind in natural writing.

FOUR

THE SELF-REFLECTIVE MIND: WORDS AND THE BRAIN

To this point we have been alluding only to the different functions of the left and right hemispheres of the brain in the creative process. Now we'll look in a little more detail at just why the right hemisphere is the fertile repository of the powers we wish to develop for natural writing and how both hemispheres must be brought into play at appropriate times for the best results.

Perhaps the best way to start is to see two powerful examples showing hemispheric specialization at work. The first is a true story told by psychologist Richard M. Jones, in *Fantasy and Feeling in Education.* (Jones was writing before the advances in brain research.)

Billy was a sixth-grader. His teacher, reviewing the previous day's math lesson, called on him to define infinity. Billy squirmed in his seat and said nothing.

"Come on, Billy, what's infinity?" his teacher insisted. He looked at the floor.

Exasperated, she commanded him again to answer, whereupon he mumbled, "Well, infinity is kinda like a box of Cream of Wheat."

"Billy, don't be silly," she snapped, and called on Johnny, who was eager to share his knowledge.

"Infinity is immeasurable, unbounded space, time, or quantity," he said. The teacher was pleased, since this was the only appropriate answer she could imagine.

Are we weaving a web that weaves us? The web of life and the web of imagination are intertwined as we create.

FRANK BARRON

Yet here's the rub: Billy had verbalized a complex right-brain image and made a nonliteral analogy. Literally, infinity is nothing like a box of Cream of Wheat, and the teacher, looking for a literal left-brain definition, understandably ignored his answer. But Billy knew something about infinity. Later, to a more sympathetic ear, he explained: "You see, on a box of Cream of Wheat there's a picture of a man holding a box of Cream of Wheat, which shows a picture of a man holding a box of Cream of Wheat—and it goes on and on like that forever and ever, even if you can't see it anymore. Isn't that what infinity is?" Billy had a rich right-brain understanding of infinity. The literal, left-brain definition fed back by his classmate Johnny meant so little to Billy that he could not reproduce it even though he had written it down the day before. Billy's and Johnny's different definitions are a striking example of two separate modes of processing the same information.

The second example is taken from *The Shattered Mind*, in which psychologist Howard Gardner of Harvard reports his exploration of the linguistic capabilities of Peter, a man with previously normal intelligence who had sustained severe right-brain damage. Left brain intact, Peter's use of language was nearly perfect despite the damage, with two qualifications: He could answer only questions that required the literal use of language, and his literal responses were spoken in a monotonic voice akin to a computer printout.

But when it came to evoking nonliteral responses, real difficulties became apparent. When Gardner asked Peter to interpret the proverb "Too many cooks spoil the broth," he was only able to answer, "Well, it means that if you have too many cooks cooking the soup, it'll spoil." Of normal intelligence and with our own right hemispheres intact, most of us will puzzle a bit and then suggest that the proverb could have something to do with raising a child, designing a building, training a dog, producing a work of art, or even writing a book! Proverbs are by nature nonliteral; they are meant to be interpreted, but Peter was unable to do this because understanding nonliteral language requires the participation of the right brain. Without it, we are left with only the denotative and literal. Interpretive meaning escapes us.

THE DISCOVERY OF CEREBRAL DUALITY

From the rich, albeit often contradictory, world of brain research over the past thirty years, two irrefutable facts have emerged: (1) the brain is dual (Figure 4-1), and each hemisphere is capable of operating independently of the other; (2) each hemisphere interprets the world through a different lens—that is, each of the two minds processes the same information differently. Using the specialized functions of both hemispheres in appropriate ways is

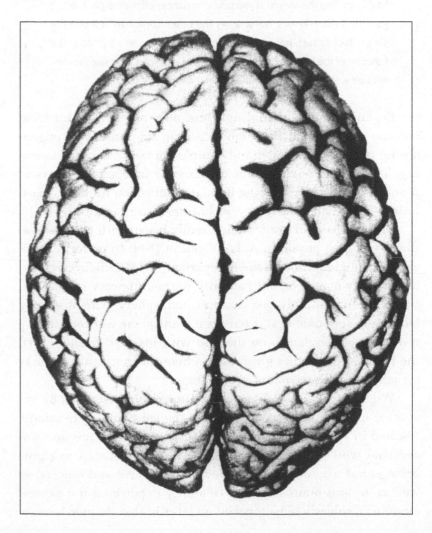

Figure 4-1

crucial to the creative act and especially to cultivating your inner writer.

In 1998, split-brain pioneer Joseph Bogen reasserted that the expansive research on hemispheric specialization yielded two fundamental lessons—and that these two facts hold today as they did thirty years ago:

> Lesson #1 is that everything is double: "Everything in the cerebrum, except for a couple of glands, is double. They're in duplicate. Is it in duplicate like the runners of a sleigh? Or is it in duplicate like a team of horses pulling the sleigh? If you take one runner off the sleigh, it won't go. But if you take one horse away the other horse can still pull the sleigh. Not as fast, not as far, but adequately. Lesson #2 is that "the function of the brain is double. Like a team of horses. Not like the runners on a sleigh" (in Judy Gilbert, *Expanding Our Vision*).

Bogen's metaphors highlight not only our two-brainedness but also the fact that they don't think in the same way, engendering two fundamental—and complementary—ways of knowing. The key here is that this capacity for independent ways of problem solving increases the human predilection for creative solutions in human endeavors—including writing naturally.

The discovery of brain duality really began with the observations of English physician A. L. Wigan in 1844. In performing an autopsy on a longtime friend and patient, Wigan discovered that his friend, whose behavior had been normal in every respect until his death, had only one cerebral hemisphere. This discovery led him to speculate that if only one hemisphere can constitute a mind—as clearly had been the case with his dead friend—then the fact that nature has given us two hemispheres means we may actually be in possession of two "minds."

Wigan's speculation was eclipsed for a hundred years by yet another medical discovery: Damage to the left hemisphere usually resulted in *aphasia*, an impairment of the power to use and understand words. Left-brain aphasia can be contrasted to right-brain *visual agnosia* (inability to recognize faces and objects) as well as to right-brain *aprodosia* (inability to perceive and express emotions), subjects to be touched on later in this chapter because

Of all the animals, we are the one least dictated to by genetics or by nature. We have the capacity to take part in our own design.
WILLARD GAYLIN

The mind is still dual, no question about it. We can be of "two minds."
JOSEPH BOGEN

they are crucial to understanding the ways in which the right brain participates in natural writing. Since an impairment of language functions represented an obvious and dramatic loss of human faculties, the unexamined assumption took hold that the left hemisphere was the "smart" hemisphere while the right was much like a spare tire—good only in emergencies and only until the "real" one was operative once more.

Such assumptions were challenged by the first epileptic "split-brain" patient. He was operated on by neurosurgeons Phillip Vogel and Joseph Bogen in Nobel Prize–winner Roger Sperry's lab at the California Institute of Technology. Vogel and Bogen, believing that epileptic seizures originated in one hemisphere and spread to the other via the connecting bundle of nerve fibers called the corpus callosum, hypothesized that if the connecting nerve cables would be cut, the "electrical storm" of epilepsy, with its uncontrollable convulsions, could be contained. Accordingly, they performed a "commissurotomy" by cutting through the 200 million nerve fibers of the corpus callosum (Figure 4-2). Their hypothesis proved correct: The electrical storm was contained, and the seizures, now confined to one hemisphere, could be treated and controlled.

The really fascinating findings began to appear as the patient was recovering from the surgery. Despite the cutting of some 200 million nerve fibers connecting one hemisphere to the other, at first glance the split-brain patient's behavior appeared to be quite normal. The disbelief and curiosity of the attending neurosurgeons led to the first of an extensive—and still ongoing—series of tests and experiments, which in turn confirmed Wigan's original speculation over a hundred fifty years ago: The human being has two minds in one head, and these two minds generate two independent streams of conscious awareness, each to some extent unaware of the other.

As experiments with these patients began to yield insight after insight, other researchers intensified the search with patients who had sustained damage in one or the other hemisphere. Still other researchers devised elaborate experiments with normal subjects, whose brain-wave patterns were measured during specially devised tasks to determine which hemisphere would show active

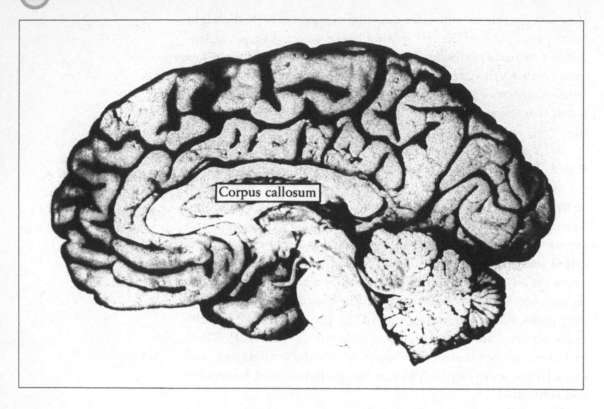

Corpus callosum

Figure 4-2

brain waves and which would maintain an idling rhythm. Out of this enormous body of published experimentation, a profile of the workings of each hemisphere emerged.

SIGN VERSUS DESIGN MIND: A COMPLEMENTARY DIVISION OF LABOR

What we are really interested in is how each hemisphere thinks, for we now know that each tends to process the world in radically different ways. As you can see from Figure 4-3, the most basic difference in how the two hemispheres see the world is that the left is specialized to process only one stimulus at a time, albeit at lightning speed, which leads to orderly sequences of thought and a focus on parts. The right brain, by contrast, can process a whole cluster of stimuli simultaneously, which leads to a grasp of complex wholes. This fundamentally different process largely accounts for the other differences delineated in Figure 4-3. The one-at-a-time processing of the left brain leads to the sequential, logical functions that produce linear thinking; they are also responsible for ordering language into syntactic units we can understand. Like a computer, the left brain's thought is rule-governed, drawing on pre-existing learned, fixed codes that were organized and stored very early in life. Like a computer, the left brain can recall complex motor sequences. In short, the left brain cultivates the repetitively predictable. And a good thing it does, because otherwise the world would forever appear to be unbearably unfamiliar and chaotic. We could not fall back on even the simplest of habitual sequences like starting a car. In writing, we could not rely on knowing the alphabet, hooking letters together to make words, correct spelling and grammar, or that words are signs having stable meanings.

However, as Figure 4-3 indicates, we have evolved two thinking apparatuses that not only dramatically increase our mental options but make creative acts possible. If the left brain governs learned sequences, the right brain takes charge of novel situations by searching for patterns. It can take in a whole face; it can connect parts of the world into fresh patterns of meaning by perceiving correspondences or resemblances; it can interpret the amoebic formlessness of intricate emotions and think in complex images (dreaming might be called clustering in images). Instead of the repetitively predictable, the right brain is superior at handling the unknown, the novel, the ambiguous, the paradoxical, the unconventional, attempting to make sense out of it all by discovering workable patterns. And a good thing it does, because with only the information-processing style of the left hemisphere our world would be rigidly classified, our actions would have unvarying sequences and consequences—and human beings would have great difficulty formulating boundary-breaking ideas.

In terms of writing, the act would be highly mechanical instead of organic. As Gertrude Stein said, "If we knew everything beforehand, all would be dictation, not creation." Words would tend not to move beyond their literal definitions, and thus we could not make word designs, metaphors, images, nor could we

Linear thinkers who persist in believing they live in a garden will find their carrots veering off to intersect the lettuce, while weeds and animals from the forest slip through the slackening fence wire. No one thing can safely be treated in isolation. Life in such a wilderness requires all the brain there is, not just the part that thrives on analytical division.

JOSEPH MEEKER

The brain has to be largely irregular. If not, you have epilepsy. This shows that irregularity, chaos, leads to complex systems. It's not a tall disorder. I would say that chaos is what makes life and intelligence possible. The brain has been selected to become so unstable that the smallest effect can lead to the formation of order.

ILYA PRIGOGINE

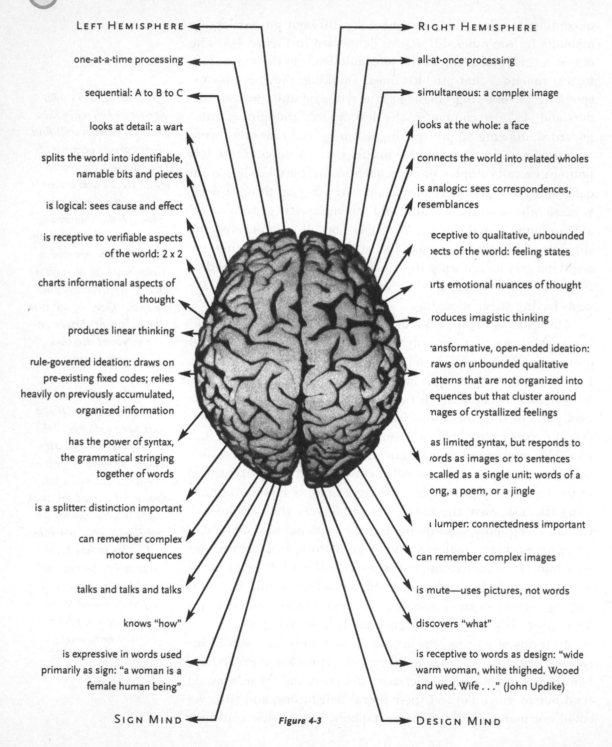

LEFT HEMISPHERE

one-at-a-time processing

sequential: A to B to C

looks at detail: a wart

splits the world into identifiable, namable bits and pieces

is logical: sees cause and effect

is receptive to verifiable aspects of the world: 2 x 2

charts informational aspects of thought

produces linear thinking

rule-governed ideation: draws on pre-existing fixed codes; relies heavily on previously accumulated, organized information

has the power of syntax, the grammatical stringing together of words

is a splitter: distinction important

can remember complex motor sequences

talks and talks and talks

knows "how"

is expressive in words used primarily as sign: "a woman is a female human being"

SIGN MIND

RIGHT HEMISPHERE

all-at-once processing

simultaneous: a complex image

looks at the whole: a face

connects the world into related wholes

is analogic: sees correspondences, resemblances

receptive to qualitative, unbounded aspects of the world: feeling states

charts emotional nuances of thought

produces imagistic thinking

transformative, open-ended ideation: draws on unbounded qualitative patterns that are not organized into sequences but that cluster around images of crystallized feelings

has limited syntax, but responds to words as images or to sentences recalled as a single unit: words of a song, a poem, or a jingle

a lumper: connectedness important

can remember complex images

is mute—uses pictures, not words

discovers "what"

is receptive to words as design: "wide warm woman, white thighed. Wooed and wed. Wife . . ." (John Updike)

DESIGN MIND

Figure 4-3

respond to the subtle shades of meaning and nuances that make language a living, dynamic, changing entity.

After reviewing an enormous body of research, two researchers—E. Goldberg and Louis Costa—proposed that these hemispheric differences exist because the two halves of the brain are "wired" differently. They say that the right hemisphere has a greater neuronal "interregional connectivity" and so can handle novel material better, whereas the left hemisphere, because of its sequential neuronal organization, has superior compact storage of well-routinized pre-existing codes. They suggest that the right hemisphere has a greater neuronal capacity to deal with informational complexity for which no learned program is readily available. By contrast, the left hemisphere relies heavily on previously accumulated, sequentially organized information. Thus the right hemisphere is specialized for the initial orientation of a task for which no preexisting routine is available. Once an appropriate system has been discovered, they say, the left hemisphere holds a leading role in its utilization. This research has much to tell us about the directionality of hemispheric involvement at different stages of the creative process or in any complex symbolic activity that moves from novel to known, such as natural writing.

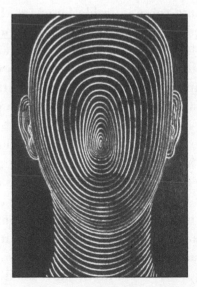

Figure 4-4

When the two halves of our brain exchange their disparate experiences, pool their viewpoints and approaches, the resulting synthesis brings to problem-solving a whole symphony of talents.

ALBERT ROTHENBERG,
The Emerging Goddess

This combinatory play seems to be the essential feature of productive thought before there is any connection with logical construction in words or other kinds of signs which can be communicated to others.... This play is, in my case, of visual and some of muscular type. Conventional words ... have to be sought for laboriously only in a secondary stage, when the mentioned associative play is sufficiently established and can be reproduced at will.

ALBERT EINSTEIN

Thus, in the human brain, the corpus callosum becomes a crucial channel of communication between two radically different thinking systems. When the specialized talents of each hemisphere are brought to bear on a given task, we can indeed make beautiful music.

ORCHESTRATING HEMISPHERIC COOPERATION

The corpus callosum connects the two brain hemispheres for two main purposes: It allows them to communicate with each other at the rate of thousands of impulses per second, but it can also inhibit this informational flow when it is more advantageous to focus the talents of one hemisphere alone on a given task. Such inhibition can be seen in examples from Einstein, who, from the age of fifteen on, engaged in what he called "thought experiments."

In one thought experiment, Einstein imagined what a light wave would look like if he were an observer riding along with it. In another, he imagined a man in a falling elevator and how that would "feel" and what would happen to his keys in his pocket. Einstein asserted that only when these images became so clear that they were voluntarily reproducible could he laboriously transform them into communicable language. Here we have a compelling example of callosal inhibition of logical "sign" information from the left brain so that the right brain can seek out, discover, and stabilize its images. (Clustering, as we saw in chapter 2, creates a similar inhibition of logical left-brain thought while the nonlinear associations of the patterning right brain are spilling forth.)

However, once images are voluntarily reproducible (or, in our case, associations are held fast in clusters), the corpus callosum shifts from *stop* to *go*, making right-brain images and patterns accessible to the left brain, which in turn can give them sequential, communicable form. At this stage we benefit from the left brain's systematic application of learned strategies, of its ability to create "signs" that can be communicated to others.

Conversely, if a task is familiar, thus coded and stored as a repetitively predictable skill, the corpus callosum may inhibit nonproductive "help" from the right brain, which would only interfere.

Here is the important point: The right brain, or Design mind, plays a critical role in the initial stages of doing something not already clearly laid out. It takes the lead in the learning of novel tasks. As skills necessary for the task are acquired and routinized, the Sign mind attains superiority. So, to engage in natural writing we move from the initial wondering, exploring, inquisitive, receptive, idea-generative Design-mind stage to the subsequent, organizing, sequential, syntactic Sign-mind stage. Both "minds" are complementary and necessary to the creative process. The only catch is the order: We explore the tenuous melody *before* we fiddle with the sequential notes precisely so that we won't tune out the larger melody in our one-by-one attention to the notes.

In effect, you cannot routinize or methodize Design-mind clustering any more than you can scramble the Sign-mind's logic of syntax. Each time you cluster, it begins in novelty, is open to surprise, discovery, new patterns. For these reasons natural writing—as do all creative acts—depends on the orchestration of both sides of the brain.

My left hand is my thinking hand (image), my right hand my doing hand (sequence).
BARBARA HEPWORTH, SCULPTOR

Free-floating RH knowledge is like a borrowed book, a snatch of melody heard in passing, a vague memory. If the felt idea—the stranger—is not given a name, it is lost to full consciousness. It goes to wisps and tatters like a half-remembered dream.
MARILYN FERGUSON

THE CHILD BRAIN'S UNFOLDING OF CEREBRAL LATERALIZATION

The corpus callosum—that bundle of 200 million nerve fibers connecting the brain's two hemispheres—exists at birth, but it is undeveloped. Our phenomenal ability to learn during infancy and early childhood may have something to do with the fact that the two brains do not as yet interfere with each other's mode of learning. Only gradually, over the first eleven years, does each of the corpus callosum's nerve fibers grow the fatty myelin sheath that enables it to conduct electrical impulses from one hemisphere to the other, resulting in the constant communication that occurs between the hemispheres in the fully developed brain.

Neurologist Jason W. Brown and psychologist Joseph Jaffe

have hypothesized that during infancy and before the acquisition of language, the right brain is dominant. Thus we are able to shape the unfamiliar, uncatalogued world around us into meaningful image patterns. Then, as language begins to be lateralized to the left brain, we begin to master the shared sign and symbol world of our culture. Overall, however, our perceptions still seem to be heavily guided by aesthetic influences. We see wholeness rather than parts and sequences; we fashion stories as unified wholes despite gaps in logic; we imagine "wild things" and fantasize playmates that are as real to us as our neighbor's dog.

In this stage of the innocent eye, ear, and hand, the critical censor of the left brain still does not have much clout, so to speak, and early efforts at writing are intensely natural aesthetic acts. We tell stories, first verbally, then written, with easy strokes, impulsively following our immediate and most intense interests. We create patterns of words that are meaningful to us and give us pleasure. We enjoy language naturally—its sounds, its rhythms, its picture qualities. This lasts for the first few years of life.

Young children are natural poets, until the left hemisphere takes over, between the ages of nine and twelve, correlating with the onset of puberty. By this time, the corpus callosum achieves full effectiveness as a conductor of information between hemispheres, and it has also begun to inhibit the transfer when the exclusive attention of one hemisphere is more appropriate to a given task. Language begins to be used largely informationally and thus becomes the specialty of the left brain. With our increased exposure to formal learning, the logical left brain is becoming dominant, with a continually expanding storehouse of words.

In school this left-brain bias is strengthened by the rewarding of left-brain skills and the general neglect of right-brain skills, as we saw in the story of Billy at the beginning of the chapter. The curriculum emphasizes parts-specific learning, and we are intensively exposed to and shaped by rule-governed left-brain thinking. This "conventional" stage of perception is both appropriate and necessary; our increasing vocabulary and command of language ground us in the security of clear and unambiguous references,

How to teach rigor while preserving imagination is an unsolved challenge to education.

R. W. GERARD, BIOLOGIST
The Biological Basis of the Imagination

How does one bring the child to his full analytic powers in a discipline while at the same time preserving in him a robust sense of the uses of intuitive thinking, both in intellectual activities and in daily life?

JEROME BRUNER,
The Relevance of Education

thus assuring us of a common framework for communication in the world.

Yet, given our left-brain education and the suppression of right-brain tendencies, many of us come to believe ourselves to be uncreative: We "can't" draw; we "hate" to write; we become inhibited in our body movements, in singing, and in other forms of creative expression. We begin to lose our spontaneity, our aesthetic sense, our trust in our natural abilities, our playfulness. And writing begins to be drummed into us as an unnatural, artificial act replete with contradictory rules, even requiring the formal breaking into parts of the language we had learned so effortlessly in our "innocent" stage. And so we stop writing.

A few of us come through this period with our ability to write, draw, and express ourselves naturally and creatively, intact. There may be two reasons for this: either such people have a very strong right-brain bias that continues to develop in spite of schooling (I believe Einstein was such a case), or they are recognized by teachers or parents and are encouraged in their creative endeavors. Many of us, however, feel stuck and creatively thwarted in this "conventional" stage of development.

From late adolescence on, the brain is fully lateralized for specialized functions, and in most cases the left hemisphere has become more dominant. The neglected Design mind, with its aesthetic predilection for wholeness, patterns, images, metaphors, its ability to reconcile logical opposites, and its receptivity to creative play and wonder, has lost its primacy. Regaining access to our Design mind and nurturing a conscious collaboration between the abilities of both hemispheres allow us to reach the cultivated stage of the eye, ear, and hand. Creative acts depend on the productive tension between right and left brain, our Design and Sign minds, which connects the rule-abiding with receptivity and play, literal language with metaphor, and the stability of form with the dynamics of process. The functions of the two hemispheres are complementary, and the foundation of creative activity lies in the collaboration between the two.

Let's focus specifically on the hemispheres and language.

My question is "When did other people give up the idea of being a poet?" You know, when we are kids we make up things, we write, and for me the puzzle is not that some people are still writing, the real question is why did the other people stop?
WILLIAM STAFFORD,
Writing the Australian Crawl

Human language [is] the epitome of flexible behavior.
STEVEN PINKER

LANGUAGE, IMAGE, AND THE HEMISPHERES

Images are not stored as facsimile pictures.... The brain does not file Polaroid pictures of people, objects, landscapes; nor does it store audiotapes of music and speech; it does not store films of scenes in our lives.... There are no permanently held pictures of anything, no microfiches or microfilms, no hard copies. Facsimile storage poses difficult problems of retrieval efficiency. Whenever we recall a given object, or face, or scene, we do not get an exact reproduction but rather an interpretation, a newly reconstructed version of the original. As our age and experience change, versions of the same thing evolve. Memory is essentially reconstructive.

ANTONIO DAMASIO

We've seen that natural writing depends on hemispheric cooperation, each side of the brain contributing its complementary capacities to the writing process at the appropriate times. Research shows that we are able to rely on the left hemisphere in writing, although the result lacks the evocative dimensions characteristic of natural writing. Predominantly left-brain writing is usually dull, often using inflated language, clichés, or jargon. It is stiff and lifeless because it lacks the Design mind's imagery, rhythm, wholeness, resonance, and other subtleties of which language is capable.

It was long assumed that, because it is largely mute, the Design mind has no language capability. However, researchers like Eran Zaidel of UCLA, whose main interest lies in exploring the linguistic capability of the right hemisphere, have shown that the Design mind has an "unexpected and unusual form of natural language"; natural because it is an inherent ability developed in infancy and early childhood in the Design mind, not one that is "learned" from the left brain. Linguistically, the Design mind responds to verbal units as whole patterns without the ability to divide and analyze them into their component parts. A unit might be a whole poem, lines of a song, a proverb, a phrase, or a word, depending on what the Design mind perceives as a *pattern of meaning*.

What the right brain cannot do well is string words together like the left brain does because it has a highly limited syntactical ability. For this reason, the right brain is not normally engaged in expressing itself in language, with a few exceptions first observed by the nineteenth-century neurosurgeon Hughlings Jackson in aphasic patients and experimentally demonstrated by Joseph Bogen, a pioneer in split-brain research. The exceptions proved to encompass emotionally charged units of language such as lines of a poem, songs, or proverbs—language that belongs to a rhythmic, imagined, semantic, or emotional whole where totality of meaning transcends grammatical components.

Zaidel calls his findings about the right brain's linguistic abilities "an unexpected and unusual form of natural language"—unexpected because brain researchers believed for so long that the right brain had at best only a token involvement in language; unusual because it is not governed by syntactic rules, as left-brain language is; natural because it is an inherent ability developed in infancy and early childhood in the right hemisphere, not one that is transferred and "learned" from the left. Herein lie many of the characteristics of natural writing, and here is our principal clue to the way the right brain helps to generate natural writing.

As we saw in Figure 4-3, the right brain, or Design mind, processes a face as a total unit, not just a small portion of it, such as hair on the chin, as the left brain does. Similarly, according to Zaidel, in the linguistic domain the right brain responds to verbal units as whole patterns without, however, having the ability to divide and analyze them into their component parts. A unit might be a whole poem, a stanza, a sentence, a phrase, or a word, depending on what the right brain perceives as a whole.

In sum, the Sign mind provides us with the solid stuff of language, including syntax, denotation, correct spelling; this language enables us to express ourselves literally, specifically, and verifiably. It deals with information that is routinized into repeatable codes. By contrast, the Design mind processes the ephemeral images we try to give language to, but it has limited syntactic skill. Patterns of meaning emerge *in a context.* So you see, our creative acts do not lie in one or the other hemisphere but in the *cooperation* of the specialized talents of both the Sign and Design minds.

Clearly, to great writers, philosophers, and pyschologists, such two-sidedness in the creative process is nothing new. Over the centuries, they have made distinctions between artistic/critical, unconscious/conscious, imagination/analysis, inspiration/perspiration, intuition/reason, restraint/passion, to name but a few. All, sometimes obliquely, sometimes directly, tie in with the findings of hemispheric specialization: and suddenly these findings underscore what creative people have "intuited" all along.

Writing teacher Dorothea Brande would have been astounded at how accurately her 1934 positing of two metaphoric "selves," which she called "the artist" and "the critic," reflects what we are discovering about the two halves of the brain today.

The thing that differentiates the human brain from the computer is the talent, or knack, or quirk, which the brain has established, of logical and also illogical relationships. Emotion, humor, fear, hate—all these come from unlikely juxtapositions of seemingly random bits in the storage banks, or the cauldron. The contents of the cauldron are not readily accessible to me until two or more random bits clot together in some associational relationship and float to the surface. Then I take these items out, a coagulation, and turn the lump this way and that until I see a pattern that may or may not become a story.

JOHN D. MACDONALD

In *Imagery and Verbal Processes*, creativity researcher Alan Paivio spoke of "interplay" between imaginal (Design mind) and verbal (Sign mind) processes.

Philosopher Susanne Langer foreshadowed hemispheric differences with extraordinary clarity when she spoke of a mind that is sensitive to forms, patterns, designs, wholes beyond mere (Sign-mind) "classification of things"—a reflection of right-brain processes.

From our current perspective, other binaries that help us understand the differences between Sign and Design processing are:

Left Hemisphere	Right Hemisphere
love of order	tolerance of chaos, ambiguity
need for routine	rage for novelty
single-minded	multi-minded
local	global
sequential	spatial
foreground—parts specific	background—holistic, allatonce, contextual, spatial
known steps	novel configuration
smaller story	the larger story
denotation	connotation
narrowing	widening
sequence	Gestalt
outsight	insight
Sign Mind	**Design Mind**

The most enviable writers are those who, quite often unanalytically and unconsciously, have realized that there are different facets to their nature and are able to live and work with now one, now another, in the ascendant.

DOROTHEA BRANDE,
On Becoming a Writer

Creativity, which is often considered the highest form of thinking, presumably involves an extraordinary degree of interplay of imaginal and verbal processes. Through its high memory capacity and freedom from sequential constraints, imagery contributes richness of content and flexibility in the processing of that content. . . . These imagistic attributes may underlie the intuitive leaps of imagination that often characterize creative thinking.

ALAN PAIVIO,
Imagery and Verbal Processes

Creativity, the Corpus Callosum, and Interhemispheric Transfer

Split-brain pioneer Joseph Bogen, in a 1998 paper, argues that interhemispheric exchange is the source of creativity. He shows that much productive thinking occurs that is not accessible to verbal output, that is, is not explainable. Such thinking often comes as a sudden insight. That insight, he suggests, takes place largely in the right hemisphere whereas later stages of creative acts depend on "greater than usual interhemispheric communication during an individual's more intuitive moments, an interaction dependent upon the corpus callosum."

The corpus callosum's central location and its large size have long made researchers suspect that it serves "the highest and most elaborate activities of the brain," that is, creative effort. Split-brain experiments of the past thirty years show it to play a significant role in transferring high-level information between the two hemisphers. According to Bogen, if "the fundamental finding from the split-brain is that the two cerebral hemispheres can function independently and simultaneously, in parallel," then "problem-finding and problem-solving, like learning, can proceed simultaneously, independently, and differently in each hemisphere" as well, giving us the ability to follow different trains of thought. Therefore, Bogen argues that the interaction of these dual memory codes, verbal and imaginal, dependent as it is on the corpus callosum, necessarily leaves interhemispheric exchange incomplete. Bogen hypothesizes that moments of creative insight (an Aha! or a dawning realization of pattern) is due to the momentary suspension of the separateness of the two brains.

Clustering and the Hemispheres

Since I specifically developed clustering as a way to gain access to the right brain, it becomes the first and most vital step in natural writing, and serves as the basis for this book, leading to— and used in—the other techniques, which also tap the rich

A mind that is very sensitive to forms as such and is aware of them beyond the common sense requirements for . . . classifications of things, is apt to use its images metaphorically, to exploit their possible significance for the conception of remote or intangible ideas.

SUSANNE LANGER,
Problems of Art

It is an approach whose medium of exchange seems to be the metaphor paid out by the left hand [right brain]. It is a way that grows happy hunches and "lucky" guesses, that is stirred into connective activity by the poet and the necromancer looking sideways rather than directly. Their hunches and intuitions generate a grammar of their own— searching out connections, suggesting similarities, weaving ideas loosely in a trial web.

JEROME BRUNER,
On Knowing:
Essays for the Left Hand

perceptions of the right brain. Accordingly, let me review clustering in view of what we have learned about our modes of thought.

1. Clustering forces the surrender of the left brain's step-by-step operation in favor of the right brain's seemingly random associations spilled nonlinearly onto paper.

2. In clustering, such left-brain characteristics of language as syntax, sequence, and cause/effect play little role. Thus words tend to shift from their customary role of *sign* toward *design*, from literal meaning toward complex and evocative images.

3. Through clustering, the right brain has the opportunity to generate the fresh perceptions and meaningful patterns peculiar to its special cognitive style.

4. Clustering generates right-brain involvement through an unimpeded flow of images, ideas, memories—all emotionally tinged—which lead to the vision of a tentative whole, enabling us to begin writing easily and coherently.

Writing Left, Writing Right

To help my students experience predominantly left-brain versus right-brain thought in writing, I often ask them to respond to proverbs—first from a Sign-mind perspective, then from a Design-mind perspective—through clustering. What characterizes Sign-mind writing is that it is logical and literal; it doesn't go beyond the dictionary meaning of the words. For example, here is a Sign-mind response to the proverb "Birds of a feather flock together":

> "Birds of a feather" refers to a number of birds of the same type, the same species or subspecies and "flock together" means staying together with their own kind—flying together, feeding together, living in the same trees, etc. So "Birds of a feather flock together" means that birds of the same type stick together.

What is of overriding importance in the matter of the brain's hemispheres is not the division between them but the unity—a synergy. The corpus callosum is a busy two-way bridge, not a Berlin wall. There is interchange and there is wholeness. The information on either side is equally important to the whole—like stereo speakers. Balance is *the key. Bring the percussion down so as not to drown out the strings.*

DENISE McCLUGGAGE,
The Centered Skier

In contrast, Design-mind writing tends to be metaphoric, re-flecting a complex image or a series of connected images. It goes beyond the literal meaning of the words. The following is one student's Design-mind response to the same proverb:

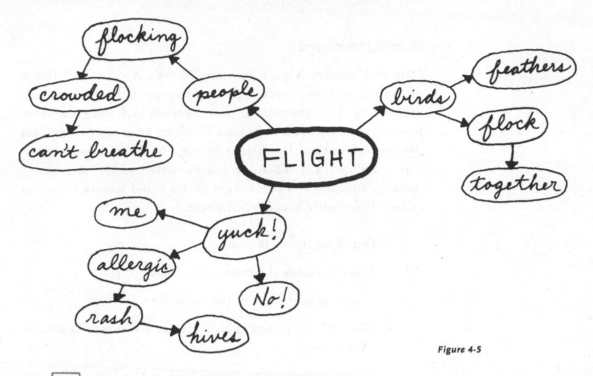

Figure 4-5

FLIGHT

When birds of a
     feather
flock around me, I
     break out in a rash.
Am I allergic to
     feathers?
Or am I allergic to
     flocking?

Proverbs are sometimes belittled as clichés, but proverbs last because they are sound bites that call up ideas and feelings we can easily verbalize or agree with. The writer Cervantes called proverbs "short sentences based on long experience." Shake-speare's plays are rich in proverbs or allusions to proverbs. The brevity of proverbs makes them stick in our mind—and they're perfect as a jumping-off point for experimenting with Sign-versus Design-mind writing.

Directing Your Hand

Date and number a page in your Writer's Notebook. Select a proverb from those below and write about its literal meaning very briefly. Turn the page in your notebook and, using the same proverb, cluster it for associations. Don't try to analyze or explain the proverb; rather, be curious to see what your Design mind wants to do with it. Then write a vignette quickly, improvisationally, knowing you can always go back and rework if you so choose. Remember to come full circle.

- Out of sight, out of mind.

- Absence makes the heart grow fonder.

- Beauty is in the eye of the beholder.

- We don't see things as *they* are, we see things as *we* are. (Anaïs Nin)

- What is grass to the lion is flesh to the horse. (Turkish proverb)

- The pebble in the brook secretly thinks itself a precious stone. (Japanese proverb)

After Writing

You probably noticed the precision with which you searched for words when you wrote the Sign-mind response. You most likely struggled to avoid simply rephrasing the proverb. Does your response offer any additional feelings or insights? Probably not, since the Sign mind doesn't concern itself with developing anything new.

Now consider your Design-mind response as you complete these sentence beginnings:

- I was surprised . . .

- I discovered . . .

- I wonder . . .

To reflect on your writing in this way helps spur your self-reflective mind, almost as if you are watching its patterns of thought. Chances are you focused on something that was not in your mind at all when you began clustering, so you may have experienced some surprise. You probably felt that your writing was out of character with what you normally produce; perhaps it came more easily, felt more coherent, more vivid, more detailed. As you compared your cluster and your subsequent writing you found that your cluster was somewhat of a self-organizing process—that is, you probably developed only one or two "arms" of the cluster rather than everything in it. Finally, you could not help but perceive the radical difference between your first literal effort and the vignette that grew out of gaining access to your Design mind.

As you write your way through this book, you will gain increasing confidence in the powers of your Design mind and the richness of the integrated creative experience. Learn once again to trust it, to be playful. The way to have one fresh idea is to have choices from among many.

A Last Word and Heading On

When Design and Sign minds work together—one making discoveries, the other giving shape to those discoveries—writing becomes a holistic, natural experience. Roger Sperry noted that an actual physiological harmony—resonance—occurs as the brain's diverse strengths work together. The reward for this cooperation is a psychological sense of wholeness. Our yearning for such wholeness can be satisfied through creative acts. Natural writing is such an act.

The brain is not something static and fixed that determines our behavior. Rather the brain is fluid, a constantly changing instrument of extreme subtlety. Each experience, action, or thought feeds itself back into the brain to modify synaptic connections and produce changes in neural networks. . . . The act of thinking changes the thinker. . . . Within consciousness there is an irreducible link between the thinker and the thought. Indeed the thinker is the thought; the thought gives birth to the thinker, which, in turn creates the thought anew. . . . Minds are the unfolding of thought. Meaning is crucial in determining the world. The unfolding of this meaning in time produces the whole gesture of the mind's dance. Within this gesture, brain and consciousness are sustained just as the fountain lives by virtue of the water that flows through it.

DAVID PEAT, PHYSICIST

FIVE

DISCOVERING DESIGN: THE TRIAL-WEB SHIFT

I n all creative acts the ancient tension between chaos and order is continuously renewed. The trial-web shift is your first awareness of a direction, an image, a thought, an idea, a vague sense of wholeness. It happens when the seemingly random associations of your clustering suddenly cohere.

Trial web: The term itself tells you much. A web is something formed by weaving or interweaving. The word suggests unity, coherence, connectedness. And complexity. The word trial (try-all) refers to an experimental act. A trial web is exploratory, not definitive. It is your Design mind's way of expressing its awareness of a tentative pattern, a whole. It is the secret of the qualitative that cannot be easily named.

This loosely floating vision of wholeness gives focus, impetus, meaning, and direction to your writing. Your Design mind produces it because of its pattern-seeking propensity. With a sense of pattern, meaning begins to emerge. We call this larger pattern context—literally, from the Latin "that which is braided together."

The global Design-mind vision gains solidity, form, and detail as you begin to write with your Sign-mind's sequencing skills. As your writing unfolds, the broad vista of the trial web is modified into a richly expanded whole. For example, for four years I was blocked in writing this book when it dawned on me, "Why not

We know more than we can tell.
MICHAEL POLANYI

From the first shock of the contemplation of a face depends the principal sensation which guides me constantly throughout the entire execution of a portrait.
HENRI MATISSE, Artist

use your own process?!" Sitting on the floor with a piece of butcher paper, I clustered around (NATURAL WRITING), spilling all associations that came into my head. The paper was full of circles and connections, and I felt a sudden shift when, in that welter, I saw at least four chapters, then six, then twelve. My momentum was so great that I re-clustered each potential chapter. That first trial-web shift had guided the discovery of the book's overall pattern.

The purpose of this chapter is to extend and deepen your understanding of clustering—the first nonlinear act of spilling and circling and connecting—through a feel for the trial-web shift, the moment when you become aware of the essence of what you want to write about. You probably already experienced this moment or "shift" when you stopped clustering and started writing the vignette in chapter 2. Now we're going to analyze in more detail what happens at that moment of transition.

THE TRIAL-WEB SHIFT: AN ILLUMINATED LANDSCAPE

The trial-web shift is movement from indeterminate form to focus. You are clustering, seemingly randomly, when suddenly you experience a sense of direction. The moment between randomness and sense of direction is the moment of shift. It occurs during any creative act. Composer Paul Hindemith described it as a flash of lightning illuminating a landscape; writer Joseph C. Pearce, as a unified instant of insight; sculptor Henry Moore, as a crystallization that determines form.

When you experience the trial-web shift it is unmistakable; it suddenly strikes you that you have *this* to write about. You suddenly perceive a direction to follow. An image or idea coheres and connects the seeming randomness of your clustering. You have already experienced this sensation in doing your first cluster; now we are simply defining it and bringing it to awareness so you can recognize and cultivate it.

I tell my students it is like looking through the eye of a camera at a total blur only to discover, as you turn the focusing mech-

> *We all know the impression of a heavy flash of lightning in the night. Within a second's time we see a broad landscape, not only in its general outlines but with every detail. Although we could never describe each single component of the picture [a Sign-mind task] . . . we experience a view, immensely comprehensive and at the same time immensely detailed, that we could never have under normal daylight conditions . . . if our senses and nerves were not strained by the extraordinary suddenness of the event. Compositions must be conceived in the same way.*
>
> PAUL HINDEMITH, COMPOSER

anism, a sudden broad vista or an expectant face or a grouping of clearly defined figures. Not only is this image focused, but it is *framed* to give you a sense that the objects you are focusing on somehow belong together. The trial-web shift is accompanied by sensations of pleasure/surprise/delight, as when you unexpectedly and gratefully recognize a familiar face in a crowd of strangers.

The trial-web shift is also inevitable, for your Design mind wants to make meaningful patterns out of whatever it encounters; thus you will, sooner or later, perceive a pattern in the seemingly random spilling of associations around a nucleus. That moment of recognition constitutes the shift to tentative trial web, and that awareness triggers the impulse to write. And you do write, usually with surprising effortlessness, since so many of your previous experiences with writing were an excruciating stop-and-go affair. The most persuasive evidence is for you to experience it directly.

Directing Your Hand

Find a quiet place. Turn to a new page in your Writer's Notebook. Breathe comfortably. Natural writing is not chore but joy.

1. Cluster the word (WEB) for a minute or two. Be receptive to everything that comes, not only words, but phrases, lines of song, snatches of poems, proverbs, book and movie titles, pieces of conversation—anything within your experience. Do not let your Sign mind interfere by censoring. I call this the phase of active quiescence.

2. As you cluster, allow yourself to enjoy this state of active quiescence by simply letting come what will without judgment. The trial-web shift will come without trying to force it. Just be open to it, be curious, and it will come.

3. The shift will happen in one of two ways. Most often, it will come as a sudden illumination of a connected complex of thoughts and feelings, but occasionally it is a gradual realization of a sense of a whole, accompanied by the urge to write. The trial-web shift is not a method; it is a phenomenon that cannot be standardized. A method

---

Only an instant is needed for insight to break through since it comes always as a single unit, not in some digital breakdown. Insight is always complete and perfect in its single instant's appearance, for it is wholeness, or a power, that can't be divided. It appears in all-or-nothing form.

JOSEPH C. PEARCE,
The Bond of Power

I sometimes begin a drawing with no preconceived problem to solve, with only the desire to use pencil on paper and make lines, tones, and shapes with no conscious aim; but as my mind takes in what is so produced, a point arrives where some idea crystallizes, and then a control and ordering begins to take place.

HENRY MOORE, SCULPTOR

can only be imposed from without; a trial-web shift always emerges from within—it is the response of your natural inner writer recognizing meaning.

4. Now simply follow the impulse to write your vignette. It will become a process of discovering and recording what you have recognized in that trial-web shift. Your Sign mind now has full access to your Design mind's trial vision. It is time to crystallize that vision. Try to stay within the ten-minute limitation for both writing and clustering, but don't leave your writing hanging. Fulfill your Design mind's need to bring your thought process full circle, but don't let your censoring Sign mind get the upper hand.

5. Now read aloud what you have written. Spend a minute or two making any changes you feel will enhance your vignette.

After Writing

Let's focus for a moment on your feelings throughout the process you just went through. Now that you've done it a few times, quite likely you've begun to feel a sense of letting go as you cluster, trusting your Design mind to come up with something that holds meaning for you. The trial-web shift probably occurred as a mild shock of recognition, a sudden awareness of tentative design, the discovery of a focus. With this delicious sense of direction, your writing came as a flow instead of a trickle, accompanied by a sense of satisfaction, perhaps even exhilaration.

If you felt somewhat neutral or even disappointed, don't conclude that clustering won't work for you. It works for *all* of us because we are all equipped with patterning right brains. It is true that some Sign minds will put up greater resistance to novelty than others. This resistance will disappear as you continue to practice, and soon you will experience flow. If you experience really strong resistance, however, try drawing circles around a nucleus and connect them with lines and arrows, as suggested in chapter 2. This doodling puts you into a state of relaxed

The turning point in the whole cycle of growing is the emergence of a focus or a theme. It is also the most mysterious and difficult kind of cognitive event to analyze. It is the moment when what was chaos is now seen as having a center of gravity. There is a shape where a moment ago there was none.
PETER ELBOW,
Writing Without Teachers

We must live within the ambiguity of partial freedom, partial power, and partial knowledge.
SHELDON KOPP

awareness. When your resistance ebbs as you begin to relax, you will begin filling those circles.

The stricter your education in composition, the longer it may take you to get past your anxiety. Just know that no one but you is evaluating or judging your efforts. Remind yourself that clustering is playful; let go enough to enjoy it. All my students eventually cluster effortlessly, with great interest in what discoveries they will make. Let me share with you a few of their reactions.

Although clustering is a phenomenon unique to each individual Design-mind consciousness, it demonstrates certain characteristics no matter who is doing it. Clustering relaxes your attention; this is like opening all the doors and windows on a summer night and then sitting in your favorite easy chair to let the night sounds pour in to your expectant ears. Relaxed attention—or active quiescence—leads to a receptive attitude, allowing you to accept anything that comes your way—words, phrases, lines of songs, anything within your experience. You can accept the randomness of clustering without feeling distressed, because you know a shift will come. Your Design mind can't help it.

And come it does. Students report the trial-web shift as a physically felt sense of unblocking often followed by a deep intake of breath, an opening up, a release of tension, a feeling that the writing simply wants to flow. They have also reported a sense of physical lightness or of timelessness, but most often they speak of feeling amazed that, in letting go and allowing *design* to happen, it actually happens! Poet Alastair Reid calls it "the moment when amazement ran through the senses like a flame," the moment of shift when the urge to write is overpowering. As Reid has written, "A word in that instant of realizing catches fire, ignites another, and soon, the page is ablaze with a wildfire of writing."

A Closer Look at an Elusive Process

The process of natural writing, then, occurs as follows: nucleus word leads to clustering, clustering to an internal pattern awareness, pattern awareness to the emotionally charged trial-web shift, trial-web shift to the impulse to write. Although the cluster itself is accessible to the senses and visible on paper, the process of pattern awareness occurs in your right hemisphere, inaccessible to your logical Sign mind, and the trial web you recognize is the designation we give to your Design mind's sudden emotionally tinged perception of pattern and meaning.

From trial web to writing is like a camera zooming in for a close-up. As you write, using relevant words and phrases from your cluster, the encompassing shape of the trial web crystallizes into sharpness, detail, and a more complex structure than was intially apparent—that is, through the writing the trial vision continues to evolve. It evolves because the Sign mind has come into play, creating a dynamic interplay between global and local focus: local detail shedding new light on global possibility, global vision generating new details. In this orchestration of talents lies the creative act.

Once you have experienced the trial-web shift, you have the answer to a paradox that has puzzled students of writing for centuries: How is it possible to structure the parts of a whole if the whole does not yet exist? The answer lies in the dual nature of the brain. The whole cannot exist in the Sign mind, which can only process parts, nor does it exist in the Design mind's shorthand cluster on the page. However, from that shorthand, as it expands into longhand, creative natural writing can happen. Creativity lies in the collaboration between pattern and syntax, between chaos and order. As one student explained clustering:

> To me, clustering is like blossoms on a branch. Each bud originates from its own main branch, sprouting and developing, yet always linked to its own source. The branch is constantly giving way to more and more blossoms, collecting them, linking them, and sending more stems out in new directions all the time. Individually, each bud can conjure up partial visual patterns in our mind, but when we see those buds clustered in bunches, we feel fulfilled, as if we had seen the whole picture.
>
> That's what clustering does for me. It groups together many ideas that sprout from one main one and, when I stop to reflect upon what has been developed from clustering, I see the whole picture emerge. It enables me to understand more fully what I had trouble arriving at in

Making a basket, or making a horseshoe, or giving anything form gives you a confidence in the universe . . . that it has form.
ROBERT FROST

the beginning, allowing the patterns and connections to spur me into a more rounded grasp of meaning.

Once you begin writing, you initiate a natural collaboration between the two halves of the brain. Your Design mind has created a tentative whole and has made it accessible to your Sign mind through clustering. Now the very act of setting the emerging parts down in sequence stimulates an ongoing interaction between your Sign and Design minds.

So you see that writing naturally and effortlessly begins with generating a trial-web vision. This sense of purpose, of knowing what you want to say, not only minimizes the anxiety so commonly associated with writing but also leads to a dynamic and absolutely essential collaboration between the two modes of thought.

Here is a cluster (Figure 5-1) around the nucleus (OPEN):

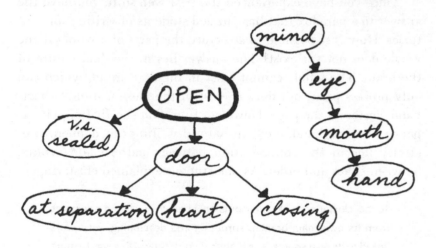

Figure 5-1

The cluster shows a reaching: Open leads to mind, to eye, to mouth, to hand. It jumps to "open—vs. sealed." The last new "grape" attached to the center is "door"—which quickly leads to "heart," to "closing," to "at separation." Notice the direction this writer takes:

I could seal my skin against you, I could close. I could close because everywhere, always, you are leaving me, leaving. You walk

away. The open door closes and I am outside, outside again. I forget
that I have a door, I am a door, fifteen bolts, I am shut tight against
your leaving and I want you to stay. We are so alike then, our doors
closing, our skin pulling apart, pretending we haven't touched. I am
open. I am closing. I want you to stay.

ANDREA SANDKE

Essentially, Andrea's Design mind shifted with the last two
strands of the cluster: "open/sealed" led to "opening/closing of
the door, the heart." She began to write in a rush of images,
quickly, rhythmically. Many of the words and images are about
closing off.

TRIAL WEBS FROM PICTURES: DOMINANT IMPRESSIONS

All visual art, no matter how vague, appeals to the Design mind's
predilection for wholeness. In looking at a work of art, while your
Sign mind focuses on specific details, your Design mind forms a
dominant impression of the whole.

Directing Your Hand

Number and date a new page in your Writer's Notebook, and
draw a circle in it, leaving the circle empty. Look at the drawing
by Walter Hilke (Figure 5-2). Be aware of your breathing as you
enter a state of active quiescence, or suspended alertness.

1. Just look. Don't judge until you experience a perceptible
   shift. Then, write in the circle whatever dominant impression surfaces. It will be your nucleus. You can think of
   the nucleus as a title, as a feeling, as a descriptor, as a
   metaphor, or whatever comes.

2. Should no dominant impression come to mind, ask,
   "How does this make me feel?" Don't strive for profun-
   dity. Let what will come come. Something always does.
   Be patient.

3. Cluster this impression as you continue to look at the drawing, until you experience a trial-web shift that gives you a sense of direction.

Figure 5-2 Walter Hilke, Celle, Germany

4. Write quickly and for no more than five minutes. Use anything that feels right from your cluster and ignore whatever doesn't fit your sense of the whole. Be sure to come full circle.

5. Read your vignette aloud and make whatever changes you wish.

After Writing

As you saw, responding to a work of art requires two shifts: first, the sudden recognition of a dominant impression, and second, the trial-web shift to a sense of pattern. In clustering, your associations are erratic, producing disequilibrium by pushing against your old boundaries. Thus, any small mind-leap becomes amplified, moving you to a new level of awareness that may lead you to an unexpected, unplanned pattern in the flux of thought. Whatever was triggered by this image was filtered through your past and present experiences and emotions. *You* created the meaning. Now, look again at the drawing. The artist explained that this image of a man and a woman was one of a series drawn in a time of great turmoil in his relationship with his wife. Can you "read" some of the signs of emotional turmoil in his drawing?

A Last Word and Heading On

In this chapter you have experienced the trial-web shift, the act that leads to discovery, pattern, and meaning in the diversity of spilled associations. When you don't begin in the fluid Design mind, which can accept the fullness of seemingly random images and feelings, you may get stuck in Sign-mind detail. You may worry about how to start and what to say, write fitfully, judge your work's rightness, and get bogged down in details of correctness that may block you from discovering a larger picture. The mind is not a straight thinker. A trial-web shift gives you a tentative design, something to put into sequence. It also gives you the heart to explore the creative landscape unfolding before you.

In chapter 6 we will explore a stunning new process, that of Re-Creations, which has helped me understand scientist Michael Polanyi's dictum, "We know more than we can tell."

To know and feel all this and not have the words to express it makes a human a grave of his own thoughts.

JOHN DONNE

SIX

THE ZEN OF IMPROVISING: RE-CREATIONS

Improvisation, writing, painting, invention—all creative acts are forms of play, the starting place is creativity in the human growth cycle, and one of the great primal life functions.

STEPHEN NACHMANOVITCH

If you search into the question of knowledge, you will find the only things you can be said truly to understand are those you have made yourself.

GIAMBATTISTA VICO

Zen, a Buddhist movement introduced into China in the sixth century and into Japan in the twelfth century, is broadly defined as enlightenment by the most direct means. What does writing have to do with Zen? In improvising you don't try too hard. When you improvise you are necessarily in a Zen state. But it's easy to tell someone to improvise, difficult to do so on command. You need a jumping-off point, a way of getting into it. In experimenting with ways to enable students to write immediately and easily, I discovered a stunning evocative process about seven years ago. I call this process Re-Creation. It is a vehicle that taps you into the Zenlike power of improvisation.

"In order to get your creative juices flowing," I told my students, "you can use a created piece by someone else as a jumping-off point and re-create it (from *creare*, to make, to do plus *re* = again, thus, "to make or do again"). Listen to it being read [▶], cluster as many words or phrases without effort or deliberation, then re-create it in two and a half minutes *in any way you wish*, on the spur of the moment. No pressure to do it a certain way. Improvisation is composing without previous preparation, from whatever is readily available, from *im* equals not, plus *proviso* equals L to see beforehand, not to prepare ahead of time."

Unpremeditated, unrehearsed, improvisation engages the Design mind first; it triggers the impulse to go for pattern first instead of detail. It doesn't wait for a given order, it focuses on the total impression.

The trigger for your improvisation can be a poem, a passage from a novel, an excerpt of nonfiction, a fragment of conversation, whatever can be read aloud, whatever can be listened to, is potential inspiration for Re-Creation. Let me give you one of my earliest examples. I read the original poem by Lorna Dee Cervantes twice to high school students. During the first reading, I simply asked them to listen and enjoy. During the second, I asked them to cluster around a blank circle any words or phrases without making any effort to plan or follow a sequence. After the second reading, I said, "Now give this blank center a name; it can be the title, it can be a feeling, it can be an image. Don't stop to think about it. Then write for two and a half minutes, using—or not using—what you jotted down."

I read the poem by Lorna Dee Cervantes once, asking them to enjoy, then a second time, reminding them to cluster inversely, that is, around a blank circle.

While I am working I am not conscious of what I am putting on the canvas. Each time I undertake to paint a picture I have a sensation of leaping into space. I never know whether I shall fall on my feet. It is only later that I begin to estimate more exactly the effect of my work.

PICASSO (in Zervos)

REFUGEE SHIP

Like wet cornstarch, I slide
past my grandmother's eyes. Bible
at her side, she removes her glasses.
The pudding thickens.
Mama raised me without language,

I'm orphaned from my Spanish name.
The words are foreign, stumbling
on my tongue. I see in the mirror
My reflection: bronzed skin, black hair.

I feel I am a captive
aboard the refugee ship.
The ship that will never dock
El barco que nunca atraca.

LORNA DEE CERVANTES

I was nervous, thinking I had asked for too much, but the room was silent with concentration. One by one pencils and pens were laid down. We all sat for a moment. When I asked for volunteers to read, several students raised their hands. They read their 2½-minute improvisations. We listened. None of us could believe what was produced.

Here are four samples of that first day:

Re-Creation #1

LOST

Sliding out of control
into the thick pudding of chaos
my mind is bungled with words
the sounds are foreign to me.
What I don't understand,
I cannot see
The ship disappears into the horizon
orange golden flashes of light spark,
my reflection appears in the water
alone, my reflection appears.
I am lost.

Re-Creation #2

ORPHAN

Remembering the corn starch smell of my grandmother's fingers as she turned phrases and pages in her Bible, I suddenly know I have been orphaned since her death. No family tree to say "you have your mother's black hair," or "your father's skin would bronze like yours—a strong summer statue." Adios, Abuela. Adios, mi familia. I slide through heavy waving water like an abandoned, sinking ship.

Re-Creation #3

TRUTH

Sliding ever downward,
I clutch at the Bible,
but the pudding of my doubts thickens
in my mouth and heart,
riding on a ship that will never dock,
except in the harbor of my own design,
the Bible's saturated pages
floating to the surface,
my skin bronzed by the sunshine of truth,
all my illusions orphaned and cast aside.

Re-Creation #4

MIRROR

The "refugee ship" reminds me of the girl I see in the mirror every day. She feels left out of the culture she grew up in. In the Hispanic culture there is big pressure from the family to retain your culture. Maybe the poet is a refugee because she forgot all her tradition. Now she just sees the Hispanic in her appearance but not in her head.

VISUAL RE-CREATIONS:
THE GERMAN EXPERIMENT

I knew I was on to something when I came across an article describing a process with visual art that was analogous to what I was asking my students to do with words. This German museum's experiment involved children in actively seeing (rather than passively looking at) and then painting—*from memory*—a work they really liked.

Children from ages four to fourteen, visiting the Kunstinstitut in Frankfurt, were asked to select their favorite painting and then to paint or draw it—*from memory*. The museum was experimenting to see whether there would be a shift in the quality of children's attention from passive to active. The children didn't have to be asked twice. Once seated before easels in the basement of the museum, they re-created their choice eagerly and unselfconsciously. They painted with fervor—and what they drew were the qualitative aspects of the original piece upstairs: a feeling, a special angle, or some ineffable quality that they zeroed in on with intuitive certainty.

For example, Tischbein's *Goethe* (Figure 6-1) was painted by five-year-old Marc (Figure 6-2). In little Marc's Re-Creation, the great poet reclines "hang-loose" in the landscape.

Expression is not an appendix to knowing but an integral part of the process by which something becomes knowing.

CHARLES M. JOHNSTON, M.D.

Pictures are never finished in the sense that they suddenly become ready to be signed and framed. They usually come to a halt when the time is ripe, because something happens which breaks the continuity of their development.

PENROSE, 1958

Figure 6-1

Figure 6-2

Five-year-old Sara re-created Lovis Corinth's Carmencita (Figure 6-3), expressing the qualities of redness/blackness, whiteness in a lushly red-lipped snowman (Figure 6-4). Sara seemed enchanted with the colors of the original painting, and in the haughty stare and white chest she saw ice.

Figure 6-3

Figure 6-4

We find the constantly paradoxical nature of creativity ... [here]: as they internalize the work of others ... creative persons are also developing their individual view of the world.

FRANK BARRON, CREATIVITY EXPERT

To sum up the lessons we can draw from this experiment:

- We bring the Design mind's natural patterning propensity to the created artifact, a painting, for example. The re-creator filters that image through her own experiential sieve and generates only what is meaningful to her at the moment.

- The artists or writers do not copy; they do not imitate but generate, in the absence of the model, a free Re-Creation.

- A Re-Creation means just that: to make again. There is no such thing as a "correct" way to do it; there is no judgment of "better" or "worse."

INVERSE CLUSTERING: ACTIVE QUIESCENCE

I have already described my first experiment. With the second class, I said, "We're going to do an improvised writing activity in a very brief amount of time. Listen to my reading of a poem with *active quiescence*, simply listen, be receptive, enjoy. Then I'll read it again. As I read, on a new page, dated and numbered, cluster *around* a blank circle. Catch any words or phrases from the poem that evoke images, or feelings, or trigger a memory. When I stop, give your center a *name* (the actual title, a dominat impression, a feeling, your own title). Now write your Re-Creation quickly. To keep you improvisational, write only for two and a half minutes; glance up at the cluster if you get stuck." I reminded them that they could re-create what they had heard in any form they wished, move in any direction the flow of the writing took them, that there was no "right" or "wrong" way to re-create. "Just hear its echoes. You don't tell *it. It* will tell you." They looked at each other as if I had asked them to swallow a spider, arguing with me that they wouldn't know what to say, wouldn't know what the poem meant, didn't understand poetry. I said, "Just watch."

This time, I collected the students' Re-Creations, and as soon as I reached my office, I scanned them—stunned at the quality of writing produced in less than three minutes. All the students had written; all had re-created a pattern of meaning; all had shown an astounding grasp of the essence of the poet's nuances, and this was a poem they had only heard twice and had never seen in print. Each Re-Creation took its own shape; each reflected one nuance of the poem; each retained a strong connection to the original. I typed six Re-Creations onto a single page, along with the original. At the next class meeting we read them aloud. Students were as astonished—and delighted—as I was.

In time, my students and I came to see Re-Creations as a dynamic improvisational interplay of an existing poem and the listener's experiential sieve through which it was filtered. We realized that Re-Creations are a way of tolerating ambiguity, paradox, and partial knowledge. My students understood that they would finish writing before they had time to worry about right or wrong, good

In quickness is truth. The faster you blurt, the more swiftly you write, the more honest you are. In hesitation is thought. In delay comes the effort for a style, instead of leaping upon truth which is the ONLY style worth tiger-trapping.

RAY BRADBURY

The arts of improvisation involve recombining partly familiar materials in new ways, often in ways especially sensitive to context, interaction, and response. . . . Improvisation can be either a last resort or an established way of evoking creativity. Sometimes a pattern chosen by default can become a path of preference.

M. C. BATESON

or bad, profound or superficial. They felt creative, as though their bodies had lifted to fly.

Here is a poem, the original, followed by the stunning Re-Creations of college students, written from a cluster without deliberation, that is, improvisationally, in less than three minutes.

THE DEATH OF MARILYN MONROE

The ambulance men touched her cold
body, lifted it, heavy as iron,
onto the stretcher, tried to close the
mouth, closed the eyes, tied the
arms to the sides, moved a caught
strand of hair, as if it mattered,
saw the shape of her breasts, flattened by
gravity, under the sheet,
carried her, as if it were she,
down the steps.

These men were never the same.
They went out
afterwards, as they always did,
for a drink or two, but they could not meet
each others' eyes.

    Their lives took
a turn. One had nightmares, strange
pains, impotence, depression. One did not
like his work, his wife looked
different, his kids. Even death
seemed different to him—a place where she
would be waiting,
and one found himself standing at night
in the doorway to a room of sleep, listening to
a woman breathing, just an ordinary
woman
breathing.

SHARON OLDS

Here are the Re-Creations of three participants in a workshop who clustered, then wrote in less than three minutes:

Re-Creation #1

UNTITLED

Was it the love of Marilyn or the love of
    Everyman
that turned men to drink
when they faced the ancient, heavy iron fist of
    death,
when the eyes of their wives gave them
    nightmares,
when flat breasts spoke to them of not
    breathing
rather than sex?
If Monroe could die, so could they.
All it is, is steps.

Re-Creation #2

THE DEATH OF MARILYN MONROE

A room where she would be
waiting,
a woman breathing.
Pulled there,
a woman breathing,
as if anything, even death, mattered,
a body gone to stone,
not breathing,
a caught hair
still breathing
as if it were she.
An ordinary woman,
a woman
breathing.

Re-Creation #3

M M

Those ambulance men,
used to it all,
shocked into recognition of death
and tenuous life,
shifted the body,
prepared her for the journey.
The body wasn't going anywhere
    special.
They were:
One to nightmares, strangeness,
another to dislike, to fear.
The last to listening.

I recall that someone in the UCLA workshop, as these Re-Creations were read, blurted, "We're all poets!" Indeed, it felt that way. Over time, I experimented with this breathtaking process. The more eloquent the language of the students, the bolder I became. It seemed there was nothing students could not re-create with immediacy and articulateness. The more involved they became in listening, the more improvisationally their own patterns evolved, yielding an immediate grasp of qualitative form.

I believe Re-Creations are a vibrant indicator of how the Design mind, with its attention to the whole, its ability to apprehend meaning with only partial knowledge, its ability to process the compression of the poetic, can step in to generate its own pattern in a fraction of the time it takes the logical brain to churn something out.

Wherever you are is
the entry-point.
KABIR

Directing Your Hand

A Re-Creation involves an immediate, brief, intuitive written response to any heard text. A created pattern that is already there ignites your spontaneity. The written piece already created allows us to have a place to jump off from.

1. Listen once to the poem entitled "Reflection on the Vietnam War Memorial."

2. Place your name, the date, and a blank circle on a new page in your Writer's Notebook. You are going to *inverse cluster*, that is, leave the center blank.

3. Listen to the poem a second time and, as you do so, jot down any and all words or phrases without worrying which are "right" and which are "wrong."

4. As soon as you've heard the poem a second time, give your cluster a name. It can be a dominant feeling, a dominant impression, the title of the original poem, an attitude.

5. Now write rapidly for two and a half minutes, using as much or as little from the cluster as feels right.

Original Poem

REFLECTION ON THE VIETNAM WAR MEMORIAL

Here it is, the back porch of the dead.
You can see them milling around in there,
    screened in by their own names,
    looking at us in the same
vague and serious way we look at them.

An underground house, a roof of grass—
one version of the underworld. It's all
    we know of death, a world
    like our own (but darker, blurred)
inhabited by beings like ourselves.

The location of the name you're looking for
can be looked up in a book whose resemblance
    to a phone book seems to claim
    some contact can be made
through the simple act of finding a name.

As we touch the name the stone absorbs our grief.
It takes us in—we see ourselves inside it.
    And yet we feel it as a wall
    and realize the dead are all
just names now, the separation final.

JEFFREY HARRISON

After Writing

Only after you come full circle do you want to go back, read what
you've written, and make whatever changes you wish. Before going on, jot down a response to the following sentences:

I discovered . . .

I was surprised . . .

I wonder . . .

A Re-Creation seems to be a bridge between visual/verbal, auditory/written, receptive/expressive, whole/part, qualitative/quantitative, implicit/explicit, in short, between Sign and Design modes of knowing. It has little to do with "what shall I write?" but much to do with what wants to be written. The little time allowed to write is so absurdly brief that the Sign mind shakes its head and allows the unfolding pattern to find you!

NUANCE

Nuance is qualitative. Nuances circulate in an ongoing fashion, from the emotional and perceptual centers of our brains. In becoming receptive to the whole of a poem, we become aware of subtle and delicate levels of meaning, branching out to create new connections. In fact, nuance illuminates the relational, the connectedness between image, feeling, and the Design mind's ability to make metaphoric leaps.

Here is what I think happens during a Re-Creation: The heard poem is filtered through *your* experiential sieve. Attention goes to the whole, to the qualitative, the metaphoric, the connotative, in short, the nuanced. The Design mind reads between the lines, synthesizes, processes the poem as a whole. It infers the whole from a few features about how things are interconnected, interrelated—even with scant information. So, the creation of *meaning* is the synthesizing of configuration. The Design mind has the ability to fill in the blanks.

THE POWER OF RE-CREATIONS

Beginning with a blank circle, inverse clustering makes you particularly sensitive to nuances of the created pattern you are hearing. Before you give it a name, the pattern begins to resonate with your consciousness, and your unique experiential sieve begins to discover its own focus—which can be a feeling, a dominant impression, the title of the poem you are hearing, or your own title. It all depends on the nuances you discern.

Inverse clustering lets you find the focus after your Design mind has had a chance to make a tenuous pattern of words, then lets you give that focus a name.

Patterns of nuance in the heard words—nuances of sound, feeling, image, idea, patterns—all resonate in the listener's mind as a totality, enabling him to write swiftly about knowings that are not logically and analytically derived but *simply understood.* The nuances of the poem are picked up and amplified into a personal expression. The Re-Creation is not a paraphrase; it is not a copy; it is not plagiarized; nor is it imitation. A Re-Creation is its own configuration. When you re-create, you move into the domain of pattern, of nuance. You let it carry you. You do not carry it. The original trigger, like the nucleus word of clustering, flits around in your mind like most dreams after we have awakened. What emerges is *your* piece.

I have often asked my students to articulate what they saw happening in their own heads as they re-created. Their responses have been illuminating:

- "Images flow in and out of consciousness. Some stand out for me, and those are the ones I jot down. When one of these coheres with the outside world as well as within me, the hair on the back of my neck stands up."

- "When I re-create, I let go, and memory, mood, and experiences flood my expression. Flow sets in. I am the vehicle. The voice is mine."

- "What jumps at me initially from the 'heard poem' are the words I love, then pictures in a physical sense that stimulate me to generate my own pattern."

- "Re-Creations come through my ears and leave through my heart, as they are internalized and personalized—and given my expression."

But I think there is more. Visual artists have always built on what other artists have done before them, just as they have used nature as inspiration, and just as they have used their own earlier

Expression is not an appendix to knowing but an integral part by which something becomes knowing.
CHARLES M. JOHNSON

The early stages of any creative product are not accompanied by certainty. Passion maybe, compulsion maybe, momentary visions of enticing clarity maybe, but certainty—that we have come to the right forest and are following the right track—rarely.
STEPHEN M. NACHMANOVITCH

Experiencing the works of others is like experiencing nature.
WASSILY KANDINSKY

work as launching pads for inspiration and variation. For example, look at the "Venus Callipyge" (Figures 6-5 and 6-6) and Picasso's cubistic experiment, rendering back and front simultaneously in "La Puce" 1942 (Figure 6-7). Look at Modigliani's famous fascination (Figure 6-8) with the stylization of African sculpture (Figure 6-9).

I believe Re-Creations are an indicator of the receptive, qualitative gifts of the Design mind that remain largely untapped in formal schooling, gifts we can utilize if we have tools to tap them, much as a match and flint became a tool to strike fire instead of having to wait for lightning to strike.

The process of Re-Creation seems to activate the mind's synthesizing ability in detecting and generating patterns of meaning. It invites you to improvise and make metaphoric leaps.

Natural writing depends heavily on the ability to improvise before you organize.

A LAST WORD AND HEADING ON

Any piece of writing in this book—or any short passage you come across in a newspaper, magazine, or book—can serve as the trigger for a Re-Creation. You can use a poem, or a passage you like from a novel, a short story, or an essay. Or, as you are watching a film, any dialogue you become aware of as a self-contained vignette can be re-created from memory—and will reveal your own unique voice.

Re-Creation is the harmonizing of the desire for certainty and the desire for risk. The process of Re-Creation, tapping as it does into Design-mind nonlinearity and nuance, short-circuits the conventional and allows us all to participate in the creative act with an immediacy that is exhilarating.

Chapter 7 introduces another important tool we can use in the process of writing naturally: recurrences. They help us to unify a vignette into a harmonious whole.

No one could possibly draw this scene of young oaks and maples, interspersed with alders and other shrubs, as it actually appears. All that can be done is to take the existing material and discard nine-tenths of it.

FRANK RINES

Knowing anything in its deepest sense means knowing how to be creative with it.

ELLIOT EISNER

What does it mean to be released into language? Not simply learning the jargons of the expected but learning that language can be used as a means of changing reality. What interests me in teaching is less the emergence of the occasional genius than the discovery of language by those who did not have it.

A. RICH

Figure 6-5

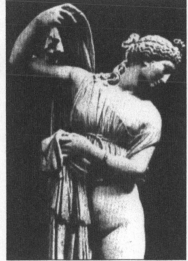

Figure 6-6

Figure 6-7

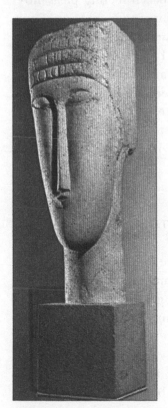

Figure 6-8

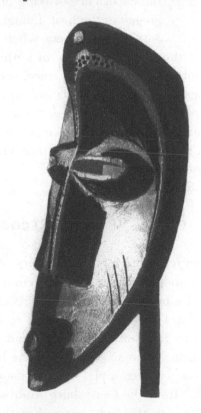

Figure 6-9

SEVEN

RECURRENCES: THE UNIFYING THREAD

For constructing any work of art you need some principle of repetition or recurrence; that's what gives you rhythm in music and pattern in painting.

NORTHROP FRYE,
The Educated Imagination

R ecurrence is a natural phenomenon. We have all had the experience of lying on a beach feeling pleasantly groggy in the heat, thoughts slipping in and out of our conscious awareness, when a sudden, inexplicable shift in attention makes us aware of nothing but the sound of waves: forward rush, momentary silence, backward sucking sound, coming again and again, not as isolated phenomena, which is how they reached our ears before, but as pattern. And we experience pleasure. Yet that pleasure comes not because the waves all sound alike, but because there is pattern, and within that pattern there is variation, irregularity.

PATTERN RECOGNITION

Pattern recognition is the province of the Design mind. In writing naturally, recurring words, sounds, images, and feelings have the same powerful effect that a recurring melody has in music, recurring foliage in a landscape, recurring colors in a painting: We react to them emotionally, and they intensify the unity of the whole. In language, we are more likely to remember recurring patterns—for example, "of the people, by the people, for the people" from the Gettysburg Address—because of their powerful effect on the right brain. For this reason, much persuasive writing, and especially speeches, contains recurrences, as do poetry and other writings with a strong emotional content. Learning to use recurrences—the *meaningful* repetition of words, images, ideas, phrases, sounds, objects, or actions throughout a piece of writing to unify and empower it—constitutes the third basic step in achieving natural writing. Beyond the cluster and the trial web, recurrence is one of the simplest and most natural reflections of your Design mind's love of making patterns, of seeing wholes rather than discrete bits and pieces.

Look at the archetypal pattern generated in Robin Nelson's poem, "Tides." Even the title tips us off to something that surges and recedes, surges and recedes, surges and recedes: recurrence. What makes this vignette really work is that this ebb and flow is underscored by the recurrences in the poet's language.

TIDES

The days curl over and become translucent
for a moment, coming from far off
to crash in a language learned on the way.
Things you never saw before wash up,
suddenly yours. A shell worn smooth.
A piece of colored glass. The usual treasure.

And then the days curl over again,
and the treasure is pulled back,
bound for another place—the swell that was yours,
going away. Even your footsteps disappear as fast
as you make them. They too are pulled away
to be imprinted on another shore.

Be children again! When the sea
lays treasure at your feet, fill your pockets with
shells and colored glass!

What fills them now?

Nothing the sea wants to carry.

ROBIN NELSON

In all of us an ancient infant responds to the rhythm of the waves as if to a lullabye.
LAVELLE LEAHEY, STUDENT WRITER

Young children's concern with words are more like that of the poet, since they are more than usually aware of their physical qualities, and show this by the way they play with sounds, making jingles and rhymes and puns and mixing in nonsense sounds.
JAMES BRITTON, *Language and Learning*

Note the recurrences of idea and image in "Tides": With each surge, objects "wash up." With each receding, "the treasure is pulled back," coming and going, appearing and disappearing, like footprints on the sand. The recurrence of the wave pattern implicit in the words of this vignette gives the last five lines their strength: A child is happy to fill its pockets with small treasures. A day curling over to the next day brings small treasures. Don't leave them, the poet is saying. In using the recurrent image of the wave to suggest something about the recurrence of days, Nelson has left us with the reminder that each day brings only "usual treasures"—and that we'd better learn to treasure them like children who value the present moment. Notice also the recurrence of particular images: translucence, colored glass; of particular words: "treasure" repeated three times, each in a different context; "days curl" twice, to emphasize ebb and flow; "pulled" used twice; of particular sounds: the repeated use of "l's" suggesting the fluidity of water—*l*anguage *l*earned, cur*l*, trans*l*ucent, sudden*l*y, she*ll*, co*l*ored, g*l*ass, usua*l*, pu*ll*ed, p*l*ace, swe*ll*, *l*ays, fi*ll*; a heavy use of "s" sounds, reflecting the hissing of water breaking—*s*uddenly, *s*hell, *s*mooth, trea*s*ure, day*s*, *s*well, foot*s*teps, di*s*appear, a*s* fa*s*t a*s*, *s*hore, *s*ea, pocket*s*, fill*s*, want*s*. It is almost as if the "l" sounds carry the wave in and the "s" sounds pull the wave out. The recurring sounds are distinct, yet they work in tandem. The recurrences in this poem help relate its theme: that if we want to enjoy life as children do, we must learn to treasure the momentary gifts between ebb and flow.

CHILDHOOD ORIGINS OF RECURRENCE

Recurrences are a natural characteristic of childhood language. Even before children can speak, they amuse themselves with a rhythmic jabbering of repeated syllables: "goo-goo," "ma-ma," "da-da." As they get older, they begin to delight in the rhythms and recurrences of such games as "Pat-a-cake, Pat-a-cake," "This little piggy," and countless others. Linguist Kornei Chukovsky suggests that the rhythmic recurrences of nursery rhymes actually grew out of children's intoxication with repetition, rhythm, and melodic lines. Children clap, chant, rhyme, and repeat words because such activity makes patterns, which produce intense pleasure.

As soon as children begin to write, recurrences find their way into their writing. An example of recurrence came from a clustering experiment I was asked to do in a second-grade class. We clustered the nucleus word (ROUND) on the board, all the children eagerly participating in filling the board with all sorts of "roundnesses" radiating outward from the center. Next I asked them to write about roundness—tell a story, describe something round, explain a "round" experience, anything they chose.

This vignette, written in twenty minutes, illustrates the extent to which the natural rhythms of language are used intuitively by a child. The repetition of "round" not only places the focus on "round things" but also ties the poem into a coherent, self-contained whole.

WHAT IS ROUND?

Round is a ball bouncing high in the air.
Round is a flea that crawls up in your hair.
Round is the earth that we're now standing on.
Round is the sun that goes up at dawn.
Round is an apple that blooms in the spring.
Round is a beautiful emerald ring.
Round is a planet up in space.
Round is a necklace made out of a shoelace.
Round is the super small moon.
Round is the head of a big baboon.
Round is a log floating down the stream.
Round is a pie topped with whipped cream.
Round is a little o.
Round is a tangerine that had a friend cow.
Round is a dime, a penny, a nickel.
Round is the end of a pickle.
Round is the doorknob that sits on a door.
Round is a table that stands on the floor.
Round is a tummy of a boy.
Round is the middle of a toy.
And that's all of this round tale
Goodbye, see ya after my bottle of ale!

As you recover the childhood "innocence of eye, ear, and hand" that took pleasure in the recurrences in language, you extend your Design mind's ability to become attuned to recurrences in nature, in art, in architecture, even in the speech of a friend. As a natural writer, you will reach the "cultivated eye, ear, and hand" stage by using recurrences in your writing. The purpose of this chapter is: (1) to sensitize your Design mind's natural affinity for recurrences, and (2) to enable you to use different types of recurrences when you write.

> *Young children's concern with words is more like that of the poet, since they too are more than usually aware of their physical qualities, and show this by the way they play with sounds, making jingles and rhymes and puns and mixing in nonsense sounds.*
>
> **JAMES BRITTON,**
> **Language and Learning**

RECURRENCE OF LETTER SOUNDS—ALLITERATION

When we repeat letters of the alphabet, we get patterns of alliteration, such as the following, which was written from a cluster with Ⓜ as its nucleus (Figure 7-1).

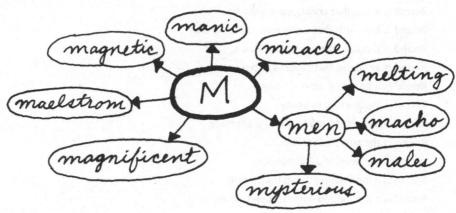

Figure 7-1

THE MALE ANIMAL

Men—
magnificent muscles moving,
mysterious yet malleable
minds like a maelstrom merging
macho yet magnetic
    and mercurial.

In the midst of a million marvelous males,
I feel a manic mingling.
The miracle of mere men—
    they make me melt.

SIMONE, 22

Directing Your Hand

Pre-cluster (ALPHABET), and keep on jotting down sounds until one takes off and you find yourself clustering words with that sound around it. Let yourself be playful, childlike. Then write for no more than five minutes, changing your vignette to suit you only after you have completed the first writing.

After Writing

Enjoy this childlike recursive process. Over time, cluster (LETTERS) again and again to see which letter it yields today and what playful vignette you will produce.

The presence of an alphabet in our heads has had profound import in our portrayal of the world.

TYLER VOLK

RECURRENCE OF WORD SEGMENTS

Repeating segments of words, as novelist Geoffrey Wolff does below, can also communicate or intensify particular feelings or ideas. In characterizing the writer, Wolff is playing with the word "out." It happens to be a preposition, one of the least conspicuous parts of speech in our language. However, since prepositions connect ideas, they are essential to thought and writing. Used as a segment and hooked up with another word, "out" generates a whole series of ideas that are, because of the recurrence, highly compressed and, therefore, effective:

The writer is an
outsider, outlaw
outcast, out-of-bounds,
out-and-out
outrageously out
of his mind.

GEOFFREY WOLFF

"Side" and "law," and "cast" and "bounds" and "rage(ously")
are, by themselves, complete words, but they take on totally different meanings once they're paired with the little word, "out,"
which changes everything by its sense of exclusion.

RECURRENCE OF "THROW-AWAY" WORDS

Some words may not look like much, especially prepositions, as
you've seen, but they seem to generate amazing creative leaps.
For years, I wondered why, but the reason always escaped me. I
kept using prepositions as nuclei but couldn't explain how or why
they produced such interesting vignettes.

One day, in an upper-division college writing class I placed
the preposition AROUND on the board, asking students to loosen
up with language by clustering, then writing for five minutes.

Here is one tongue-in-cheek memory, triggered by AROUND
(Figure 7-2), from an accounting major, which becomes humor-
ously significant by the time you reach the conclusion of the
vignette:

[▫▬▫] AROUND

I don't think I thought about anything as much in my eighth-grade
year as Eileen. You see, word was out that Eileen had been "around."
Lord knows I wasn't sure what that meant, but I just felt I'd like to be
there once Eileen decided to go around. Gym class was a great place to
find out who had been "around." Seems as though everyone except
me knew at least two or three girls who had been around THEM.

By the middle of my eighth-grade year, I too, had boasted my
share of girls I'd personally found to have been around. There were
only 48 girls in our class. There were only 45 guys, and each of us had
3 or 4 girls we *knew* had been around. 45 guys by 3.5 girls = 150?

Eileen sure must have been around!

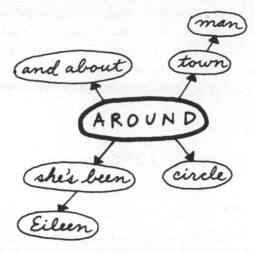

Figure 7-2

Such wonderful examples as this made me realize that, not only are words like prepositions malleable, used in any number of contexts, but they are temporally and spatially archetypal. Say "underneath" out loud; there is almost a bodily sensation of movement. Say "beyond" out loud, and there is an almost physical reaching toward something, something . . . not quite there. Indicating time and space with words is central to how human beings orient themselves in the world. No wonder the Design mind taps into the power of these small words.

Directing Your Hand

In your Writer's Notebook, number and date a new entry. By clustering (UP/DOWN), play with words and ideas to see what comes up. Be curious; be outrageous. As you write your vignette, repeat "up" and/or "down" as often as possible without forcing it. It is not necessary to attempt to force both words into your vignette. Let your Design mind choose; allow whatever interplay presents itself.

After Writing

Prepositions never fail to elicit rich writing. It took me years to figure out why. Basically, prepositions connect us in space and time, one of the most fundamental orientations of survival.

The Design mind takes "out" and "in" and, instead of seeing "preposition," interprets an almost physical external/internal shift, puts an emotional spin on it, and associates things like "in-group, out-group." If we're out, we're excluded. If we're in, we're accepted and safe. These small prepositions carry much of that meaningful weight.

RECURRENCE OF CONCEPT

Directing Your Hand

"Maybe" is a concept that suggests indecision or ambivalence or ambiguity. Cluster (MAYBE) using as a guide two very different examples of the concept of MAYBE below. They will give you permission to go in whatever direction your Design mind wants to go.

MAYBE

If I planted a bushel of Maybes,
nothing would grow.
If I planted one Yes,
I'd have a large tree full of fruit.
Yesses are not free;
they cannot be bought.
Someone has to give one to you.
I try and I try.
No one has given me one yet.
Meanwhile I collect Maybes.
They are as empty, as dusty
as they sound.
I will die with the world's largest collection of
        Maybes—
A gigantic pile of
        plastic fruit.
STUDENT

MAYBE

How idiotic sixteen years old and never been
kissed well not really maybe tonight I like the
way this Johnny smells and the feel of his arms
his collar turned up and maybe he likes me too in
the dark in the color turquoise he slows down on
the dead streets of my neighborhood maybe my
mother and father are asleep maybe the lights
will be out Johnny turns off the engine a half a
block from the house maybe we will glide to
just under the street lamp or just past it to the
black shadows of the neighbor's magnolia tree
Johnny knows maybe I should say something
maybe I should duck my head and maybe maybe I
won't appear too stupid or unappealing maybe I
have the Indian princess look especially here in
the dim glow of the light from the radio that
he's clocking off now so maybe oops its all dark
maybe its time to get out thanks it was really
nice maybe Friday maybe oh please stop me don't
let me go so quickly maybe you know exactly
how I feel so flustered there's your arm maybe
you love me in some way maybe I love you well
maybe I love your mouth in the shadows the
smell of roses from my mothers little garden my
mothers little garden along the edge of the lawn
your mouth maybe it would fit on mine like my
drawings of couples kissing what happens do I
tilt my head like this oh oh I thought it would be
drier I have to go my parents will be angry
maybe they're right maybe you're not supposed to
do that what I just did Christ it was only a kiss
in the dark I am a fool maybe I'll look different
in the light in the mirror maybe he thinks I'm an
idiot maybe I am.

JOAN BAEZ

The concept "Yes" affirms. "No" negates. Maybe hedges. These concepts exist in all cultures. Cluster one of these three words, and, as you write, watch a pattern unfold. Write quickly for no more than five minutes without stopping. Then go back to the completed vignette and make whatever changes you want to.

THE RECURRENCE SANDWICH

Listen with your inner ear to the rhythms of language. Pay attention not just to *what* is being said, but to *how* the words say it. In the following poem, hear how the words come full circle: beginning and end repeat, like two pieces of bread in a sandwich. The interface between bread and the contents of the sandwich make both bread and contents more than each was separately. This is the Recurrence sandwich.

LEARN TO BE WATER

Learn
to be
water

direction is any
way
you can
travel
your shape
whatever
you naturally
become

let the
moon
strum
belly
the planets

beckon
and
tug

learn
to be
water

MORTON MARCUS

Directing Your Hand

In your Writer's Notebook, date and number a new page and cluster (LEARN TO BE . . .) Reach for learnings you are hungry for. Give yourself several so that the one that is just right for this moment, now, at this time in your consciousness, can appear. Re-cluster the one that speaks to you. When you begin writing, fill in what this learning means to you, says to you, gives to you, then come full circle by re-stating it. This activity can be clustered again and again and will reveal evolving insights as we change.

RECURRENCE OF IDEAS

A provocative example of idea recurrence is Lisel Mueller's poem, "Eggs."

EGGS

Mothershape, how we love you!
In a dream we almost remember
the floating cushions, the waterbed,
in nightmares, we hack our way
out of the calcium walls
which refused to expand with us.

When we eat eggs, we return.
It's a matter of beginnings.
Heart attacks are forgotten
when the delicious, dangerous yellow

is rich and smooth as paint in the can
and the tasteless, foam-rubber white
transformed by a pinch of salt,

when we sit down for picnic lunches
and peel our way back inside,
the shell falling under our fingers
to reveal the gleaming rim,
the oval promise through which we come
to the holy of holies,
the green-tinged, golden, solid sphere,
a child's first model of the moon.
                    LISEL MUELLER

Mueller turns the concept of corners this way and that, exploring the archetypal, the fearsome, the delicious, in eggs. Here is an attempt to make sense of a simple word that suggests so many things and carries so many emotional nuances. Most obvious is her use of egg-related words like "calcium walls," "delicious yellow," "gleaming rim," and "oval promise," but when we get into the poem, we begin to discover the rich layers of connotations in the idea of "eggness" and what we humans read into it.

Directing Your Hand

In your Writer's Notebook, cluster (ROAD), coming up with as many associations as you can. Without trying to sequence your vignette in a particular way, quickly write a sentence or so for several of the associations. Write no more than five minutes. Only when you run out of things to write, go back and order your sentences into some kind of sequence that pleases you. The sequence may turn out to move from small to large, from personal to public, from things to ideas, or any other organization that emerges for you. The pattern should please only you until you venture out into the complexities of the recursiveness of language patterns.

A Last Word and Heading On

Recurrence is one of the simplest and most readily apparent natural strategies leading to powerful writing. Continue to experiment and have fun with it as you do the writing activities throughout the book. Remember that any element of language can become a recurrence: the sound of a particular letter or group of letters, a word segment, a phrase, an image, a concept, an idea. Recurrences reflect your Design mind's awareness of patterns, and using them will make your writing more rhythmic, more inviting, more unified.

Now that your ear has become more attuned to recurrences, you are ready to explore the more subtle techniques described in the following chapter: recurrences that make language become musical.

EIGHT

LANGUAGE RHYTHMS: THE MUSIC IN WORDS

I only have twenty-six letters of the alphabet; I don't have color or music. I must use my craft to make the reader see the colors and hear the sounds.

TONI MORRISON

Robert Louis Stevenson called the rhythms of sentences "the pattern of sound in time." Before our birth we were attuned to the rhythms of our mother's voice, an influence that continues after birth. As infants we were rocked, sung to, talked to. As babblers we were enchanted with the sounds we made just for the sake of sound. As toddlers we became familiar with the strong, regular rhythms of chants and nursery rhymes such as "Peter, Peter, pumpkin eater," counting rhymes, such as "One two, buckle your shoe," and jump-rope rhymes such as "Lady bird, lady bird, turn around," long before we could jump rope. We are born with a hunger for the harmony, melody, and rhythms of language.

The music in words is Design-mind territory. In this chapter we focus on *cadence*, the rhythmic flow of sequences of sounds, words, phrases, sentences that provide the aural sense of continuity in writing. You'll relearn to recognize and use language rhythms as expressive and melodic patterns. Sound and sense: Cadence reminds us that the sounds of words arranged in particular ways and their sense go together.

LANGUAGE RHYTHMS WITHIN SENTENCES

Recurring rhythms within the same sentence please the Design mind's ear. For example, one of the simplest rhythmic forms lies in parallel structures. The principle behind parallel forms is logical: Let words or phrases seek their own kind—noun with noun, verb with verb, adjective with adjective, adverb with adverb. In a sentence, when a noun is parallel with another and then another, the ear picks up a rhythm that helps us gather meaning: "I sing of shoes, of ships, of sealing wax." Without grammatical analysis, we recognize the threeness of objects sung about; they are alike in some way at a level below logic.

Our Sign mind, on the other hand, knows that things named are nouns and that, when we have items in a series, they have to match. For example, most of us can pick out the three nouns—*things*—which, according to the author of *The Rubaiyat of Omar Khayyam*, are necessary for happiness: "a loaf," "a jug," and "thou":

 A *loaf* of bread, a *jug* of wine, and *thou* beside me in the wilderness . . . (nouns). Our Design mind responds, too, though not by labeling the nouns but by hearing the cadence, the intonation, and the emphasis on those three words, the "threeness" of happiness, and not a single thing more. To be happy, one needs three things: something to eat, something to drink, and someone to love. That is parallel form, and it has powerful emotional overtones for the Design mind's sense of not only *what* but *how* something is said.

Here is a sentence that uses a series of verbs/actions to create rhythm:

 "Peace is not something you *wish* for, it's something you *make*, something you *do*, something you *are*, and something you *give* away!"

ROBERT FULGHUM

In the next sentence, the series of adjectives—"hard, tight, controlled, tensed . . ."—which qualify what the "I" is feeling— creates the rhythm:

[▭] I am tired of being *hard, tight, controlled, tensed* against
    the invasion of novelty.

SAM KEEN

Our Design mind doesn't label; it hears the *pattern* words make. In this case, it hears four words piled one next to the other, which qualify—and amplify—what this writer is *tired* of. Parallel rhythms make us aware of the recurrent nature of events, feelings, actions, qualifiers. Once you become more aware of the power of parallel structures on the human mind, you will see them everywhere. For example, Sharon Olds wrote that one of the ambulance men in "The Death of Marilyn Monroe" "had nightmares, strange pains, impotence, depression." One of these maladies would have been enough, but the piling up of four becomes serious, and we *hear* the seriousness in the rhythm of the list—even without focusing on the meaning of the words. Similarly, in Jeffrey Harrison's "Reflections on the Vietnam Memorial," the wall is described as "an underground *house*, a *roof* of grass, one version of the *underworld*." The recurrence of nouns describing where the soldiers now live sets up a rhythm that pulls us into the poem and helps to communicate a particular meaning. Parallel rhythms have the ability to compress meaning for us because their impact is felt viscerally and thus cancels the need for lengthy explanation.

Directing Your Hand

Now it's your turn to play with rhythm. Each of the following excerpts—only one sentence long—contains a distinctive rhythmic pattern. Read them out loud. Then choose the rhythm that appeals to you most and, using it as a model, write your own sentence with a similar rhythmic pattern. For example, the first excerpt, from the first lines of a poem, is followed by student sentences using a similar rhythmic pattern. Read them aloud to hear the rhythms:

There is a sadness to this world, a grimness, a nastiness in the throat, a foulness of breath, a slackening of the penis into sorrow, a chill in the bloodstream that hurts.

AL YOUNG

 There is an electricity to the touch, an intensity, a shivering through the arm, a feeling of the unknown, a surge of power that is erotic.

STUDENT

 There is a gloom about that house, an awfulness, a bizarreness, an icy-to-the-boneness, a smell of evil riding on the fluttering of grey wings, the terrible ending of someone who was young and who shone.

STUDENT

Now quickly write one or more sentences using parallel rhythms. Only afterward stop to shape it to sound even better. If you need a nudge to jump-start your Design mind, quick-cluster (THERE IS A . . .) to give you options.

Other sentences from which to model your own are:

 Wanting too much, wanting the wrong thing, wanting what you can't have is one definition of the human condition; we all have to learn how to make some livable compromise between the always insatiable self and the always insufficient reality principle.

EVA HOFFMAN, Lost in Translation

 Learning to live with a person you do not love and respect, learning to live with a person who neither loves nor respects you, is merely learning how to die, how to walk around as a shell, how to deny what you feel, how to hate without showing it, how to weep without tears, how to declare that the sham you live is the true reality and that it is good.

JULES HENRY

You might want to take the first phrase from the excerpt you've chosen, substitute your own parallel words, and use those as a quick-cluster if you want to explore options. For example, the "wanting too much" phrase in the Hoffman piece could become (BUYING TOO MUCH . . .) or (SLEEPING TOO MUCH. . . .) And from the "learning to live" phrase in the Henry piece, you might cluster (WISHING TO . . .) or (DARING TO . . .)

OTHER WAYS OF JOINING SOUND AND SENSE

Parallel rhythms can take entirely different forms as balanced juxtapositions, the invisible durability behind many proverbs: "Speech is silver; silence is golden." This juxtaposition evokes the image of a scale: a chunk of meaning laid on the left is counter-weighted on the right. Each part of the sentence has a similar de-sign, and its two balanced halves create wholeness. Balanced rhythm brings compression, texture, and cohesion to writing. When the thoughts of a balanced sentence are in agreement, there is a sense of mutual reinforcement; when in contrast, a source of tension.

Directing Your Hand

In your Writer's Notebook, play with your own combination of balanced rhythms, following any or all of the models below. You may want to quick-cluster a double circle e.g., (GREAT) (SMALL), to remind you of the tension of juxtaposition, the balance of rein-forcement.

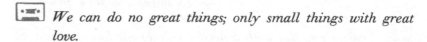 *We can do no great things; only small things with great love.*

MOTHER TERESA

Loneliness is like sitting in an empty room and being aware of the space around you. It is a condition of sepa-rateness. Solitude is becoming one with the space around you. It is a condition of union. Loneliness is small, solitude is large. Loneliness closes in around you; solitude expands toward the infinite.

KENT NERBURN

After Writing

How does the previous writing activity work? Your Design mind hears the totality of a given sentence's rhythmic pattern. Then your sequencing Sign mind writes your own sentence, governed by the pattern's echo. This collaboration results in numerous rhythmic juxtapositions, making you increasingly sensitive to, then aware of, the rhythmic aspect of language.

You can also become more sensitive to rhythm when you read. If you come across a particular cadence that strikes you, copy it in your Writer's Notebook for later language rhythm play. The following rhythms, for example, exemplify stop and start, stop and start rhythm:

We misunderstand love because we have chosen to worship power; we fail in compassion because we have become obsessed with control; we silence the reasons of the heart because we have chosen to follow a path of heartless knowledge, no matter where it takes us.

SAM KEEN

At times the whole sky was ringed in shooting points and puckers of light gathering and falling, pulsing, fading, rhythmical as breathing. All of a piece. As if the sky were a pattern of nerves and our thoughts and memories traveled across it. As if the sky were one gigantic memory for us all.

LOUISE ERDRICH

LINE PLACEMENT AND RHYTHM

The form that poetry takes on the page appeals to the Design mind due to its rhythmic as well as its visual aspects. Some poems have such a distinctive pattern in the way the lines are placed on the page that they nudge us to read it in a certain manner. The poet e. e. cummings is so sensitive to cadence that he wants to make it visual. Take "Portrait VIII," for example: Because of the way cummings places the poem on the page, we tend to read it a

certain way. We notice that "onetwothreefourfive" are run together, so we read it rapidly and then realize that this quick
rhythm relates to the speed with which Buffalo Bill hit targets
(he was famous for hitting clay pigeons tossed into the air). Because some lines are nothing more than single words, we tend to
emphasize those words by pausing before and after. Gradually,
we become aware that the rhythms inform the ironic sense of the
poem, which yokes the sounds of awestruck idolatry to the ironic
satisfaction of the speaker that he is still alive while the famous
"blueeyed boy" has landed in Death's hands.

PORTRAIT VIII

Buffalo Bill's
defunct
            who used to
            ride a watersmooth-silver
                        stallion
and break onetwothreefourfive pigeonsjustlikethat
                        Jesus
he was a handsome man
            and what i want to know is
how do you like your blueeyed boy
Mr. Death

In the modelings below, the writers sustain cummings' visual
spacing as well as his language rhythms.

PORTRAIT III

Jerry Garcia's
    dead
            who used to
            play a custom rosewood
                    guitar
    chubby   fingers   onetothreefourfive

winding   justlikethat
        up   the   fretboard   WOW!
he was a weathered   man
        and what I want to know is
is the fat man finally grateful
Mr. Death

SIMONE

PORTRAIT 10

Princess   Di
is   dead
        who   used   to   sport
onetwothreefourfive million dollar dresses
on a 10 million dollar body
                        Damn
did she have a death-defying
                        smile
When I consider   the billion dollar price of fame
I wonder, will   she   out-shine   you in the Hall   of legends
            Norma Jean?

STUDENT

Directing Your Hand

Your turn to play with e. e. cummings' exquisite timing by writing about someone famous and "defunct." Pre-cluster (PORTRAIT OF . . .) just to discover what names pop into your head and which beckon you to write. Preclustering gives you choices, often of subjects your Sign mind would never have thought of: Edison, Picasso, Lincoln. Briefly recluster the name that speaks to you at this moment for any and all associations that emerge. Now, play with your content and enjoy the process. Humorous or serious, you will gradually mesh rhythm with the person that clicked in your head. Read your creation aloud, making any changes you wish.

After Writing

This activity is playful. If you had difficulty with it, don't worry about it. All of us are equipped to be sensitive to the cadences of language. Sometimes we try too hard, blocking the Design mind, which does not function well under brow-furrowing effort. Ease up and allow the cummings cadences to sink in by re-reading and listening to the poem several times. Think of yourself as a child playing with a language that holds infinite surprise.

USING LANGUAGE RHYTHM TO EVOKE EMOTION

Simply enjoy "Laughter" below and notice that the whole of it is one long sentence stitched together with eight "&'s." This simple, single memory is summed up in the title as "laughter," but the language reveals the headlong rush of a totally unexpected, improvised moment.

LAUGHTER

One night my father yanked a tablecloth
from under my face & plates spun like meteors
as he wrapped it over his shoulders & his bald head lit up
like a pumpkin as he waltzed my mother round our crooked house
& tears soaked my collar & my stomach jumped into my mouth
as they flew chair over sofa & the world was a moment so full of us
I think of the Samurai playing with a daisy as he waits for his enemy
& only the daisy & the bright summer sun in his smile & I ask you
if at a time like this you would wonder if there was a beginning or end
with angels gathering on the roof to fear such loud tearing
at the fiery curtain of human delight.

PHILIP SCHULTZ

Read it again and note that the whole vignette brings an unforgettable moment of high emotion into dramatic relief, an infinite moment of explosive laughter, a moment of emotional "togetherness," which Schultz calls the "fiery curtain of human delight."

The rhythm is urgently forward moving, the "ands" creating a pulsing extraordinary picture simultaneously ecstatic and bottomlessly sad. There is no explanation—only the impulsive act that the poet never forgets. A Samurai is a Japanese warrior of the sixteenth century who has entered the moment of "now" in total surrender to that moment—and therefore cannot experience fear of the danger around the bend in the near future. How does the Samurai fit into the picture?

Another emotion-filled, rhythmically-charged piece of writing connects the ecstasy of new "snow" with the ecstatic play of "brothers." The event, the first snow in childhood, evokes emotions of "dizzy pleasure," both then and in the retelling. The rhythms of action, verb after verb of things the three brothers *do* in the snow, are piled up like snowballs until the reader feels almost like a participant in this ecstatic game.

 **THREE BROTHERS IN THE SNOW**

Winter has its pleasures.
GERARD DE NERVAL

Snow immediately comes to mind—
those mornings our hearts leapt (and they still do)
when we looked out at another world, another
planet. We'd stumble out all bundled up
like astronauts, kicking through lunar dust
whose sparkles made you fall in dizzy pleasure,
then roll over and make a snow angel.
Or if it was pouring down you'd really feel
like someone walking on the moon, falling
upward, gravity releasing you.

And sleds that had been hanging all year long
unnoticed on the wall of the garage
came down: toboggans, Flexible Flyers
(their runners, orange with rust, would shine again!),

and flying saucers dented from rough landings.
No hill was too steep for us; we tried them all,
crashing into thickets, plunging through creeks,
then standing up and laughing at each other,
our faces white with thick and stinging beards—
three crazy snowmen that had come to life.

We kicked it, packed it, threw it at each other,
ate it (I still do), and if we could
get through all those layers, pissed on it:
yellow acid etching a crooked line.
But despite those blasphemies we worshiped it.
Snow! It had the power to call off school.
I never doubted that it came from heaven.

JEFFREY HARRISON

Read the poem aloud ⬛. Notice how the rhythm is rough-and-tumble, the accent on the first syllables of many of the words: *kick*-ing, *stum*-ble, *spark*-les; *morn*-ings *plan*-et *bund*-led *lun*-ar *diz*-zy *pleas*-ure *ang*-el *pour*-ing *real*-ly *some*-one *walk*-ing *fall*-ing *up*-ward; *hang*-ing; *Fly*-ers *run*-ners *or*-ange *land*-ings *sau*-cers *den*-ted *crash*-ing *thick*-ets *plung*-ing; *stand*-ing *laugh*-ing *o*-ther *fac*-es; *sting*-ing. Other words that add to the choppy rhythm of excitement are the one-syllable words, like *snow*. See how many you can count. Note also the single-syllable action verbs, such as kicked, packed, threw, ate, pissed).

Directing Your Hand

1. With Philip Schultz's "Laughter" in mind, quick-cluster (A MOMENT OF NO FORGETTING) for options, then cluster the one moment that wants to be written about here, this minute. Now, do so. Write rapidly with an eye to using as many "&'s" as possible in order to reach an emotional peak.

2. Cluster (I REMEMBER . . .) until you retrieve an event that has particular emotional significance for you, that will say, "Write about me!" Name the event's nucleus and

recluster it for the specifics, which will create the rhythmic rush. Without working on it too hard, keep your language simple by using as many one or two syllable words as possible, stringing everything together with &'s. Write without stopping. When you have come full circle, you can go back and make revisions to hone your vignette until you are pleased with it.

A Last Word and Heading On

Rhythm is one of the constants in human life: our beating heart, our breath inhaled and exhaled, night and day continually giving way to each other. Language, whether spoken or written, is rhythmic as well. The more we attend to its rhythms, the more expanded our options as writers. Similarly, when we become aware of the strength of images in shaping patterns of meaning, the subject of chapter 10, we create yet another series of options for natural writing.

NINE

IMAGES: INNER EYE DIRECTING WRITING HAND

I began Play It as It Lays *just as I have begun each of my novels, with no notion of "character" or "plot" or even "incident." I had only two pictures in my mind: one of white space, and the second of a young woman with long hair and a short white dress walking through the casino at the Riviera in Las Vegas at one in the morning.*

JOAN DIDION

Virginia Woolf revealed that her novel *The Waves* unfolded from a single image—that of a "fin turning in a waste of water." Henry James called these images "germs." Joan Didion says that pictures in her mind have been the beginning of every novel she has written.

Much of what we remember is stored as images, and these remembered images are always emotionally charged. For example, have you ever placed a certain food in your mouth, and suddenly the taste flooded your senses with images from your childhood? Images are multisensory.

We all have the ability to conjure up images. That is your Design mind's special province, the ability to bring forth complex patterns even in the absence of sensory stimuli. An image is an internal whole in the mind's eye. Images are probably the main content of our thoughts, regardless of the sensory modality in which they are generated and regardless of whether they are about a thing or a process involving things; or about words or other symbols, in a given language, which correspond to a thing or process.

Images reconstructed in words represent a human effort to re-create—to "real-ize" or "real-eyes"—a picture in the mind so charged with feeling that we are compelled to translate it into verbal language.

Since we have access to a written code, we can "hold" our

images in words on a page. For example, consider how the following words by D. H. Lawrence pull us into the emotion-filled image of a sunset:

> She went to the fence and sat there, watching the gold clouds fall to pieces, and go in immense, rose-colored ruin towards the darkness. Gold flamed to scarlet, like pain in its intense brightness. Then the scarlet ran to rose, and rose to crimson, and quickly the passion went out of the sky. All the world was dark grey.

In this passage, Virginia Woolf steeps us in images of darkness:

> So with the lamps all put out, the moon sunk, and a thin rain drumming on the roof, a downpouring of immense darkness began. Nothing, it seemed, could survive the flood, the profusion of darkness which, creeping in at keyholes and crevices, stole round window blinds, came into bedrooms, swallowed up here a jug and basin, there a bowl of red and yellow dahlias, there the sharp edges and firm bulk of a chest of drawers.

And in this excerpt, John Hawkes entangles us in extraordinary images of wind:

> But the wind, this bundle of invisible snakes, roars cross our wandering island—it is a wandering island, off course, unlocated in space and quite out of time—and seems to heap the shoulders with an arm-like weight, to coil about my naked legs and pulse and caress the flesh with an unpredictable weight, a consistency, tension of its own. It drives, drives, and even when it drops down, fades, dies, it continues its gentle rubbing on the skin.

An image tells us more than pure fact: "The sun went down," "night came," "the wind blew." It makes us experience the crumbling of a multicolored sunset, the gobbling darkness, the sinuous island wind, through carefully chosen words that strike the tuning fork of our senses and resonate through intellect, emotions, and body to reclaim a childlike innocence of eye. Like language rhythms and recurrence, images make writing

We are what we imagine. Our very existence consists in our imagination of ourselves. Our best destiny is to imagine who and what, and that we are. The greatest interpretation, a newly reconstructed version of the original. As our age and experience change, versions of the same thing evolve. Memory is essentially reconstructive.

ANTONIO DAMASIO

So the point of my keeping a notebook has never been, nor is it now, to have an accurate factual record of what I have been doing or thinking. . . . Perhaps it never did snow that August in Vermont; perhaps there never were flurries in the night wind, and maybe no one else felt the ground hardening and summer already dead even as we pretended to bask in it, but that was how it felt to me, and it might as well have snowed, could have snowed, did snow.

How it felt to me: *that is getting closer to the truth about a notebook.*

JOAN DIDION

memorable. They stimulate our minds to see better, understand more, play with ideas, wonder, and to interpret emotional nuances.

Language scholar James Britton tells of reading a poem to eight-year-olds about a night watchman in winter, another about cold wind. When he looked up, a boy in the back was hugging himself, pleading, "Please, sir, would you read us a *warm* one?"

In chapter 8 we reawakened the ear's sense of rhythm. In this chapter we will reawaken the noverbal inner eye. The purpose of this chapter is to help you tap these reservoirs of remembered or imagined experience, then to make them accessible to your Sign mind for verbal expression.

THE CHILDHOOD ORIGINS OF IMAGING

Before words, there are images. When we are infants, our mother is our primary image, representing security and nourishment. "To the infant," wrote developmental psychologist Jean Piaget, "the world is a thing to be sucked." Our earliest images were all-encompassing. Only gradually did they become separated out into discrete entities.

In the stage of the innocent eye, ear, and hand, emotional states are translated into the visual images that people the world of fairy tales. These images and the accompanying feelings are unforgettable precisely because they reflect the child's inner state. For both children and adults, images are made manifest in nightmares. Maurice Sendak's *Where the Wild Things Are* attests to the idea that children find comfort in externalizing these dream images.

Impressive testimony of children's imaging powers comes from children's strong impulse to make meaning even of something written in a language they do not understand or read. I asked my youngest daughter Simone, then nine, to "translate" a poem in German. She looked astonished at my absurd request: "I don't *know* that language!" "Just say the words to yourself and just write what you *think* it means," I told her. Both original poem and Simone's "mis-translation" follow. Read her very creative translation aloud, watching for images generated by a language meaningless to her.

SCHNEEWINTER	SKIWINTER
Nun, da die Daecher schneeumkleidet liegen,	Noon on the deck. You ski in drunk light, lie down,
der Winterstrum durch leere Heiden irrt,	but winterstorms are here, hiding out
dass sich die nackten Baeume seufzend biegen,	and, such, die naked. But Sue's friend, Bigger,
Da sehn' ich mich an eine Brust zu schmiegen	will send her much envy, bursting with a smidgeon,
an der mein wildes Trauern stiller wird.	and it's mine, wild, drawn into stiller worlds.
Nach Fingern, die nur meine Stirne streifen	No fingers die, mine are still striving.
und aller Gram und Unlust flattertfort.	An alarm, grained, and an unjust flattered fort
nach Blicken, die mir and die Seele greifen,	will look and see death in steel grief.
bis mir dann neue Fruehlingstraeume reifen	But as dawn knows, feeling some brings grief,
aus einem einz'gen leisen Liebeswort.	and enemies are gazing on your sword.
STEFAN ZWEIG	SIMONE RICO

Out of words totally meaningless to her, Simone had created a coherent whole. The strange words suggested images to her that her mind struggled to fit into a pattern of meaning, however absurd.

Although all children graduate to the conventional stage of eye, ear, and hand, as adults we can reach the stage of the cultivated eye, ear, and hand by relearning to tap the imaging gift of our Design mind: Poets and artists like Picasso are people who have reclaimed this authentic vision.

Directing Your Hand

Have some fun! Here are two poems in two different languages. Choose the language you do not know and see if you can feel your Design mind search for meaning. Don't spend much time. Who knows? It might lead to a wonderful vignette. It will most certainly lead to an expanded sense of image, playfulness, creative urge.

The image cannot be dispossessed of a primordial freshness, which idea can never claim. An idea is derivative and tamed. The image is in the natural or wild state, and it has to be discovered there, not put there, obeying its own law and none of ours.

JOHN CROWE RANSON

HERBSTTAG

Herr: es ist Zeit. Der Sommer war sehr gross.
Leg deinen Schatten auf die Sonnenuhren,
und auf den Fluren lass die Winde los.

Befiehl den letzten Fruechten voll zu sein;
gieb ihnen noch zwei suedlichere Tage,
   draenge sie zur Vollendung hin und jage
die letzte Suesse in den schweren Wein.

Wer jetzt kein Haus hat, baut sich keines mehr,
   wer jetzt allein ist, wird es lange bleiben,
wird wachen, lesen, lange Briefe schreiben
   und wird in den Alleen hin und her
unruhig wandern, wenn die Blaetter treiben.

RAINER MARIA RILKE

ALLA NOIA

Quiete, quando risorse in una trama
Il corpo scerbo verto cui m'avvio.

La mano le luceva che mi porse,

Che di quanto m'avanzo s'allontana.

Eccomi perco in queste vane corse.

Quando ondeggio (accent grave on o) mattine ella si
   stese
E rise, e mi volo dagli occhi.

Ancella di follia, noia
Treppe pez(r)o fosti ebbra e dolce.

GIUSEPPE UNGARETTI

After Writing

Remember that as adults we are not as open to playing as we
were as children. These activities are a good way to reconnect
with the sense of novelty, surprise, and wonder characteristic of
the less emotionally bound world of childhood.

CREATING IMAGES WITH COLOR

A direct way to tap into your store of images is to play with color,
as Peter Meinke has done in this wonderfully zany poem:

BLUE GIRL

because you wore blue yesterday
today I am in love with everything blue
The blue books on my shelves smile at me:

TEN GREEK PLAYS and CONVERSATIONAL FRENCH

Que j'adore le bleu!
Bleu, blau, azul, azzurro . . .
words popping like blueberries in my mouth
My indigo wastebasket too pure for use;
applecores fly out the window
When I close my eyes
visions of violets and sapphires blow them open
bluejeans & bluebells, blueback trout leap from the walls
No good telling myself
it's only a wavelength of energy
so many radiant millimicrons zapping my eyeballs:
one man can handle only so much blue
I'm writing this with a red ballpoint pen
using blue only for punctuation
at my age even the semi-colon is risky
but I hate being careful
I feel like ending it all
Looking for you
I'll dash out in this blue October day
and let those bright blue chips
fall
where they may

PETER MEINKE

During a session on color imagery, "red" announced itself to Joan Baez in her cluster, then led her to a memory, which she released into words. Her warm-up vignette captures a luminous moment of childhood, making us nod in recognition of its elegant simplicity.

RED

How fascinating the sight of blood, the small prick following the starchy nurse's "This won't hurt" as she takes your first finger firmly in her grasp and steadies her hand and jabs you and it DOES hurt, and the tiniest red dot grows into a bubble of solid red blood and you push and push with your other fingers on the outside so the blood spills

over and trickles down in a red rivulet and then you can suck it clean
and it is always warm, as warm as fresh cow's milk.

JOAN BAEZ

Directing Your Hand

1. In your Writer's Notebook, quick-cluster the word (COLOR)
   to see what color begs for attention. Watch for a shift that
   says, "Here I am! Write about me."

2. Cluster this color for associations, paying attention to
   whatever images arise. Cluster a lot in order to get
   beyond the obvious (red-Valentine), allowing yourself
   to be open to more subtle imagery. Cluster until you experience a trial-web shift that gives you a sense of direction.

3. Write a focusing statement or two, bringing your Sign
   mind into the act.

4. Now write quickly for five minutes or less, focusing on
   images of the color in your mind. Be aware of the possibilities for recurrences, parallel forms, language rhythms—
   without trying too hard.

5. Come full circle with your vignette and revise as you
   wish.

6. Read it aloud, perhaps to a friend, and see how far your
   writing has come since you began writing naturally.

After Writing

Did your color imagery vignette take the form of a poem, or was
it prose? Where did it take you? Present, past, or future? Was it a
personal description, a tiny slice of your life as you recall it, or
was there a broader connection between the color that chose you
and the world at large? Baez focused on a tiny memory flash of a
moment involving blood, and Meinke on blue as a reflection of
feeling exuberant—the opposite of what we conventionally asso-

ciate with "blue." The following student writer leaps from "brown" to a political statement of affirmation:

BROWN

When I was small, I thought—like everyone else—brown was a drab, boring color. My brown hair and brown eyes were dull, unexciting, compared to blue, green, blond. But brown has changed for me— now, it is warm, rich, deep, kind, intelligent, knowing. The brown eyes and hair that seemed so common when I was small now reflect the richness and endurance of many, many—Asian, Mexican, Indian, African. Brown is real, solid, the color of the earth we have worked and struggled upon for generations. Brown is the color of our skin and of our hands that worked the farms and fields to make this country grow. Our eyes, hair, skin are brown like the roots of the tree we have planted here, brown like the sturdy growing bark and limbs of the future. Brown is beauty, strength, history, survival—brown is the future.

STUDENT

WHERE DO IMAGES COME FROM?

Images come from three interrelated sources: (1) external reality directly presented to the senses; (2) internal daydreams, fantasies, and dreams and nightmares; (3) imagery from myth, religion, and the arts, sometimes called archetypes, meaning that they are common to all humanity.

The External World as a Source of Images

Although our world is full of images, our senses are often dulled to them. We often go about the familiar patterns of our daily routines ignoring the powerful images that surround us. Attention is key; we need to cultivate a kind of active quiescence so that the marvels of the world around us startle and excite our consciousness. Only when we really open the mind's eye to see everyday experiences from a new angle can we write about them as moments of illumination. Karen Nelson clustered the word (WAKING) and came up with lovely, surreal images of a forest—and birth—in her bedroom: Figure 9-1 clusters around (WAKING).

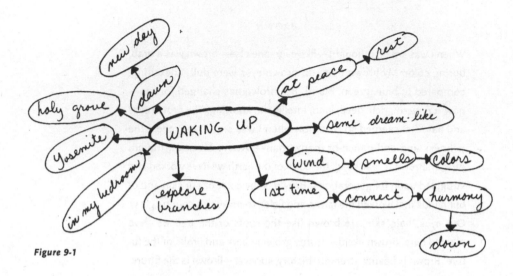

Figure 9-1

AROUSAL

Dawn-dappled ceiling
Yosemite in my bedroom
holy grove where I
awake for the first time.
I watch life's kaleidoscope
branching, and in my reverie
I see a sun being born.

KAREN NELSON

Can you recall when the discovery of the first furry caterpillar sent you into shivers of fear/pleasure? Remember when kicking crunchy leaves in fall on the way home from school made you happy inside? Well, do it again—today: really observe the face in the car next to you at a red light or a child playing with blocks, totally absorbed; look steadily at the inside of a flower, not just at its color or shape. The world brims for us. Here is Paula Jones Gardiner whose "Pear Tree" is like no other: It is *her* tree in *this* particular setting:

PEAR TREE

This is the tree I thought I'd prune
into manageability and ripe fruit,
the way my mother pruned me, hands
folded in my lap, my wiry hair cut short.
But I like it the way it is, a constellation
outside my window, its dreamy limbs in a tangle
from the second-story roof to the clothesline,
a dusting of lichen, like talc, on its skin.

Directing Your Hand

Quick-cluster (THIS IS) and in five or fewer minutes write a vignette of an object that means something special to you, showing how it is special.

Dreams as a Source of Images

Dreams are the Design mind's way of expressing itself in images. A student once told me, "A dream is clustering in images." And so it might well be. As early as 1844, neurologist A. L. Wigan suggested that our two brains are relatively independent during sleep, with a suspension of the power of the Sign mind over the Design mind. His hypothesis has been confirmed by studies showing greater electrical activity in the right brain during dreaming. Many researchers since then have suggested that the most complex dreams are done by the right brain, hence the nonsequential, nontemporal nature of the dream, with its overlapping images drawn from different time periods and locations. Brain surgeon Wilder Penfield found that mild electrical stimulation of a patient's right temporal cortex produced visual illusions of vivid memories—images—while probes of the left temporal cortex did not.

Great writers have always recognized the potency of dream images, using them as inspiration, among them Poe, Coleridge, and Hermann Hesse. Doris Lessing's *The Golden Notebook* is filled with dream images.

> I dreamed marvelously. I dreamed there was an enormous web of beautiful fabric stretched out. It was incredibly beautiful, covered all over with embroidered pictures. The pictures were illustrations of the myths of mankind but they were not just pictures, they were the myths themselves so that the soft glittering web was alive. In my dreams I handled and felt this material and wept with joy.

Since the advent of psychoanalysis, all therapies have included interpretation of dream images as keys to our mental states. For Freud, dream images were, at their root, sexual symbols. For Jung, they reflected the archetypal concerns of the collective unconscious. And for Gestaltists, they represent parts of ourselves, often in conflict.

Our Design mind designs our dreams without logical cause and effect. Each night, whether we recall them or not, we receive vivid images, complex and compelling stories from our Design mind. Pay attention to your dream images, and you will be in contact with the mystery of your life, for dreams are a form of communication from ourselves to ourselves. To ensure that you'll remember your dreams, record them by clustering as soon as you awaken. When you cluster, think of your dream as a painting. Begin with a dominant impression, an overall feeling of the totality of the dream. Was the dream frightening, disturbing, joyful? Dominant impressions could be named (TERROR) or (LAUGHING). There was a time when I had recurring "house" dreams. The houses were all different, from Victorian mansion to contemporary redwood homes at the ocean's edge, but each house brought with it differing degrees of negative feelings. One I named (APPREHENSION); another, (CURIOUS); a third (ANXIOUS). These were my dominant impressions. I could also have clustered dominant images from the dreams, for example, (COBWEB-FILLED EMPTY ROOM) or (CURVED STAIRCASE) or (DIM CHANDELIER).

Directing Your Hand

1. Dream-cluster for at least a week, then choose a dream that was most compelling.

2. Recall the dream as you look at what you've clustered, adding any other images you recall.

3. Now write your dream in the first person and in the present tense as though it were happening here, now. Even if your dream recall is fragmentary, re-create these fragments in words and see what happens. As you write, remember recurrences, language rhythms, and parallel structure to stack image on image ("floating, sticky cobwebs, worn wooden stairs, dirty light speckling the floor below") in order to achieve the compressed quality of a dream.

4. Come full circle by returning to your dominant impression that constellates these images. It doesn't have to be logical; for example, it can be a feeling (of dread?) or a total picture (of a bedraggled, turreted mansion).

ARCHETYPES AS IMAGES

Dream-clusters can lead to a discovery of archetypal aspects of our consciousness. Archetypes recur over and over in human consciousness, irrespective of culture. According to Jung, these images are preserved in the memory of the species because of innumerable repetitions of certain experiences: images of birth, love, death; images from nature—the sea, a mountain, the desert, a tunnel, valleys. We respond so powerfully to archetypal images because they reveal truths that are universal, and they appear in stories that cross all cultural boundaries.

Water, for example, is associated with life and birth in all cultures, just as the desert suggests sterility. Archetypes touch on our deepest wishes and fears: death, sexuality, abandonment, freedom. The monster, in all cultures, signifies what we fear most, possibly something in ourselves. The image of flight is also archetypal. Flying allows us to transcend gravity, the body's limitations. Flying suggests moral or spiritual ascent. In the myth of Icarus, flight suggests the need of an adolescent to break away and the consequence of such disobedience. For the writer below, flying and writing share similar imagery: Both are risky enterprises.

The Eskimo have the ability to walk around images in their minds like holograms. Because their environment could float away, they had to have remarkable visual memory in order to survive.

JEAN HOUSTON

Archetypal images bring us into touch with communal experience, general truths which have eternally bound humankind together.

C. DAY LEWIS

FLYING

For me, writing is lately like flying, in the risk it involves—the letting go whenever I fly, and a part of me does love to fly, first for the sensation of taking off, and second for the sense of adventure—I come face to face with all that I can lose. I fly and I fly over an abyss, I fly suspended above all that is uncertain and breakable in my life. I fly, and a thousand times I experience a small moment of death, of the plane lurching, exploding, falling down. I fly and experience loss. Lately, picking up this white and blue pen is a lot like flying. I cluster—I'm circling on the ground. I'm not lifting off, not letting go, every connection brings to me a new sense of the abyss, the abyss which Hamlet stared and stared into, the abyss that is loss of home—of my small family of friends and relatives who accept me (however little I ask). I write a word and circle it, and the word is like Paris or Copenhagen to me—I hear the clopping of the King's horse's feet on cobblestones, I smell diesel fuel and stare up at the face of Notre Dame—the world is reaching out, and still I touch down. I don't want to lose my home. I'm afraid to lose my home. If I leave, I will lose my home. And so, when I try to write these days, I hesitate—I'm afraid to leave the ground.

ANDREA SANDKE

Directing Your Hand

Develop your image-making powers by discovering your own associations with flight.

1. In your Writer's Notebook, cluster the nucleus (FLYING). Practice active quiescence; widen your attention as though squinting your eyes to get a fuller picture. Cluster for 30 seconds to a minute until you experience a trial-web shift to a sense of direction.

2. Now write quickly for five minutes or less. Be aware of the qualities of natural writing that give your writing richness and authenticity—rhythm, recurrences, openness to wonder.

3. Only after you come full circle should you think about going back to reshape what you've written. Read the whole out loud, then add to or subtract from the pattern of meaning on the page.

IMAGE AND ART

Lascaux, France, is the site of cave paintings that are more than 30,000 years old (Figure 9-2). In his poem, William Stafford imagines himself *in* that cave, imagines himself as that first cave painter, imagines his mind making the connection between image and actuality, between mental image and the real thing, between image and self, and image and act—and pictures the sense of empowerment in this early ancestor. The "I," "the animal," "the bow," and "the arrow," all come together as an imagined whole. The image rendered on the wall "hold(s) still." Stafford is reverent before the unfolding of the imaging human mind and the stunning artifacts that spring from this impulse.

Figure 9-2   Lascaux, France

AT LASCAUX

It came into my mind that no one had painted there
deep in the ground: if I made a beast,
an arrow into the heart, then above ground
it would come into my mind again, and
what I hunted, wherever it was, would fall.
Now where I go, daylight or dark,
I hold something still. Before I shoot,
whatever the bow does, and the arrow, and I am
the animal, all come true down deep in the earth:
all that I am comes into my mind.

WILLIAM STAFFORD

Directing Your Hand

Your turn to experience what your Design mind will do with art images.

1. Take a few moments to bring your body and mind into active quiescence. Now let your eyes take in the entire painting. Your Design mind accomplishes this in microseconds. Be alert for a dominant impression. The first is most often the best. Trust it.

2. Name that dominant impression in a word or phrase and write it inside the circle on the page.

3. Cluster around this impression what you see, feel, interpret, associate. Be curious to see what will turn up.

4. Notice the trial-web shift, signaling a sense of direction.

5. Experiment with one or two focusing statements before writing, bringing your Sign mind into play.

6. Write quickly, oscillating between global whole and emerging detail. Let it take whatever shape it wants to.

7. Read your vignette aloud and listen for full-circle whole-ness, recurrences, language rhythms, images. Make any changes you would like.

After Writing

Although any external visual image exhibits a pattern of meaning, when you filter it through your experiential sieve, you generate your own pattern of meaning. Very likely your strongest experience during this activity was the feeling of being pulled in a particular direction as your Design mind struggled to create its own meaning from this image. You also probably experienced a strong positive or negative pull resulting in a dominant impression.

A LAST WORD AND HEADING ON

Images are the Design mind's way of constructing patterns and weaving context. The impulse to create images is basic to human cognition and can be stunningly enhanced. Nadia, an autistic child, at the age of three and a half, suddenly showed an amazing capacity to draw. She drew horses especially, in the manner of a skilled adult artist (Figure 9-3). This child, with devastating cognitive and emotional deficits, apparently skipped the various scribbling and tadpole stages, right away demonstrating skill with perspective. Interestingly, she did not draw from a model but from memory of pictures she had once seen. But the pictures were merely the point of departure, as she varied her versions almost at will, experimenting with different forms until she hit upon a product that satisfied her. Cognitive psychologists now know that the "normal" learning curve can sometimes occur in great leaps and, in the case of autistic children, in certain islands of skill, such as musical or mathematical systems.

Poet Lisel Mueller apparently came across Nadia's work (Figure 9-3) and was moved to write a poem expressing her amazement at the human impulse to make patterns of meaning:

Figure 9-3   Nadia, Age 5½, Horse

THE ARTIST

The girl who never speaks
draws a horse like you've never seen,
a horse with feathers,
with eyes cut into diamonds
like the eyes of a bee,
with a tail of braided grasses
and a man of waterfalls.
Its ears are lilies
and its nostrils homes for swallows,
but its fine hooves and ankles
are what they always were,
because there is no greater beauty.

Where she lives there are no horses,
but she has seen them in books
and watched them rear and whinny
on television. She understands

their patience, day after day,
in the land of the flies. In a dream
she encountered a solitary
blue horse in a field. He came close
and ate an apple out of her hand.

She draws him over and over
in absolute silence. She is afraid
language will fritter away the world,
its gleam and thunder,
its soft, curled lip,
the flying back which only
she dares to ride.

LISEL MUELLER

The brain's islands of skill—in Nadia's case, the recollection of an image and the ability to draw it creatively—say something about its astonishing flexibility to express its knowing, despite stifling deficits. And, if Lisel Mueller's delicate rendering of Nadia's gift is any indicator, the creative process is essentially a re-creative pattern-making process, triggered by nature or by our own or others' images, ideas, or feelings. As plentiful as images are, many are fragile, fleeting, insubstantial. They are Design-mind associations that reflect emotional nuances, which we can't fully understand with our Sign mind. To fully cultivate your natural writer, become receptive to the images of your waking and dreaming worlds. Even if you have no time to write, record images as a cluster in your Writer's Notebook. Held on the page as a cluster, they are easily accessed.

This chapter on images leads naturally to the next chapter on metaphor, for metaphor can come into being only through the mediation of images and can be understood only by building a bridge between Design-mind image and Sign-mind idea.

TEN

WEDDING WORD TO IMAGE: METAPHOR

I n F. Scott Fitzgerald's *The Great Gatsby*, Gatsby, referring to the wealthy Daisy, tells the narrator:

> "Her voice is full of money."
>
> That was it. I'd never understood before. It was full of money—that was the inexhaustible charm that rose and fell in it, the jingle of it, the cymbals' song of it. . . .

Fitzgerald could have written "Daisy gives the impression of being very rich," but the author's metaphor goes far beyond the givens of literal language to resonate and suggest, creating shock waves of deeper meaning.

Metaphor consists of images connected to something they literally cannot be. Literally speaking, a voice cannot be full of money, yet the fusing of these dissimilar entities into one new image tells us something about Daisy's personality that is inexpressible in denotative language. Metaphors create tension and excitement by producing new connections, and in so doing reveal a truth about the world we had not previously recognized.

Images, as we have seen, are word pictures that give language power and richness by involving our senses in the experience. When we wed an image to something totally unexpected, a provocative new pattern—metaphor—is created. For example, if an instructor told a skier, "The mountain is a dish of vanilla ice cream and you are hot fudge—flow down the slope" (as Denise McCluggage did in her book, *The Centered Skier*), the skier would have an image of gliding and connectedness that would convey something important about a skier's proper relationship to a hill. Consider the Sign-mind alternative, which might go something like this:

> Now plant the pole on your right, then swing your body and skis around it, keeping your skis parallel and shifting your weight to the downhill ski as you go into the turn. Ski downhill a few yards to gain momentum, skis parallel, and then plant your pole on the left; swing around your pole, paying attention to the parallel of your skis, and then shift your weight to your right, the downhill ski.

Of course, the mountain is *not* ice cream and a person is *not* hot fudge, yet the advice communicates the proper feel of skiing, the sense of a whole fluid movement, more directly than a sequence of technically correct instructions can.

This chapter focuses on yet another aspect of natural writing: the Design mind's ability to make fresh connections, to see, hear, and feel metaphorically. Metaphors bring additional dimension to your writing and help to train your thinking in Design-mind ways. Metaphor generates new means of expression when the conventional or denotative will not suffice, thus extending your power over language and expanding your inherent creative potential. Since each of us has the natural potential for making connections and seeing relationships in our own unique way, metaphor-making is a highly personal, richly creative phenomenon.

An experiment with split-brain patients described by Robert Nebes (in *The Human Brain*, edited by Merle Wittrock) underscores the Design mind's metaphoric view of the world, contrasting it with the Sign mind's stolidly logical view. A picture of a round cake on a plate is flashed on a screen to a split-brain patient's right visual field, which feeds into the logical left brain. The patient is then instructed to choose an object from a large array that is pictured with the cake. The left brain invariably makes a logical choice, such as a knife or fork, for naturally you

To a wholly new experience, one can give sufficient organization only by relating it to the already known, by perceiving a relation between this experience and another experience already ordered, placed, and incorporated.

JAMES OLNEY

We pay for the exactitude of factual language with the price of being able to speak from only one point of view at a time.

ALAN WATTS

need the one to cut the cake with, the other to eat it with. But when the same round cake on a plate is flashed to the patient's left visual field, which feeds into the right brain, the patient invariably chooses—a round straw hat with a brim! Perceiving similarity of shape in dissimilar things is certainly not logical, but it strikes us as ingenious—and that is the power of metaphor: to surprise us, make us catch our breath, illuminate an aspect of the world that is totally at odds with the conventional way of seeing it.

In chapter 4, I described Sign-mind thinking as computerlike. In a government-funded automatic-language-translation project, researchers discovered that even the most sophisticated computer is utterly baffled by fairy tales and metaphors. Translating "The spirit is willing, but the flesh is weak" from English to Russian and then back to English, the computer wrote "The wine is agreeable, but the meat has spoiled." When given the proverb "Out of sight, out of mind," the computer decided it meant "Blind and crazy." We can get beyond the literal and conventional only through Design-mind participation. In the last eighteen years we still have no software programs that can decipher metaphors.

Let me use another visual illustration. In Figure 10-1 you see a pair of bicycle handlebars; in Figure 10-2 you see a bicycle seat. When you logically process these two objects with Sign-mind expectations, you see the parts and think "bicycle." But if, like Picasso, you see from a Design-mind perspective, bicycle handlebars and bicycle seat do not add up to bicycle, but rather to the

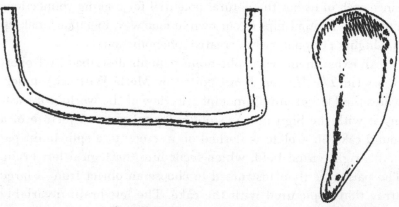

Figure 10-1   *Figure 10-2*

head of a bull (Figure 10-3). For Picasso, the literal bicycle parts coalesced and were transformed into something each was literally not: The seat was not a head, nor the handlebars horns. Yet, combined, the two elements created a strong new image that cast each element in a new light.

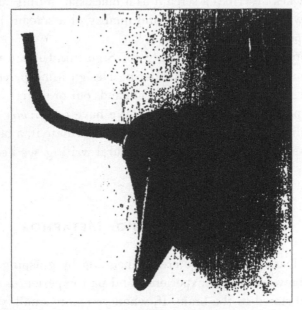

Figure 10-3 Pablo Picasso, Tête de taureau, © Spadem, Paris/Vaga, New York, 1982

Art is the most compelling combination of metaphor and image. When art is successful in metaphorically "bearing" us "across and above," there are no transitions. It is an all-at-once quantum jump.
LEONARD SHLAIN

All language is fossil metaphor.
R. W. EMERSON

Picasso's bicycle bull is a visual metaphor. Let us turn now to linguistic metaphor, which is equally grounded in image and which graces all potent writing.

METAPHOR: A BILINGUIST FOR THE BRAIN

Linguistic metaphor is simultaneously sign and design, and, as a consequence, it has the power to connect our two modes of knowing. Denise McCluggage, in *The Centered Skier*, suggests that metaphor is a "bilinguist" for the brain, drawing on the power of both hemispheres: verbal for the left and image for the right. When we use a metaphor, she says, a spark arcs from Design to Sign mind, making a connection. The metaphor as image resonates in the right brain with pictures, or complex wholes, which the left hemisphere expresses in words that imply a similarity in dissimilarity; in joining word and image, a sudden illumination takes place, a perception or insight that sheds new light on a familiar feeling/idea/event. For example, in *Second Skin* novelist John Hawkes describes a scream as a black bat, telling us something new about the character and quality of a scream by joining unexpected image to idea.

Metaphor does not substitute for Sign-mind meanings but adds to those meanings by articulating Design-mind perceptions. In so doing, metaphor enormously expands our ordinary resources for both perception and expression. We have to *perceive* a similarity in dissimilar entities before we can articulate it, a talent we have possessed since childhood. In natural writing, we need only reawaken these perceptions.

CHILDHOOD ORIGINS OF METAPHOR

Children learning language create meaning by grasping a relationship between a new experience and past experiences already coded and stored in the brain. If, when you were small, your existing repertoire did not fit a new situation, you tended to generate metaphors—or their first cousin, simile. (Both metaphor and simile originate in the ability to perceive similarity in dissimilarity; the difference is that simile has "pointers"—*like* or *as*—to explicitly signal that we are joining logically unjoinable entities. Metaphor dispenses with these pointers, simply asserting a likeness between two unlike things, thus making a metaphor richer, more open-ended, more resonant.) In *Language and Learning*, British scholar James Britton gives an account of how this works. Presented with the first strawberries of her life, his two-and-a-half-year-old daughter examined them and said: "They are like cherries." As she tasted them, she said, "They are just like sweeties [candies]." Then she summed it up: "They are like red ladybirds." To bring novel experience into meaningful focus, she borrowed qualities already familiar to her—redness, sweetness, roundness, and spottedness, from cherries, candies, and lady bugs—and

The scream ... that was clamped between my teeth was a strenuous black bat struggling, wrestling in my bloated mouth and ... I, with my eyes squeezed tight, my lips squeezed tight, felt that at any moment it must thrust the slimy black tip of its archaic skeletal wing into view.

JOHN HAWKES, *Second Skin*

Metaphor builds a bridge between the hemispheres, symbolically carrying knowledge from the mute right brain so that it may be recognized by the left as being like something already know.

MARILYN FERGUSON,
The Aquarian Conspiracy

applied them to strawberries. Thus, new meaning emerged from her metaphoric play.

Children in the stage of the innocent eye, ear, and hand make metaphors because they don't as yet have sufficient fixed and literal terms for all the ideas they want to express; they substitute words and concepts they do know. Once when I was playing gin rummy with my five-year-old, Suzi, she asked in all seriousness, "Mom, in a run, do all the cards have to be the same sex?" In due time she learned the proper—albeit less imaginative—word *suit.*

In my own study of children's metaphoric abilities, I found not only the metaphoric responses came easily and naturally but that these responses were derived primarily from the shapes of the images they conjured up. Four-year-old Simone, for example, readily answered questions metaphorically as each object was pointed out to her:

What is that star like?	It's like a flower without a stem.
What is the moon like?	It's like a smiling mouth.
What is your shoe like?	It's like a little boat.
What is your nose like?	It's like a tiny, tiny hill.
What are my eyebrows like?	They're like two bridges over two swimming pools.

In contrast, children in the stage of the conventional eye, ear, and hand created virtually no metaphors. As the following examples from nine- to eleven-year-olds show, they tend to respond either with rudimentary definitions or the overly familiar.

What is this book like?	It's like reading about something: a lot of words.
What is this TV like?	A movie screen that is close up.
What is this mirror like?	A weird piece of glass; something that makes another of you.
What is this star like?	A light in the distance.
What is the sun like?	A big ball of fire burning in the sky.

Metaphors are the threads by which the mind holds on to the world even when, absentmindedly, it has lost direct contact with it, and they guarantee the unity of human experience.

HANNAH ARENDT

What is the moon like?   A shining piece of something in
                                the atmosphere; a big glow-
                                ing thing in the sky.

*When we attempt to
express living experience
with words, logical
speech quickly
becomes permeated
with metaphors.*
CHARLES M. JOHNSTON

*Without metaphor,
language would lose
its lifeblood and stiffen
into a conventional
system of signs.*
ERNST CASSIRER

As our repertoire of fixed and reliable Sign-mind categories increases, our metaphoric power seems to diminish and we readily observe the boundaries imposed by the literal-minded and formal education. And perhaps necessarily so, for we have to learn to function in a world in which shared and conventional Sign-mind systems are the prime means of communication and expression. But we don't want to get stuck in the conventional mode without the tools necessary to move into the third stage—the cultivated eye, ear, and hand of the natural writer.

Even though our metaphor-making has been somewhat eclipsed by constant exposure to the literal use of language, none of us is purely literal-minded. When we dream, we naturally make metaphors. In my dreams, for example, the house images that have recurred again and again seem to be metaphors for my life and perhaps, even more specifically, for my psyche; the unfamiliar rooms I opened with curiosity and wonder were parts of me I was just discovering.

When we are stuck for words to describe accurately what we mean, we say, "You know, it's like . . ." or "Well, it's as if . . ." or "It feels as though . . ." Not finding in our Sign mind what we need to express a thought or feeling, we shift to Design-mind images to help us out, and, in articulating them, we make metaphors.

This tiny poem by W. S. Merwin creates an unforgettable metaphor that requires little commentary.

ABSENCE

Your absence has gone through me
Like thread through a needle.
Everything I do is stitched with its color.

The expressive power of natural writing lies in the ability to reawaken our talent for metaphor-making. If we speak and write with only our left brain, without this reawakening, we tend to sound like Northrop Frye's insistently cliché-obsessed scholar.

Success with metaphors depends on whether the Design mind is allowed to get into the act. Clustering, once again, is the key to effect a conscious shift to nonliteral, non-cliché Design-mind processing. Allow your Design mind to make spontaneous connections, and it will produce images that can be transformed into metaphor.

Before you direct your own hand in writing metaphoric vignettes, let's practice by using the simplest, most natural way of developing metaphoric insight: perceiving similarity between shapes.

SEEING SHAPES INTO THINGS

The secret of metaphor lies in letting the quality of your attention shift from Sign- to Design-mind processes. Sign mind says: "Yes, a cloud—cumulus, I think," while the Design mind sees a profile of Abraham Lincoln.

The trigger that lets us make this shift lies in the words "like" or "as." As soon as we say one thing is *like* another, we are letting go of Sign-mind insistence on the literal; it gives us license to compare apparently unlike things. For example, in this phrase by poet Nils Peterson—"our bodies wait patient *as* horses"—*as* tends to block the bossy, logical Sign-mind policeman to give metaphoric insights a chance to surface. True metaphor dispenses with these signposts, further extending and deepening the potency of an image, as in another Peterson line: "Those masters gone they turn/nuzzle, and flank to flank speak to each other." In simile, bodies are compared to horses; in metaphor those bodies have *become* horses.

Now read Nils Peterson's poem and see how he extends his initial simile into a sustained metaphor.

BEDTIME

—for Judith—

If we have quarreled our bodies wait
patient as horses for their owners' huffy

... listening to a speech by a high authority in the field, I know him to be a good scholar ... Yet his speech is a muddy river of cliches. ... The content of the speech does not do justice to his mind; what it does reflect is the state of his literary education. He has never been trained to visualize his abstractions, to subordinate logic and sequence to the insights of metaphor and simile, to realize that figures of speech are not ornaments of language but the elements of both language and thought. ... Nothing can now be done for him: there are no courses in remedial metaphor.
NORTHROP FRYE

A leaf swept along by the wind often looks like a bird.
GOETHE

departure. Those masters gone they turn,
nuzzle, and flank to flank speak
to each other all night long
the eloquent touching language of the dumb.

It is not the role of metaphor to draw our sight to what is there, but to draw our vision outward to what is not there and, indeed, cannot be anywhere. Metaphor is horizontal, reminding us that it is our vision that is limited and not what we are viewing.

J. P. CARSE

For our purposes, we will make no further distinction between simile and metaphor. Both figures of speech serve the same end—to shift to nonliteral ways of seeing, thus giving our writing its richer texture and greater expressive power.

METAPHOR MADNESS

As you regain a feel for playful Design-mind connections, you will realize that anything can be expressed metaphorically. And if one metaphor packs a punch because it delivers an image in a new context, several metaphors piled one on top of the other can be great fun:

I was dizzy as a dervish, as weak as a worn-out washer, as low as a badger's belly, as timid as a titmouse, and as unlikely to succeed as a ballet dancer with a wooden leg.

RAYMOND CHANDLER

Directing Your Hand

1. Using Chandler's sentence as a model, play with multiple metaphors to make a point. Record your work in your Writer's Notebook.

2. Play with images resulting from an activity you know well: carpentry, horseback riding, jogging, dancing, cooking.

3. Quick-cluster your own nucleus, such as:

I/HE/SHE WAS AS _____ AS _____.

HER HOUSE WAS AS _____ AS _____.

WRITING IS AS _____ AS _____.

After Writing

In these student examples, see how each writer processed particular images to create amusing and original metaphors:

- My brain was as dead as a used battery, naked as a plucked chicken, dormant as a dried pea, and empty as Old Mother Hubbard's cupboard when I searched it for the answers to the exam.

- I felt as faded as the paint job, as dented as the bumpers, as flat as the tire, as empty as the gas tank, and as cooperative as the ignition which refused to do anything but groan.

- I was as witty as Lewis Carroll, as crazy as the Mad Hatter, as transient as the Cheshire Cat, as hurried as the White Rabbit, and as perplexed as Alice in Wonderland.

- I was as happy as a cat in a cream pitcher, as smug as a rat in a delicatessen, as silly as a penguin playing the piano, and as unlikely to succeed as a rooster with laryngitis.

Notice that each writer used different connecting strategies to achieve wholeness, such as using all images from *Alice in Wonderland*.

THE "WHAT AM I?" METAPHOR

For years I have asked my students on the first day of class or in writing intensives to choose an animal they would like to be that day, because the association helped me recall their names. After a time, I asked them to experiment in writing by clustering their animal to see what associations came up. Fresh, insightful metaphors emerged. For example, student Lisa Ricks clustered (WHAT AM I?) (Figure 10-4), which yielded a metaphoric leap to an animal shape, her vignette describing qualitative aspects of herself as a starfish.

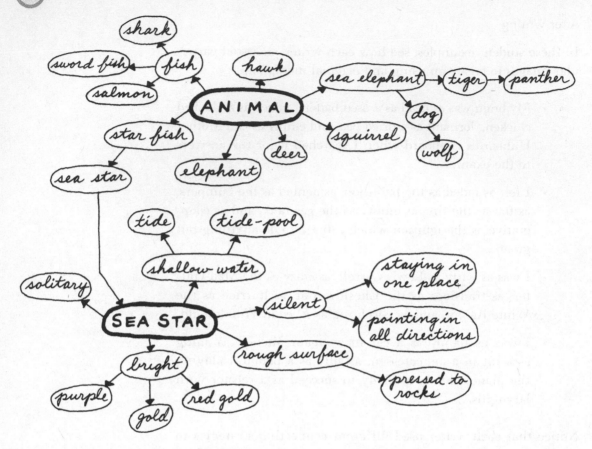

Figure 10-4
Pre-cluster and Re-cluster

WHAT AM I?

The rough purple arch of my back glows,
bright splash against dark rocks.
I suck the sand, foam, water—
stretch my salt-slicked arms
pointing in all directions
while the hulk and bulk of my soul
hunches in secret,
clinging to a single
smooth place in the rock.
Giving you directions,

I remain unmoved,
I stay still with my silence
where I can absorb and interpret
vibrations of water, changes in tide.
Fed full with my silence,
I am alone, carrying the center of my solitude
in the center of a star.

The metaphoric leap led to new ways of seeing and enabled students to break the imagined boundaries of reality or accuracy. Metaphor is improvisation.

Metaphorically we can become anything we wish, disclosing much more than we could if we said, "I am a woman," "a mother," "a professor," "an author," and so on. Student Tiffany Darrough describes herself here as a pair of Levi's:

WEAVING

I am my favorite worn-out,
torn-up,
just getting-broken-in
Levis.
I am these jeans bought when we staggered out of Death Valley
and spent New Year's Eve living it up in Las Vegas.
I won a hundred dollars on the slots in these jeans.
I am stained and torn and used and comfortable.
I am the black boots and silk blouse
that decorate them on Saturday.
I am the wooly socks and college sweatshirt
that frame them on Sunday.
I am the patches that say frugal but artistic.
I am the frayed and bare ass that says loyal but sexy.
I am baby spit and little league grass stains.
I am museums and holidays and poetry and parties.
I am an archive of all my body has lived in these jeans,
I am just hinting at possibility to come.

Directing Your Hand

In your Writer's Notebook, pre-cluster (WHAT AM I?) and reach for metaphors that characterize you. Cluster until you experience a trial-web shift, then cluster the thing that says, "Hey, this is it!" Then write quickly, knowing you can always come back and shape the initial expression. The more improvisational you are, the more true and expressive your metaphors.

THE METAPHORIC IN ALL CULTURES

All cultures seems to speak metaphorically to express essential truths in their songs, their speech, their stories. Look at the Nahuatl Indian poem about their staple food, corn; this chant was used by workshop participant Jan Egry as the basis for her extended metaphor.

EAR-OF-CORN

You　are　a silver bell
You　are　a child's teeth
You　are　a sea shell
　　　white　white
You　are　a　crystal
　　　white　white
You　are　a　green　stone
You　are　a　bracelet
You　are　perfection
You　are　our　flesh
You　are　our　bones.

NAHUATL POEM (MEXICO)

FOR DON

You are my staff—
my treble, my bass.
My notes trail out upon you.
You set my rhythms.

You encourage my rests, my trills,
my rubatos.
I improvise on your steadiness,
your trueness,
your endless lines and spaces.

You play music
more beautifully than it was written.
We read the score and
sing the songs
together.

J. P. EGRY

Linguist Suzette Elgin asserts that the more metaphors you have for something, the more indexes it will have in your memory, with a direct payoff in greater understanding and ease of access. Popular metaphors are like holograms—any recognized part will serve to carry the information of the whole. If this is so, then the Nahuatl will certainly never forget their corn!

Making Feelings Tangible through Metaphor

The elusive world of feelings becomes tangible through metaphoric leaps. Take "sadness" for instance. The dictionary tells us sadness is "a melancholy state of mind," but that Sign-mind definition does not tell us much about the nuances of each individual's experience of sadness. Most of us reach for clichés—metaphors or similes that have lost their edge from overuse: brokenhearted, blue, down-in-the-dumps. Fresh metaphors trigger a flash of recognition in us, such as the vibrant metaphors poet Lisel Mueller "paints" in "Imaginary Paintings" to make abstractions such as "happiness" or "nostalgia" or "THE FUTURE" real for us.

IMAGINARY PAINTINGS

1. HOW I WOULD PAINT THE FUTURE
   A strip of horizon and a figure,
   seen from the back, forever approaching.

2. HOW I WOULD PAINT HAPPINESS
   Something sudden, a windfall,
   a meteor shower. No—
   a flowering tree releasing
   all its blossoms at once,
   and the one standing beneath it
   unexpectedly robed in bloom,
   transformed into a stranger
   too beautiful to touch.

3. HOW I WOULD PAINT DEATH

White on white or black on black.
No ground, no figure. An immense canvas,
which I will never finish.

4. HOW I WOULD PAINT LOVE

I would not paint love.

5. HOW I WOULD PAINT THE LEAP OF FAITH

A black cat jumping up three feet
to reach a three-inch shelf.

6. HOW I WOULD PAINT THE BIG LIE

Smooth, and deceptively small
so that it can be swallowed
like something we take for a cold.
An elongated capsule,
an elegant cylinder,
sweet and glossy,
that pleases the tongue
and goes down easy,
never mind
the poison inside.

7. HOW I WOULD PAINT NOSTALGIA

An old-fashioned painting, a genre piece.
People in bright and dark clothing.
A radiant bride in white
standing above a waterfall,
watching the water rush
away, away, away.

Directing Your Hand

For Mueller, a lie is a pill, but not just any pill; it is "deceptively small." It is an "elegant cylinder." It "goes down easy." And it is poisonous! Cluster (HOW I WOULD PAINT . . .) until something rings a bell—let's use as an example (LOVE) (which Mueller would not paint). Recluster (HOW I WOULD PAINT LOVE) and reach for metaphors; what does love look like, taste like, wear? Then write quickly for five minutes or less. Now go back and shape what you've written. If you used "like" or "as," drop it and make the comparison directly. Add and subtract details that will make your metaphor display its multiple attributes. Make your "painting in words" vivid.

After Writing

This is an activity you can return to again and again. You can make any abstract word come to life by imagining how you would paint it: for example, anger could be a rabid dog. Or you could paint some of Mueller's abstractions the way you envision them. Our language is full of abstractions that can be brought to life through metaphor.

PLAYING WITH PERSONIFICATION

Another way to take a metaphoric leap to find similarity in dissimilarity is to personify—that is, to make an abstraction into a person. Sometimes discovering metaphors is best done collaboratively. I often refer to J. Ruth Gendler's personifications in her wonderful *Book of Qualities* and then have workshop participants get into groups of four and improvise. Here are three metaphors using personification, written by groups of workshop students. Each group pre-clustered (FEELINGS), then agreed on one, and set to work:

- Greed
  Greed is a blowsy woman who layers herself in soiled luxury while her pale brother, Deprivation, sits on a city street,

holding a tin cup in his bony arm. Greed is married to Speed. She has fingers that don't remember the hand they belong to. She spends her life accumulating a ransom for tomorrow. Greed gorges herself on chocolate-chip cookie dough and insecurity. She gossips about her neighbor, Abstinence, behind her back.

- Resistance
*Resistance is a cop to stop, block, deny, impose
and say, "No, no, no, OK, OK, no."
Neurotic and proud of it,
Resistance slow dances with Superiority
—and hates how Courage does her hair.*

- Resentment
*Resentment does the dishes while everyone else is eating
      dessert.
She hoards old clothes, keeps old letters and scraps of con-
      versations in a trunk in her attic.
She appears as a grey shadow in family photographs.
She smokes but always sits in the nonsmoking section.
When she dines with her friend, Anger, Anger sends back
      the soup.
Resentment eats hers cold.*

Directing Your Hand

Whether you do this activity alone or with others, begin by quick-clustering a (QUALITY), then cluster the one that wants you to pay attention to it for detail, without censoring. Then personify your quality as male or female and write for two or three minutes.

After Writing

Play with your vignettes if you still are not satisfied. Metaphor expresses truths we neither recognized nor had words for in literal language.

Metaphors of the Body

Most of us think about our bodies metaphorically. For some of us, our body is a doormat to be used and abused until it finally wears out; for others, the body is an adversary, causing aches and pains; others think of their body as something physical that merely gets in the way of the spiritual; for still others, the body is a friend to be treated lovingly. In this poem, high-tech metaphors for the body give the piece its original and lighthearted perspective.

BODY SHOP

I've been real lucky,
considering my body came
without extended warranty
and cannot be returned.
It came by mail order
and had to be purchased
sight-unseen, as-is, no-return.
A big risk,
but I was lucky:
All the parts are in the right place
    —auditory receptors, two visual remote sensing units,
    monophonic voice component
    wall-to-wall skin.
My body comes on-line regularly at around
6–7 A.M. and goes off-line
anywhere from 9 P.M. to 1 A.M.
I carry insurance on it, of course.
Just one problem: I can't find the slot
    for the memory upgrade.

STUDENT

Directing Your Hand

1. Precluster (BODY, MY . . .) for any possible metaphors that strike you.

2. Select one of those metaphors and cluster it for associations and detail until you experience a trial-web shift.

3. Write a focusing statement or two that includes the metaphor you will develop.

4. Now write rapidly, beginning with "Body, my . . ." Play with the metaphor.

5. Read your vignette aloud. Rework it until you are satisfied with the developed metaphor and its rhythms.

After Writing

For many writers this activity is a revelation. The metaphors that unfold first as images from your Design mind, then as evocative words and phrases, most likely tell you much more about yourself than you ever knew. In the past fifteen years, many of my students have been surprised at the radical differences in the metaphors that seem to choose them, from one month to the next, one year to the next. Do a body metaphor once or twice a year to see how your metaphors change.

A Last Word and Heading On

In this chapter you discovered that metaphors spring from your Design mind's predilection for seeing pattern. Every metaphor reflects similarity in dissimilarity—and as natural writers we can play with the countless connections between dissimilarities we notice every day. A tree is not a face. And yet, when you walk in the woods and come across a "face" in a tree stump, your Design mind gives it a name. Metaphors amplify our language resources and invite creativity. Without the creative insights of metaphor, our perceptions would be shaped and limited by the familiar. Metaphor extends our means of knowing.

Just as metaphor opens new dimensions for natural writing, so does an awareness of the nuances of voice—the subject of chapter 11.

ELEVEN

NUANCES: THE MANY VOICES IN THE ONE

In the Eskimo language, the words "to breathe" and "to make a poem" are the same. Remembering that has been wildly helpful to me. It means a freeness to plunge in, almost like doing a finger painting. It's a free flow, suspending fact, meaning, sanity, then seeing, in what pours out uncensored, what can be shaped, fashioned, pared down or enlarged to become a poem.

LYNN LIFSHIN

Long before human beings made marks on paper, the instrument of story was voice. Voice, coming from the Latin *vocare*, to call, is the sound of living creatures. *Vocables* are soundings-out; we *vocalize* with our *vocal* chords, which are animated by our breath. "Let me breathe of it," says the Inuit who wants to tell a story. And so we utter, express, articulate, enunciate, pronounce, deliver, emit, emphasize, exclaim. *Vocabulary* refers to our treasure hoard of words by which we throw thoughts, feelings, images, outside ourselves and into the world.

When we are *voice*less, we are mute, silent. We are aphonic. Sometimes we feel muzzled, throttled, choked off, cut short, drowned, smothered, struck dumb, put to silence—speechlessness is close to breathlessness. So, to me, voice is a resonant archetypal expression of the sacred breath. When we have a voice, we can speak for ourselves, for others, with others.

ONE VOICE OR MANY VOICES?

In writing, voice is generally defined along these lines: it is the authentic sound, rhythm, texture, nuance of a unique consciousness on the page. The prevalent belief, that only the great writers have a unique voice, is championed by those who study and support the idea that voice is tied to genius. But writers of stature spend most of their lives developing that unique voice—which we recognize only because we have read or heard their writing. Milton's voice was rich and resonant; Frost's, relaxed, conversational; Hemingway's, masculine, no-nonsense; Emily Dickinson's, spare, cryptic; Faulkner's, flowing, meandering. What we rarely read about is that they reach uniqueness only by taking on many voices. For example, Picasso insisted that the very attempt to recreate another artist's pictorial "voice" ultimately leads you to your own. We can reach our unique voice only in circuitous ways.

In fact, we all have the potential to develop a voice in words on a page. So we grow into our own voices by trying on many voices, not just the voices outside of us but the multiple voices within us.

> *You should constantly try to paint like someone else. But the thing is, you can't! You would like to. You try. But it turns out to be a botch. . . . And it's at the very moment you make a botch of it that you're yourself.*
>
> **PICASSO,** *Parmelin, 1965*

> *This is the feeling for syllable and rhythm, penetrating far below the conscious levels of thought and feeling, invigorating every word.*
>
> **T. S. ELIOT**

The Voices of the Multimind

Robert Ornstein, student of how the mind works, calls the human mind a "multimind" because he sees it as being many-minded. Linguist Stephen Pinker calls this multimind the *combinatorial* mind, which "opens up a world of words and sentences."

The contemporary understanding of consciousness, according to Ornstein, is that "we do not have access to all of our talents at once. Our consciousness is clearly limited to only a few items at a time." Moreover, he argues that we are not like computers possessed of a single kind of knowledge or remembrance. Rather, our minds change as they learn, and are *altered* to work differently with experience. "That we are consistent and single-minded is a built-in delusion," says Ornstein. "The multimind idea explains why we have so many conflicting thoughts about ourselves, about specific people in our lives, and about human nature itself. There are diverse, divergent, and multiple minds, and contradictions come with the territory of being human."

Our view of others is partial, oversimplified. We pass each other like ships in the night; we send out a small and partial signal to each other, and we receive it with a part of our minds. We are not able to know others completely in all their complexity. And our own selves are hidden from us as well. Ornstein insists that the mental diversity within and the diversity of our personalities must be understood and made use of as far as we can go. "All our separate minds know about each other is what they observe to be happening. They do not have the intimate access one would assume."

Since we are multiminded, we are many-voiced. It is part of our gift as language-producing animals. In order to become more conscious of the multi-voices of our multimind, we can experiment with taking on many different voices in different ways. Therefore we will play with the *monologic* voice (the "I" search), the *dialogic* voice (the "you" search), and the *multilogic* voice (the "we" search).

The monologic search is inward, speaking from one place and trying to sustain it. The dialogic search is outward, trying to reach out to someone and adjusting and altering as the dialogue shifts and changes direction. The multilogic search moves in several directions, like Picasso's cubistic paintings and Toni Morrison's fiction.

As we grow out of our separateness from monologue through dialogue, we hear the multilogic voice, the voice of multiple angles of vision taking into account multi-perspectives, multi-ways of seeing, being, doing, having, feeling, thinking. It is what makes us most human. These multilogic voices may not agree, but they allow each other their space, inviting alternative perspectives. Openness to multilogic voices opens us to growth, development, insight, evolution, and, ultimately, transcendence. What this chapter focuses on is strategies for tapping into and using these voices in our writing.

The multivoiced multimind lets us discover that all the voices you try on are aspects of your Self; the many voices that compete for your attention in the middle of the night, the voices of do and don't, the voices of self and other, the voices of male and female, are all attempts to express the totality of who you are. When we expand our own repertoire of being-in-the-world, we begin to see how and why other voices do what they do, see what they see, hear what they hear. Voice allows you to picture, to imagine, to empathize.

We learn about "voice" in writing by taking on many voices, by experimenting, by allowing our imaginations to express this voice, that voice. In the process, we find the writer's voice that is most authentically our own. It took me half a lifetime to discover my voice by allowing myself to become improvisational and by playing with multiple voices. Only by playing can you discover authenticity of voice. No one can do it for you.

Since we are multifaceted as human beings, why write with only one voice? What are your different voices? There are archetypal voices, such as the trickster or the wise woman, the voices of nature—a river or a pebble. We can become the voices of feelings, like insecurity or anger. Our voices can be both tough and vulnerable. We can become the voices of our friends and acquaintances, putting ourselves into their shoes, empathizing, imagining what it would be like if they spoke.

Begin to foster your "cultivated ear" by reading aloud three excerpts by writers with distinctive voices. The first is a passage from Hemingway's *For Whom the Bell Tolls:*

> He would not think about that. That was not his business. That was Golz' business. He had only one thing to do and that was what he should think about and he must think it out clearly and take everything as it came along, and not worry. To worry was as bad as to be afraid. It simply made things more difficult. . . . Think about them being away, he said. Think about them going through the timber. Think about them crossing a creek. Think about them riding through the heather. Think about them going up the slope. Think about them O.K. tonight. Think about them traveling, all night. Think about them hiding up tomorrow. Think about them. God damn it, think about them. That's just as far as I can think about them, he said.

The famous Hemingway voice, first of all, is "masculine"—that is, it contains little description, no long, flowing lines. Second, Hemingway's words are often simple. Third, he uses recurrences almost to excess: "think about" is repeated thirteen times in the above passage. Fourth, the sentences are generally short, the

And while stars and waves have something to say It's through my mouth they'll say it.
VINCENTE HUIDOBRO

whole piece reflecting the hard-driving, punctuated rhythm of a trapped man in danger of his life. In those staccato rhythms we sense a macho, thickly controlled panic.

Faulkner's voice is nothing like Hemingway's. Instead of Hemingway's staccato sentences, we hear the flowing cadences of Faulkner's inordinately long sentences. In fact, the following paragraph is one long sentence:

> He was a man past middle age, who with nothing to start with but sound health and a certain grim and puritanical affinity for abstinence and endurance had made a fair farm out of the barren scrap of hill land which he had bought at less than a dollar an acre and married and raised a family on it and fed and clothed them all and even educated them after a fashion, taught them at least hard work, so that as soon as they became big enough to resist him, boys and girls too, they left home (one was a professional nurse, one a ward-heeler to a minor country politician, one a city barber, one a prostitute; the oldest had simply vanished completely) so that there now remained the small neat farm which likewise had been worked to the point of mute and unflagging mutual hatred and resistance but which could not leave him and so far had not been able to eject him but which possibly knew that it could and would outlast him, and his wife who possibly had the same, perhaps not hope for resisting, but maybe staff and prop for bearing and enduring.

Each voice is absolutely distinctive; it is nearly impossible to confuse Hemingway's voice with Faulkner's voice.

A third voice is Pulitzer Prize–winner Toni Morrison's. She, too, has an immediately recognizable voice for anyone who has read her work. In this scene from *Beloved,* Sethe, an escaped slave and mother, is talking to a man she had known eighteen years before when both had still been slaves. Her lyrical language is evocative without being sentimental. Written in an experimental style of vignette after vignette of unfolding and overlapping images through which Sethe's memories are expressed, Morrison's voice is simultaneously hypnotic and elusive, nudging us to ask ourselves what we really mean by the words "love" or "freedom." Poetic vignette is layered into poetic vignette; image

Conversation is air. One can't control it; foolish germs escape one's lips and contaminate the air and one cannot draw them back. Whereas if you write you can change, reflect—re-flect. . . .

CYNTHIA OZICK

overlaps with image, giving us, according to one reviewer, "the most haunting and moving passages in modern American Fiction."

> "I got a tree on my back and a haint in my house and nothing in between but the daughter I am holding in my arms. No more running— from nothing. I will never run from another thing on this earth. I took one journey and I paid for the ticket . . ."
>
> "What tree on your back? Is something growing on your back? I don't see nothing growing on your back."
>
> "It's there all the same."
>
> "Who told you that?"
>
> "Whitegirl. That's what she called it. I've never seen it and never will. But that's what she said it looked like. A chokecherry tree. Trunk, branches, and even leaves. Tiny chokecherry leaves. But that was eighteen years ago. Could have cherries too now for all I know. . . .
>
> "Them boys found out I told on 'em. Schoolteacher made one open up my back, and when it closed it made a tree. It grows there still . . ."
>
> "They used cowhide on you?"
>
> Behind her, bending down, his body an arc of kindness, he held her breasts in the palms of his hands. He rubbed his cheek on her back and learned that way her sorrow, the roots of it; its wide trunk and intricate branches. Raising his fingers to the hooks of her dress, he knew without seeing them or hearing any sign that the tears were coming fast. And when the top of her dress was around her hips and he saw the sculpture her back had become, like the decorative work of an ironsmith too passionate for display, he could think but not say, "Aw, Lord, girl." And he would tolerate no peace until he had touched every ridge and leaf of it with his mouth, none of which Sethe could feel because her back skin had been dead for years.

Morrison's unique voice resides in her dreamlike poetic quality. Although she writes novels with plots that unravel, much of the effect she achieves is at the metaphoric level. The chokecherry tree may bear fruit, but it is astringent fruit, a fact made all the more poignant by Sethe's aside, "could have cherries too now, for all I know." As we read we become enveloped in the truths she is trying to get at with this poetic voice. She doesn't mince words,

but the stark and ugly truths are seen through a remarkable confluence of the actual and the dreamlike. The house may be
haunted, but the "tree" on her back is real. It is a "chokecherry"
tree, which puckers the membranes of the mouth and chokes the
one who eats of this bitter fruit.

MODELING VOICE

By experimenting with the voices of others, we begin to hear the
sound of our own. Joan Baez, attracted to Faulkner's flowing cadences, clustered (ABSTINENCE), and came up with the following
very long, single sentence, a compressed story of generational dimensions:

ABSTINENCE

He was abstinent now, and it was a constant battle to stay abstinent,
as his mother and father had been "heavy drinkers" ending their lives
early due to it, his father dying grey-lunged and inarticulate in a hos-
pital ward of men in pain, who coughed and spat the life out of themselves or just faded quietly into ghosts in the early dawn, as did he,
and his mother within two months, driving the big green Packard off
the hairpin turn that followed all the warning signs—five of them at
least (SLOW DOWN, DANGEROUS CURVE AHEAD, 15 MPH, SLIP-
PERY WHEN WET, TRUCKS USE LOW GEAR)—on the scenic route
to the city, the one lined with scotch broom and poppies and bottle
brush and oak trees which she had taken so seldom during all those
years but now without knowing it she groped for something beautiful
to present itself to her as a reason to go on through the depressing
business of post mortem details, and she had not really felt her husband for many years now, since the drinking had settled in on a grand
scale, though she had loved him very much in the first few years, in
the shining days of laughter and touching, but the son, after the second bit of news, the news of his mother, had poured all the liquor in
the house down the toilet and thrown the bottles and the smell of
them away in plastic sacks and sworn to all the angels in heaven never

to touch a drop of alcohol again, and only later, when the vow became a reality, did the sorrow of it all hit him like a fast-moving train, and he saw with terrible clarity that the sorrow was generational and had killed them both and was eating away at him, too, but he did not drink he would not could not drink but wept instead and cleansed himself in the salt water and he does so still and for that perhaps the angels owe him some special kindness.

JOAN BAEZ

Directing Your Hand

1. Like Baez, try on a voice for size. Choose any of the voices here: Hemingway's, Faulkner's, or Morrison's. Read your choice aloud once again ⌈▪▭▪⌉ so your Design mind can internalize its distinctive rhythm. Then, in your Writer's Notebook, cluster around a word or phrase taken from one of the passages, such as (THINK ABOUT), (LAUGH ABOUT), (ENDURANCE), or (NO MORE RUNNING).

   Cluster for a minute or so until you experience the trial-web shift signaling your discovery of a direction. Write quickly with conscious attention to the voice of the writer you chose. Write for five or so minutes. If you are still going strong, don't feel you must stop, but come full circle.

2. Read aloud what you wrote. Make any changes you wish, and then share with a friend or family member.

NUANCE

Nuance refers to a complexity of feeling, perception, or thought, which is difficult to put into words or categories and which therefore speaks through the interstices of words and patterns. Nuance is the subtle shading that gives a voice distinction. It is discerned by the Design mind but ignored by the Sign mind.

Nuance amplifies idea or image, according to science writer David Briggs:

For a creator, nuances are full of a sense of the "missing information." The impressionist Claude Monet was inexhaustibly sensitive to nuance involving the shifting of sunlight. Virginia Woolf responded strongly to any nuance involving wavelike movements. . . . A nuance is at first a very private affair. . . . To express his or her experience of a nuance, the individual has to create a form which will get the nuance across.

Voice is nuance-laden. Nuances roam from the emotional centers of our brains to become rapidly simplified by our cortex into fixed thoughts. Wondering, uncertainty, and questioning are filled with nuance.

You can't methodize nuance. As you involve yourself in the creative process, nuance evolves into image, idea, metaphor.

THE MONOLOGIC VOICE

The monologic voice comes from a uni-vocal perspective: We have been led to believe we are one person, have one brain, speak with one voice. However, our brain can imagine being another, a thing, or a quality. You can speak through it, thereby accessing ideas and convictions that might otherwise be inaccessible to you.

Directing Your Hand

 Read through "What the Wing Says" by David Swanger. In your Writer's Notebook, date and number a new page. Then cluster (WHAT THE _____ SAYS). As soon as you experience a trial-web shift of some sort to something that wants to speak, re-cluster for detail, then write quickly for five minutes or so. If, after that time, you want to go on, do, but don't forget to come full circle.

WHAT THE WING SAYS

The wing says, "I am the space behind you,
a dent in the fender, hands you remember

In nuance lies our sense of the wholeness and inseparability of experience.
JOHN BRIGGS, SCIENCE WRITER, AND DAVID PEAT, PHYSICIST

Write fast, write close to the bone. Don't waste any more of your life on what does not matter to you.
BONNIE FRIEDMAN

People often lack any voice at all because they stop so often in the act of writing a sentence and worry and change their minds about which words to use. They have none of the natural breath in their writing that they have in speaking.
PETER ELBOW

for the way they touched you. You can look
back and song will still throb. I am air
moving ahead, the outermost edge of desire,
the ripple of departure and arrival. But

I will speak more plainly: you think you are
the middle of your life, your own fulcrum,
your years poised like reckonings in the balance.
This is not so: dismiss the grocer of your soul.
Nothing important can be weighed, which is why
I am the silver river of your mornings and
the silver lake curled around your dark dreams.
I am not wax nor tricks stolen from birds.

I know you despair at noon, when the sky overflows
with the present tense, and at night as you lie
among those you have wronged; I know you have failed
in what matters most, and use your groin to forget.
Does the future move in only one direction?
Think how roots find their way, how hair spreads
on the pillow, how watercolors give birth to light.
Think how dangerous I am, because of what I offer you."

DAVID SWANGER

After Writing

You gave the wing a certain voice, a certain content, a certain seriousness or playfulness, a certain conclusion. Just as Swanger allows the wing to speak in a voice he created, the object/thing you
clustered is speaking through you. The object/thing is *you* imagining what it would say if you were it.

Listen to the monologue in the following poem by Lisel
Mueller and then to my students' monologic Re-Creations. In the
original, the voice of Monet, the painter, is philosophic, expansive, almost pleading to be understood. In the first Re-Creation,
the voice is stubborn, almost hostile; in the second Re-Creation,
the monologic voice shifts to a diametrically opposed angle of vision, to the doctor who has been listening to the patient.

MONET REFUSES THE OPERATION

Doctor, you say there are no haloes
around the streetlights in Paris
and what I see is an aberration
caused by old age, an affliction.
I tell you it has taken me all my life
to arrive at the vision of gas lamps as
angels,
to soften and blur and finally banish
the edges you regret I don't see,
to learn that the line I called the horizon
does not exist and sky and water,
so long apart, are the same state of
being.
Fifty-four years before I could see
Rouen cathedral is built
of parallel shafts of sun,
and now you want to restore
my youthful errors; fixed
notions of top and bottom,
the illusion of three-dimensional space,
wisteria separate from the bridge it
covers.
What can I say to convince you
the Houses of Parliament become
the fluid dream of the Thames?
I will not return to a universe
of objects that don't know each other
as if islands were not the lost children
of one great continent. The world
is flux, and light becomes what it
touches,
becomes water, lilies on water,
above and below water,
becomes lilac and mauve and yellow
and white and cerulean lamps,

small fists passing sunlight so quickly to
one another
that it would take long, streaming hair
inside my brush to catch it.
To paint the speed of light!
Our weighted shapes, these verticals,
burn to mix with air
and change our bones, skin, clothes
to gases. Doctor
if only you could see
how heaven pulls earth into its arms
and how infinitely the heart expands
to claim this world, blue vapor without end.

LISEL MUELLER

Re-Creation #1

MONET REFUSES THE OPERATION

Doctor—
    you tell me that
    haloes don't exist
    around the streetlamps,
    that nymphs do not swim
    among the waterlilies,
    but that is *your* vision.
You tell me my vision
    is an illusion.
I could say the same to you.
Your analytic world
    believes in dimensions,
    in parallelograms, in divisions,
but the world is flux,
    and objects know each other,
    embrace each other,
    have no end in themselves.
Doctor—do not fix my eyes;

leave my vision as it is,
and keep your own.
Doctor, I refuse—
    I refuse.
    STUDENT

ANOTHER LOST PATIENT

    The poor sap!
I saw that painter today.
He's been sniffing them oils
    for too many years.
Now he cannot see—
and he likes it that way!
He talks about colors,
    he talks about blurring—
I say they're symptoms, symptoms
that can be corrected.
Then, he starts talking some strange
    mystical language.
So I tune out,
another lost patient.
I was so mad, it put me off my lunch.
    STUDENT

The first voice echoes the original poem by also giving the view of the painter but is more to the point, ending in a manifesto of sorts. "Doctor: I refuse. I refuse." The second voice is the voice of the doctor, silent in the original poem, a cranky, know-it-all who can't see beyond a disobedient patient, cannot empathize. The word "lost" is interesting because we can read it as "the patient is lost to his potential to see properly," or "I lost the income from another patient because the idiot is nuts."

The Dialogic Voice

To experiment with dialogic voice, you can express two sides of yourself or two aspects of an idea or emotion through the voices of two different people. The writer in this example clustered two voices as follows (Figure 11-1). The clusters were already a virtual dialogue as though the writer had thought about what might have transpired between these two people for a long time. Imagined or real, this vignette focuses on an explosive imagined telephone conversation, laden with anger, sadness, and cultural discord.

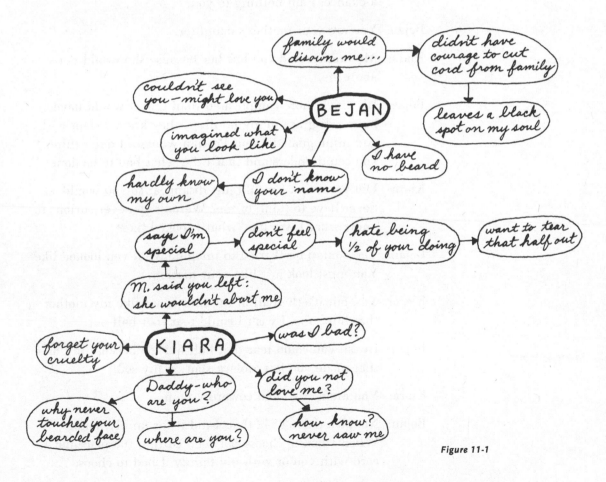

Figure 11-1

TELEPHONE CONVERSATION

Kiara: Daddy, who are you? Where are you? Why have I never felt your bearded face?

Bejan: My face is beardless.

Kiara: Why were you never here so that I could sit on your lap and feel special?

Bejan: I couldn't ever see you because I might love you.

Kiara: So, you don't love me, even though you never gave me a chance. I am nothing to you?

Bejan: You are your mother's daughter.

Kiara: My mother said you left her because she would not abort me.

Bejan: It's much more complicated than that. I would have been a disgrace to my family if they knew I slept with and impregnated a non-Persian woman. I don't think you could understand that I did what had to be done.

Kiara: Did you think I would just disappear so you would never have to think of me? Weren't you ever curious to know what I was like, what I looked like?

Bejan: Yes, sometimes I tried to imagine what you looked like. You must look just like your mother.

Kiara: Yes, but it's the half of me that is not like my mother that hurts me. I wish I could tear that half out.

Bejan: I wish you could tear that half out too because my half that made you left a black spot on my soul.

Kiara: You are a cruel and cowardly man.

Bejan: No, please don't say that. I did it for family honor. When I had to choose between cutting the placental cord with you or with my family, I had to choose . . .

Kiara: Don't say it. I hate you for . . .

Bejan: Please . . .

Kiara: I'm sorry I ever heard your voice.

Bejan: Please don't . . .

Kiara: You've never even asked my name.

Bejan: I can't even listen to my own.

Using the dialogic voice, this writer created two voices in conflict with one another. The unfolding dialogue, although written by one of the two people represented in the fictional scene, yielded profound insight into the other person's view of the world. The process of imagining and expressing both voices expanded the writer's horizon of understanding.

Directing Your Hand

1. Cluster (DIALOGUE) and let your multimind wander over conversations you've had, would like to have—and with whom. Pre-cluster pairs of names, such as (MY FATHER AND I); (JOHN WAYNE AND I); (MY BROTHER AND I), (PLATO AND SOCRATES).

2. As soon as one pair of names beckons with a flash of recognition, recluster those two names for snippets of dialogue, attitude, feelings.

3. Now write for five to ten minutes until you can come full circle. Go back only afterward to hone if you want to.

After Writing

What always amazes my students is that, as they are writing, they are not aware that both sides of the dialogue are generated by them. "Where did these voices come from?!" they will ask in puzzlement. "From your multimind" is the answer.

Remember that anyone or anything can dialogue, not just people. Dialogue with parts of yourself, with the two sides of your brain, with objects you love or dislike, with feelings, parts of the body (you and your aching back, for example), your computer, anything that *you* think you can give voice to. You will find that entering into dialogues stretches the imagination in ways you never thought possible.

THE MULTILOGIC VOICE

If the monologic voice is like chanting a single Gregorian melody and the dialogic voice is like a round for two voices, the multilogic voice is like a polyphonic Bach fugue. A multilogue offers a creative way to realize that our identity is always in the process of changing and expanding, leading to an ever-increasing richness of self.

As writers, becoming explicitly aware of our own multimind allows us to activate the three provinces of the multilogic voice:

1. *To re-cover our innocent eye, ear, and hand* through which we can suspend disbelief and pretend to be a rabbit, talk to an imaginary friend, hear the voices of the wind, of flowers, of stones.

2. *To un-cover empathy*—the ability to *be* in someone/something else's shoes, to feel what it is to *be* that person, to speak like that person, alive or dead or nonexistent, and to give him or her voice.

3. *To dis-cover that our writing voice is really many voices*—because we are part of the human family encompassing different cultures, genders, ethnicities. We discover that our particulars—our individual voice and story—echo universal human experience.

Recover the imagination of the innocent eye. Uncover empathy and become "other" through your writing. Discover the multilogic nature of the authentic voice.

Only in the particular can the universal take on meaning. The speaker is the I of all the metaphors in the poem—the I that stands solid on the earth, the molten metal molded into the steel beam, the one sperm, the Roman soldier, who arrives triumphant to fertilize the egg to make HER. This is multilogic voice at its finest and most profound.

The following student clusters and poems done in response to looking at photographs of the Greek sculpture, "The Venus of Cyrene" (Figure 11-2), show how the multilogic voices of each writer vary one to the next. The writing is not just about the sculpture, it is about each writer's perception of him- or herself, and it incorporates as well the feelings of and interactions with the many people with whom each writer has come into contact throughout their lives.

Figure 11-2

APHRODITE OF CYRENE

She should be covered,
protected.
She is tender;
she vibrates.
Careful—
she is enticing
as well as vulnerable,

sensual.
Are you aware
of the silkiness of her skin?
Can you restrain yourself
and still respond to the invitation?
Don't hurt her.
She is young,
graceful,
almost untouchable.
Are you experienced enough
to be soft,
or do you lust enough
to break her?

STUDENT

The dominant impression of the cluster in Figure 11-3 is "vulnerability." But the poem is also about the writer's conflicting views on lust and love. Bigger social questions are embedded in this little piece, general things, made fascinating by this particular voice, these particular details, these particular questions. In the details of this vignette, bigger things happen: the interplay of the multiple aspects of the writing self and the outer world.

By contrast, the dominant impression in Figure 11-4 is the feeling of JEALOUSY, leading us to a different multilogic voice.

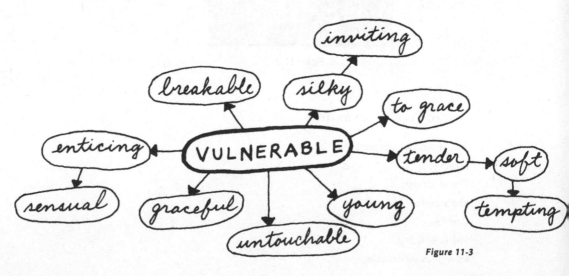

Figure 11-3

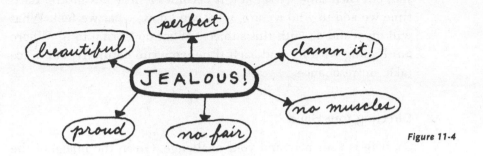

Figure 11-4

APHRODITE OF CYRENE

Now, this is simply not fair!
Just because she's a goddess she can have
an absolutely perfect body?
No strange muscles appearing as she works
off her third serving of ambrosia?

How did you do that?
Perhaps a three-mile jog around the heavens?
A Richard Simmons Angel?
No smelly pair of socks and Nikes—
no offense to your fellow goddesses intended—
cluttering up the clouds?
Oh, that's right! Marble doesn't sweat, does it?
What did you do? Just chip off the extra pounds?

STUDENT

We laugh because the multilogic voices within the poem juxtapose
allusions to classical art, contemporary culture, body image, and
mythology. These broader connections transcend the "facts" con-
cerning the statue itself and result in a marvelously funny question addressed to this perfect Aphrodite.

Even when we are describing the same object or addressing
the same theme, our unique multilogic voices mysteriously come
up with their own rhythms, images, and ideas. We write, always,
from partial knowledge, partial information, a partial sense of

self, but each time we set out, it becomes a little adventure. Each time we add to who we are, what we know, what we feel. What will my mind do with this subject? What do I bring to it? Where am I going with it? And each time we write naturally, our voice takes on resonance.

Directing Your Hand

So, here is your play and your challenge. Given the image of the Aphrodite (Figure 11-2), and the two vignettes you have read, as well as your own knowledge, or lack thereof, of mythology or Greek art, what is *your* dominant impression when you look at the image of the Venus of Cyrene? You don't have to make an effort to exclude what you've read here; just cluster your dominant impression. Your Design mind, the part of your brain that constantly integrates and re-integrates larger patterns of meaning for you so that you can see a bigger picture, will guide you to a pattern that lets you write—and to write in your own voice, given your history, your experience, your emotions, your mind-set, your angle of vision. Look at the Venus of Cyrene again, name a dominant impression, cluster, and write for three, ten, fifteen minutes. The point of this activity is that you don't have to exclude what you've read or seen or remembered, you can include it all or leave it all. The multilogic voice is precisely the voice that embraces the hodgepodge of what comes up, is not afraid of it, transforms it into a new form, into a different angle, into a transcended image of the past— and lets us know we are all explorers here. As natural writers, we can *bridge* our inner and outer worlds, our need for reaching in and reaching out simultaneously, our desire for autonomy with our yearning for connection, our Sign-mind sense of logic and order with our Design-mind vision of what it means to be human, our evolving, multifaceted voices with our desire to identify with one particular voice. Significantly, Pulitzer Prize–winner Toni Morrison wrote that "I write about things I have no resolution for."

Our true voice emerges out of that uncertainty, that indecision, that partial understanding. And, paradoxically, when we write in the multilogic voice, the web of language, the web of culture, the web of personal insight, help us to expand our understanding.

Directing Your Hand

It seems fitting that we end the chapter on "Voice" with a mono-logic moment in which you address only yourself. Make it a manifesto, a strong statement of your deepest desire and/or your greatest aversion. This statement may seem like a monologue, but the reason it will resonate not only with you but also with those who might read it is that certain generalizations fit every human being, despite the fact that the particulars may point only to our small selves in a big, uncertain universe. By clustering (NEVER), create your own manifesto, however profound or shallow, of something you would never, never, never do or be or think or live, as this student did:

NEVER

I will never be stuck in a small pink house
on an endless street without trees.
I will live in a house
barn-open to light and voices.
I will not be locked in—not walls or your will
can hold my green reaching.
I will fly the coop, climb the wall,
dare to fall into the hard and soft
soil of my choosing.

STUDENT

Punctuation is a matter of care. Care for words, yes, but also, and more important, for what the words imply. A comma can let us hear a voice break, or a heart. Punctuation, in fact, is a labor of love.

PICO IYER

A LAST WORD AND HEADING ON

When we explore different voices, which I have attempted to characterize as monologic, dialogic, and multilogic, we are increasingly aware that our own voice is only one among many and that there are as many points of view as there are people. Our own angle of vision is not necessarily another's; one person's truth is not another's. Opening ourselves to the diversity of voices, we can step into the river of uncertainty and write about things and events that we, like Toni Morrison, have no resolution for. The tension of moving into the unknown, which is also creative tension, is the subject of chapter 12.

TWELVE

YIN YANG: POLARITY AND CREATIVE TENSION

Philosopher Peter Koestenbaum insists that only when we accept the "dynamic tensions" of life can we mold this protean world into a meaning we can actually grasp:

Each idea and each conviction gives rise to the truth of its opposite idea, belief, and conviction. That is because reality is polarized, is paradoxical, and contradictory. . . . All life oscillates, vibrates, and is symmetrical, with a right and a left side. All life is confrontation and the stress of opposites. If you want conflict removed, you are asking for the unnatural. . . . The conflict of polarity is the weight that moves the ocean's waves and the ocean's tides. Polarity is the cycles of the planets and of the seasons; it is the alternation between night and day, sleep and waking, tension and relaxation. You deal with polarity not by choosing between opposites but by riding and rocking with the swing of the cosmic dialectic. Reality, and life within it, is a dance, a conversation, a series of echoes; that is the meaning of being alive instead of dead. Your heart, as it pumps, knows that.

In this chapter, we will learn how to ride the push and pull of creative tension in writing through the use of polarity, paradox, contraries, and similar word pairs. Polarity, the father of creative tension, is a philosophical concept that literature, religion, art, and science have been obsessed with for centuries.

The dictionary defines polarity as "the presence of two opposite or contrasting principles or tendencies." However, polarity implies much more than opposition. To say opposites are polar is to point to more than the chasm between the two: It is to point to their relatedness, to their existence as extremities of a single whole. In short, polarities are inseparable. In order to know one, you must know the other. Therefore, polarities are reciprocal, mutually sustaining relationships of events and forces usually considered opposed to or basically separate from one another. Polarities are aspects of the same thing; one side only exists in relationship to the other. Heraclitus said:

> It is by disease that health is pleasant; by evil that good is pleasant; by hunger, satiety; by weariness, rest.

And writer Evan Pritchard illuminates for us why the human mind can process something both as opposite *and* as related:

> The whole is made up of opposites that are part of the same thing— thesis and antithesis, point and counterpoint, yin and yang. From this unity comes wonderful diversity, but put that perception of unity in words and out comes paradox. The rational mind speaks in contrasts while the intuitive mind speaks in metaphor. But when they merge they often speak in paradox, for paradox is the language of balance. There are cold countries and hot countries, but the earth as a whole is lightly dark, coldly hot, vastly small, and now triumphantly in trouble, but we can't put it into words.

When I speak of "creative tension" I don't mean the negative anxiety you may feel when writing an essay exam or project report or short story. Tension, from the Latin *tensio*, means "stretched," as in "extension," a stretching out, a reaching for ways to join opposites and connect contrasting patterns. When I speak of creative tension, I mean the tension you produce in your writing *through* oppositions, juxtapositions, and resolutions of seemingly contradictory ideas or feelings. The purpose of fostering creative tension is to evoke a kind of conceptual elasticity to help you—and whoever reads your writing—to see seemingly irreconcilable opposites in a new light.

All things we usually consider irreconcilable, such as cause and effect, past and future, subject and object, are actually just like the crest and trough of a single wave, a single vibration. For wave, although itself a single event, expresses itself through the opposites of crest and trough, high point and low point. Reality is not found in the crest or in the trough alone, but in their unity. Crest and trough—indeed all opposites—are inseparable aspects of one underlying activity.
KEN WILBER, *No Boundary*

Paradox, the child of polarity, is a linguistic construct by which we express our polarized human existence. Albert Rothenberg, a psychiatrist and student of the creative process, calls the simultaneous recognition of opposites "Janusian thinking," after the Roman god Janus, whose two faces point in opposite directions. In Janusian thinking, two or more opposites are conceived simultaneously as equally operative and valid. The study of physics shows us that, depending on how we look at it, light can appear sometimes as electromagnetic waves, sometimes as particles. This paradox was the thrust that led to the formulation of quantum theory, the basis of modern physics.

In written paradox—the deliberate statement of seeming impossibility—there is an emphasis on contradiction that leads to another level of truth. When Juliet calls Romeo "beautiful tyrant," logically we see the contradiction, but in the tension between the two words we understand Juliet's state of mind. Such irreconcilable terms contain a common element of truth that demonstrates something profound.

Prophets such as Christ frequently spoke in paradox to show that truth is not obvious. In leaving us hanging, a paradox forces us into a confrontation and a shift to Design-mind consciousness in order to resolve it, since it cannot be resolved by logic.

Anhedonic perception is either/or thinking; the world and the self appear fragmented, dichotomized, polarized. The shift to inner joy is also a shift away from this dichotomized perception toward a unified frame. You'll find it possible to accept yourself and others as selfish and unselfish, compassionate and indifferent, individual and social, rational and irrational. From the either/or vantage point, the polarities in the world and in the self appear to struggle toward release of tension and finally death. From the vantage point of inner joy, the tension between opposing forces produces energy for growth.

HAROLD H. BLOOMFIELD, M.D.
AND ROBERT B. KORY, "Inner Joy"

DESIGN MIND'S ACCEPTANCE OF TENSION

I have purposely placed this particular Design-mind skill toward the end of the course because—with your Design mind now awakened and developed, enabling you to write naturally—you will find tension acceptable and will be able to work with it and through it, thus energizing your writing. Moreover, creative tension allows you to utilize the other elements of natural writing in new and unexpected ways: You can generate surprise, create clashes that turn into insight, bring in juxtapositions that catapult both you and your reader into illuminating perceptions.

Since your Design mind is not constituted to see things as one way *or* the other, its predilection is always toward patterns; it focuses on complementarity rather than contradiction, on possible ways to connect opposites, to unify meaning. Thus it rejects the categories of either/or and accepts and plays with both/and. This notion of complementarity is essential to Chinese thought, as seen in the yin yang symbol (Figure 12-1).

In natural writing the tension between opposing forces becomes a creative principle because it stimulates fundamental and surprising innovations. Creative tension brings new lifeblood into seeing and writing, producing effective surprise and reflecting connectedness. To the Sign mind a polarity is the presence of two irreconcilable opposites. To the Design mind a polarity represents the ends of a single, indivisible whole. The focus is on unification of opposites.

Figure 12-1

Writers use paradox to express this unifying focus, as poet Theodore Roethke has:

> In a dark time, the eye begins to see . . .
> And in broad day the midnight comes again!

Literally, the eye cannot see "in a dark time," nor can midnight come "in broad day." Yet our Design mind perceives a truth beyond logic in Roethke's words.

The function of creative tension in writing is precisely to reflect the profound truth of the both/and, rather than only the either/or, nature of life. We can perceive both perspectives because we have two brains, which process the flux of the world in radically different ways. Our Sign mind tends to focus on the either/or, making judgments and establishing rules. Our Design mind tends to focus on the both/and, with its ambiguities, its malleability, its flow.

In Robert Newton Peck's starkly beautiful novel *A Day No Pigs Would Die*, the climax focuses on the adolescent Robert's dramatic epiphany of the both/and aspects of human experience. His father has just killed Robert's beloved pet pig because the pig is barren, but we learn that the father had to kill the pet so that his family could survive. The killing hand is thus also the loving, protecting hand, and this reconciling of a terrible contradiction alters Robert's view of life forever.

The test of a first-rate intelligence is the ability to hold two opposed ideas in the mind at the same time, and still retain the ability to function.
F. SCOTT FITZGERALD

Consciousness is born in the realm of opposites.
CHARLES M. JOHNSTON

I felt his big hand touch my face, and it wasn't the hand that killed hogs. It was almost as sweet as Mama's. His hand was rough and cold, and as I opened my eyes to look at it, I could see that his knuckles were dripping with pig blood. It was the hand that just butchered Pinky. He did it. Because he had to. Hated to and had to. And he knew that he'd never have to say to me that he was sorry. His hand against my face, trying to wipe away my tears, said it all. His cruel pig-sticking fist with its thick fingers so lightly on my cheek.

I couldn't help it. I took his hand to my mouth and held it against my lips and kissed it. Pig blood and all. I kissed his hand again and again, with all its stink and fatty slime of dead pork. So he'd understand that I'd forgive him even if he killed me.

Without the paradox, this story would be at best a sentimental tale of a young boy's pet pig and at worst a novel of senseless brutality. Instead, it is a sensitive portrayal of one of life's realities, and both protagonist and reader are immeasurably enriched by this insight.

Directing Your Hand

Here is poet W. S. Merwin's classic expression of being of "two minds." We all have opportunities to move forward into growth or stay in our warm nest, to dive into a cold ocean or stay on the shore, to take a job that's beyond us or to look for something safe.

This plant would like to grow
and yet be embryo,
succeed and yet escape
the doom of taking shape.

W. S. MERWIN

Cluster (SUCCEED/ESCAPE) and be curious about where it takes you. When you experience a sense of direction, write quickly for five or so minutes. Only after you have written, go back, re-read, and make whatever changes that feel right.

After Writing

Don't worry if you're still too much on one side of the equation or the other. Reconciling polarities isn't learned overnight. Every day there are new opportunities to make connections between seemingly disparate ideas or values or feelings, and doing so in your writing will bring unexpected discoveries.

CHILDHOOD ORIGINS OF CREATIVE TENSION

Young children possess the ability to cut across the customary categories . . . to appreciate usually undiscerned links among realms, to respond affectively in a parallel manner to events which are usually categorized differently, and to capture these original conceptions in words.

HOWARD GARDNER,
Artful Scribbles

When we are very young, our logical Sign-mind categories are still limited, and so the conventional way of splitting the world into either/or is not yet our way. In the stage of the innocent eye, ear, and hand, the world is a kaleidoscope of possibility, a mosaic in which everything is potentially related. In childhood we juxtapose improbable elements, invent unlikely events, juggle semantic nonsense, all the while maneuvering in a natural sea of creative tension.

However, as soon as language enters the picture, children begin to organize concepts and words into pairs of opposites. In *From Two to Five* Kornei Chukovsky, Russia's most popular children's storyteller as well as an expert on the speech and learning patterns of children, has observed that, at around the age of three, children naturally look for the polar complement of a word they have just learned. The child, says Chukovsky, "assumes that every word has a 'twin'—an opposite in meaning or quality." Thus, if a parent refers to "running water," a child might ask, "Is there sitting water?"

Because children's Sign-mind reasoning powers are not developed, they respond naturally to the creative principle of tension inherent in a both/and awareness of life. Most of their encounters with the world are filtered through the Design mind, which is superior to the left at handling new and logically contradictory tasks.

Take the following story by my daughter Simone, written before she was six. Observe the tension created by logical impossibility and the effortless way in which she reconciles it: There is a marriage of ladybugs, but suddenly the scene shifts to a radical discontinuity; a human hand appears and the two ladybugs

become a ring on a finger of the hand. First the ladybugs behave
like humans, and then they become an inanimate ring on a real
human being's finger. Simone had no trouble reconciling these
two events in her narrative.

THE LITTLE LADYBUG

Once apon a time there was a little boy ladybug. He met a girl ladybug. So he asked her if she and him wanted to get mired. So she said
o k so they got mired. Then they found a hand so they asked the person if they could be there. So she said o k so they climbed on her finger and pertended to be a ring. The end

As our left hemisphere is strengthened by schooling, our literal outlook prevents us from entertaining contradictory notions,
and the creative tension that can produce insightful writing becomes buried under conventional wisdom.

In the stage of the cultivated eye, ear, and hand, however, we
rediscover the experience we had as a child, thus enhancing our
ability to use creative tension in our writing.

Directing Your Hand

Read the following piece by Tim McCrory:

Because I need to change my sense of self,
   I must write this.
Because I am afraid to share myself with others,
   I cannot write this.
Because others need to know me and what I care about,
   I must write this.
Because I am afraid to change,
    to alter the status quo,
    to upset the apple cart
   I cannot write this.
Because I need to be in life
    to BE alive,

to find meaning,

to act,

I have written this.

TIM MCCRORY

Notice how the both/andness of McCrory's argument is resolved in the closing lines, through a leap of insight.

Cluster ("BECAUSE . . .") until you experience a trial-web shift. Then write quickly for five or so minutes, striving to acknowledge opposite points of view in some way. Think improvisation. Only after you have come full circle do you want to go back and rework until you are satisfied.

After Writing

You can do this activity as often as you choose to. "Because" is one way we often rationalize a behavior. When you write about your awareness of opposite points of view, you acknowledge two-mindedness, an essential ingredient of natural writing.

CREATIVE TENSION THROUGH SIMILAR WORD PAIRS

A word pair—related terms, such as LOOK/SEE—confronts us with obvious likenesses. "Look," the dictionary tells us, means "to employ one's eyes in seeing," while "see" is "to perceive with the eye." When, through clustering the two words together, you engage the Design mind, blocking literal meaning, you tap levels of nuances between the two words. The resonance generated by the proximity of these related words has a peculiar tension and power. Were you to cluster each word singly, there would be no tension, but when your Design mind sees them *in relation* to one another, you often discover the unexpected.

Directing Your Hand

Explore your own word pairs by letting your Design mind discover relations.

1. In your Writer's Notebook cluster (PLAY/GAME). Anything goes. Be curious. You may cluster similarities and in the process discover differences you had never thought about. You may even discover off-the-wall perceptions as the words rub against one another. The freedom to associate is the key to clustering.

2. Associations may appear random, but you will soon recognize a meaningful pattern. That is your Design mind reaching a trial-web shift. Let it happen.

3. Write quickly, without stopping, for five minutes or less.

4. When you finish, read your vignette aloud, listening for full circle wholeness, recurrences, language rhythms, images, metaphors, voice, and creative tension.

5. Now reshape and change anything you wish to fit your bigger vision.

After Writing

Try other similar word pairs, such as

(SKY/AIR)   (FIRE/FLAME)   (WALK/MEANDER)

CREATIVE TENSION THROUGH "CONTRARIES"

Poet William Blake wrote, "Without contraries there's not progression." Contraries, like polarities, contain paradox. When Romeo says, "Parting is such sweet sorrow," he suggests that even though parting brings sadness, it also contains sweetness. In parting lies the hope of reunion, so in parting, the experience of loving is intensified.

Using the Shakespearean contrary (FROZEN HASTE), Anne Halley generated this surprise vignette:

FROZEN HASTE

In my haste
to unburden my passion,
in my desire
to move, lithe and beguiling,
I hopped into some man's bed
and lay frozen there
waiting for the thaw.

ANNE HALLEY

Directing Your Hand

1. In your Writer's Notebook, select one of the following contraries and cluster them in the same circle:

CRUEL KINDNESS   HONORABLE VILLAIN

SERIOUS PLAY

INFINITE LIMITS

FRUITFUL TENSION

QUIET TURBULENCE   ACTIVE QUIESCENCE

Be curious; cluster any way you wish. Perhaps you'll be attracted first to one word in the phrase, then to the other. Watch for the trial-web shift. Trust your pattern-seeking Design mind.

2. Write your vignette rapidly, using your cluster as reference only if you need to. Remember that reaching for metaphor allows you to expand meaning, recurrences can unify, language rhythms please the ear, and that coming full circle brings wholeness.

3. When you have finished, read your vignette aloud and re-work it until the whole feels right, sounds right, looks right.

After Writing

Running and standing still at the same time is the whole truth.
HOWARD NEMEROV

Because your Sign mind's resistance was blocked by clustering, your Design mind was allowed to respond creatively to the creative tension inherent in the suggested contradictions. What did you learn from these contraries that you didn't know before? At the bottom of the page, jot down your response to

- I was surprised . . .

- I discovered . . .

- I wonder . . .

CREATIVE TENSION THROUGH RECONCILING POLARITIES

And so we come full circle, back to polarities. Polarities can be seen as antagonists or as related, depending on whether we view them through our Sign mind or our Design mind. For example, do you have trouble seeing these polarities as being connected in some way?

Death/Life	Embodiment/Spirituality
Freedom/Bondage	Creativity/Convention
Aloneness/Togetherness	Beauty/Ugliness
Meaning/Meaninglessness	Love/Indifference
Home/Homelessness	Risk/Security

The world is ambiguous, unclear, open to many interpretations. The same world is perceived by different people, often in fundamentally divergent ways. To one, physicality is the ultimate reality. To another, the world of spirit is fundamental. Meaning is soft, pliant, malleable. Perception comes in layers. You are responsible for designing your world so that it becomes a meaningful concept with which you can live. Life is a constant stream of opposites. Sometimes we see the connectedness; sometimes we do not.

Let's examine an archetypal polarity, SEPARATION and UNION, to see how many shapes it can take:

Separation	Union
Losing a friend, mother, brother, lover	Intimacy; growth of friendships
Alienation by argument	Reconciliation by communication
Physical, geographic separation	Physical, geographic connectedness
Emotional separation; divorce	Emotional bonds; marriage
Fragmentation	Integration

What initially strikes us is that the left column seems negative, and the right column seems positive. Reconciling polarities means seeing both the positive and the negative in separation and union. For example, in what ways can divorce be positive? In what ways can marriage be negative? In what ways might alienation be a plus? Intimacy a minus?

Artists and writers prize their awareness of polarities, primarily because they see them not as separate categories but as ends of a single continuum. They value polarity as a fundamental quality of all natural processes. Think of waxing/waning, day/night, inhale/exhale, creation/destruction, motion/rest, sun/moon, chaos/order.

Directing Your Hand

In your Writer's Notebook, cluster (SEPARATION/UNION) in a single circle with a slash. Don't worry about making logical connections. Associate for one or the other term, or for both. The idea behind

To know one thing, you must know its opposite . . . just as much, else you don't know that one thing.

HENRY MOORE

Whether exploring the depths of the human soul or the depths of matter, artists, mystics, and scientists have come face-to-face with chaos and disorder. But the opened mind thrives on difference and remains open to the contradictory.

FRANK BARRON

this activity is to help you become aware that you can't have the idea of separation without the concept of union, that each is an end point of a single continuum. As soon as you experience a trial-web shift to an image or example or event, write quickly, coming full circle before you stop. Then go back if you wish to add, subtract, or change.

After Writing

You may want to experiment with more of the pairs listed below. I promise that each time you do this exercise you'll be given at least a small surprise—and, sometimes, the shift in consciousness will be huge.

LITTLE/BIG   LIGHT/DARK   STILLNESS/MOVEMENT

beginning/end   wide/narrow   Cain/Abel

chaos/order   hard/soft   sun/moon

manage/evoke   separate/connect   man/woman

add/subtract   inspire/expire   space/time

create/destroy   surface/interface   inhale/exhale

question/answer   cooperate/compete   individual/community

This may be the first time you have been conscious of polarities as being connected. You also may have found yourself reaching for metaphors, images, and recurrences to express the relatedness of your polarity. Go back to the other polarities as writing prompts and write as often as you wish. Each time you will be in a different frame of mind, at a different place in your life, so you will come up with different vignettes.

A LAST WORD AND HEADING ON

Creative tension brings new life to seeing and writing. The concept of polarities shows us that all life can be viewed through one pole or its opposite—or the two poles can be variously reconciled. Paradox and contraries are linguistic constructs by which you can express your polarized existence. Doing so, you gradually move away from simplistic either/or modes of perception and expression to a more complex awareness of both.

By now you have attained considerable skill in writing naturally. Next, we'll see how less can be more, the subject of chapter 13.

THIRTEEN

Brevity and Re-Vision: Less Is More

Less is more" was the paradoxical doctrine of the famous Bauhaus architect Mies van der Rohe, whose aesthetic philosophy of austere elegance, clean lines and clarity, elimination of extraneous decoration, visual simplicity, and jewel-like precision have something to say to writers.

Of course, sometimes less is truly less and more is better. But almost always less is a way of revealing the essence, the heart of a piece of writing, as we see in this centuries-old Japanese Haiku in which seventeen syllables speak of a fragmentary, fleeting moment. Basho relies on succinct descriptions of three images to communicate the totality of an experience:

> Winter desolation.
> In a world of one color,
> the sound of the wind.
>
> BASHO

So powerful is this form in its simplicity that, not only do many people today use it, but it can also be parodied. Think how it would be if, instead of geeky text strings, your computer wrote error messages in Haiku, like the ones below:

Three things are certain,
Death, taxes, and lost data.
Guess which has occurred?

You step in the stream,
but the water has moved on.
This page is not here.

All arts, big and small, are the elimination of waste motion in favor of the concise declaration . . .
RAY BRADBURY

Let thy words be few.
ECCLESIASTES 5:2

Writing is more like a sculpture where you remove, you eliminate in order to make the work visible. Even those pages you remove somehow remain.
ELIE WIESEL

Yesterday it worked.
Today it is not working.
Windows is like that.

First snow, then silence.
This thousand dollar screen dies
so beautifully.

Less certainly can be more!

Our goal in natural writing is not to revise in the conventional sense, but to re-envision what we've written by shifting between our global vision of the whole and the details of the parts. True revision is an intensely cooperative process between both hemispheres of the brain, a process of ongoing modification toward some envisioned whole.

Actually, in the writing of your vignettes, you have been learning to do this all along. All natural writing begins with an awareness of a tentative configuration that gives your Sign mind a sense of direction as it begins to sequence the trial web. The very act of sequencing is a sorting, selecting, grouping process, guided by the trial web. Shifting from designing to sequencing is like a camera zooming in, making the features of blurred shapes clearer. You have already experienced re-reading and making initial changes in your work. In this chapter, we will make the re-envisioning process more explicit.

If you skim through the filled pages in your Writer's Notebook, you will note that your vignettes are mostly still "first draft" material, even when you have made changes. You've learned to trust your Design mind by producing abundantly and with relative ease—with a host of strategies at your fingertips. It is time now to move from immersion to perspective.

Redesigning is seeing again, from a fresh angle. It is recalling the first vision, reading what you've written, then paring it down through one or more drafts until you are truly satisfied. Children writing in the innocent stage never revise; to them their first try is beautiful as it stands. Some of yours will be, too, as you shall see. Generally, however, writers in the cultivated stage almost always revise. In that second envisioning they hone and sharpen, bringing the specialized talents of both Design and Sign minds into the act.

Every artistic endeavor or creative act involves two broad phases—the generative phase during which the original vision is discovered and expressed, and the paring and polishing phase,

A sentence should contain no unnecessary words, a paragraph no unnecessary sentences, for the same reason that a drawing should have no unnecessary lines and a machine no unnecessary parts. This requires not that the writer make all his sentences short or that he avoid all detail . . . but that every word tell.

WILLIAM STRUNK

during which the whole piece is reworked. Painters do it; composers do it. Great writers are notorious for re-visioning the whole. D. H. Lawrence, for example, rewrote *Lady Chatterley's Lover* three times, and Hemingway wrote the last page of one of his novels thirty-seven times. There are many strategies for re-visioning.

Poet Laura Chester describes how the re-envisioning process works for her:

> When I first begin writing a poem, the words come quickly and I don't try to censor myself. Then I immediately type up what I have, regaining control for gradual revision, pressuring the poem while trying not to lose that initial blood beat. I type draft after draft almost obsessively until that first soft clay shapes itself into the poem it has become. When I rewrite I have to retrieve that original urge, otherwise it becomes mere correction and something vital is lost. True revision can be as exciting and "creative" as the first attempt. I love to feel the poem as a malleable substance that I can push and reshape on the page.

And there is the key to re-designing: "True revision can be as exciting and creative as the first attempt." In the initial stage of re-designing, your Design mind sweeps across the form of your vignette, just as you might scan the features of a face, keeping the whole in mind. Resist your Sign mind's efforts to dominate this stage of the process; stay focused on the forest, for now ignoring the individual trees. In natural writing re-envisioning the aesthetic whole must occur before detailed error correction.

Professor Diane Middlebrook of Stanford University defines revision as making a poem more true to its own terms. She tells us that the poem below originated in a dream out of which she woke full of anxiety, sleeping in a house that stood near a forest. Her first draft reads as follows:

> Winter; the woods
> Empty; the axe
> Buried in a stump
> Its fall become a sob in the sleep
> Of the dreamer waking, calling out
> Where am I? Who is there?

What I like to do is to treat words as a craftsman does his wood or stone or what-have-you, to hew, carve, mould, coil, polish, and plane them into patterns, sequences, sculptures, fugues of sound expressing some lyrical impulse, some spiritual doubt or conviction, some dimly realized truth I must try to reach and realize.

DYLAN THOMAS

In this earliest version, Middlebrook explains, the line endings were arbitrary, sometimes coinciding with units of syntax, sometimes not. Then she chose the syllabic form—four syllables to a line, except for the last line.

"The demands of the syllabic form, once I decided on it, helped me purge the poem of dead language: 'become,' 'in,' 'the,' 'out.' 'Buried' became 'sunk,' discarding a syllable and gaining force in the process; 'become' was exchanged for 'startling.' The rhythm produced by shortening the lines enhanced the feeling in the poem of being suddenly awakened into a terrible sort of questioning clarity." Here is Middlebrook's final version:

WRITING A POEM IN SYLLABICS—LOSING YOU

Winter; the woods
empty; the axe
sunk in a stump;
its thud a sob
startling the sleep
of the dreamer
waking, calling
Where am I? Who
is there?

In this chapter you will be playing with various strategies of paring and reshaping. We'll be exploring:

- re-clustering and several re-visions

- writing within shaped borders (like circles, rectangles, squares, etc.)—in order to discover the most essential shape of your subject

- thumb-nail sketches—to help you paint portraits in words using only the most crucial detail

- brevities and nutshells—to facilitate the paring-down process and make it a playful, enjoyable experience

Of course, you can always return to your first version if you still feel it is just the right version, but even if you do, you will have become more aware of your own natural writing process, and chances are you will discover ways of saying some things better.

The little anonymous poem at the left was pared to a mere twenty-one words from thirty-six. The excess verbiage of the first version buries the essence of the poem, whereas the words in the second version practice what they preach: not one superfluous word.

Re-Design through Re-Clustering

Re-clustering does two things: It crystallizes your focus, and it provides an additional burst of images and associations, reimmersing you in the wholeness of your first vision. Thus, your idea continues to evolve as you re-involve yourself in it.

I wrote the nucleus word CIRCLE on the board and asked students to cluster it, then write their vignette within the boundaries of a circle. Figure 13-1 shows this student writer's discovered options, which focused on "sacred image," which then triggered the following vignette:

The spoken or the written word
Should be as clean as is a bone,
As clear as is the light,
As firm as is a stone.
Two words will never serve
As well as one alone.
ANONYMOUS

The written word is clean as bone,
clear as light,
firm as stone.
Two words are not as good as one.
ANONYMOUS

Poetry began as song. Language is a living thing. It feeds on the living language of a community.
QUINCY TROUPE

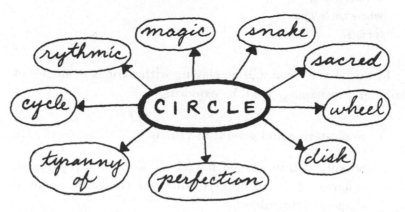

Figure 13-1

#1

Sacred image
wheel of Karma
Atom/disk, Host/God.
Perfection/equipoise.
Tasteful cycle, binding rhythm
rolling serpent, saintly halo.
Setting limits, making magic
Instinctive pathway of
confusion. How to
break your tyranny?

She re-clustered (TYRANNY) and wrote again. Her second vignette was about half the length of the first version.

#2

Everlasting
repetition, sacred
image, serpent wheel.
Tempting pathway
of stagnation
How to break your
tyranny?

Yet, she was still not satisfied. In the second version she had produced a sign-song rhythm and rhyme that was not right for her. So she re-clustered (SERPENT WHEEL) and came up with a very different vignette from the first two:

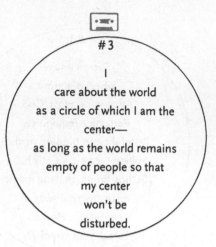

#3

I
care about the world
as a circle of which I am the
center—
as long as the world remains
empty of people so that
my center
won't be
disturbed.

Still too many words that don't add anything, she thought. She re-clustered (CENTER) and wrote

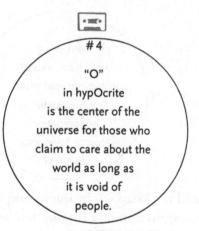

#4

"O"
in hypOcrite
is the center of the
universe for those who
claim to care about the
world as long as
it is void of
people.

You can see the progression of this writer's thoughts. Leaping here, leaping there, the mind is not a straight thinker. Yet there is a self-similarity in each piece. Ideas are added, subtracted, substituted. And a different, though related, vignette emerges.

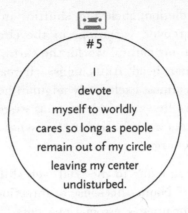

Still not quite satisfied, the writer pared a little more.

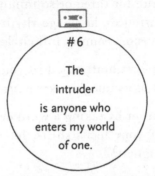

This is not just revision; it is not just compressing. As the writer searches for essence, the ideas shift and change, each version adding to and subtracting from the whole, each new version articulating a subtle change, giving direction and focus for the next change. As Elie Wiesel suggested, even the words you have removed remain on the page. Most important, each of your versions acts as a catalyst for new versions, and each of these could be revised to become its own vignette. Now it's your turn to play at re-visioning.

Directing Your Hand

1. In your Writer's Notebook, precluster the word (CIRCLE), keeping in mind that the circle is an archetypally recursive image in human experience. A circle encompasses natural cycles, such as night and day; it is a natural image

for completion, enclosing, shutting in as well as shutting out. Moreover, variations of the circle shape make up much of our natural world: the earth, the sun, the moon, the human head, fruits, eggs; whereas the human-made world is almost exclusively angular: houses, windows, tile, rooms we live and work in, cribs we're put into as babies, the caskets we're buried in. See what associations unique to you emerge.

2. When you come to the trial-web shift, ask, "What triggered it?" Name this sense of direction and circle it; now cluster for images, associations, detail, lines of song, titles, whatever will come.

3. As you write for three or so minutes, keep in mind your focus, recurrences, language rhythms, images, metaphor, creative tension, coming full circle.

4. Read your first draft aloud so you can hear its rhythms, feel the fit of its images, recurrences, full circle wholeness.

5. Now re-cluster by taking a word or phrase from your first version. If your focus shifts, let it. Write your #2 re-visioned vignette.

6. Read it aloud and ask such questions as: Do any recurrences serve a purpose? What words need to go? Is there creative tension? Do I come full circle? Am I satisfied? Depending on your answers, re-design as many more times as you wish, each time paring or adding, each time rereading the whole, then examining and clarifying its parts. Do this until your vignette feels aesthetically unalterable. Some of you will re-vision six times, some only three.

After Writing

We re-vision until we feel we have reached a point beyond which we can change nothing more—or we have run out of time. After the re-visioning process, we may find we like an earlier version better than the last one. Still, experiencing our mind re-designing and re-configuring our thoughts and words on the page teaches us

We invent [borders] as easily as fish swim, from highway lane dividers to Jefferson's call for a wall between religion and government . . . in certain lines of chalk, paint, and tape lie the purest expressions of our fondness for edges.

TYLER VOLK

creative flexibility. Since the essence of intelligence lies in our mind's flexibility, re-visioning is always time well spent.

RE-DESIGN THROUGH WRITING WITHIN BORDERS

Life at the smallest scales boasts a cornucopia of protective edges.
TYLER VOLK

For some of your vignettes, you may want to impose physical borders as you re-design, to uncover the heart of a vignette. Borders, says biologist Tyler Volk, are the "bulwarks against forces of disruption." Borders define a space in which we can experiment. They become a frame for our creative output. Borders can be of your choosing—a rectangle, a triangle, a number, a letter shape, the shape of an object—imposing their own limitations on length and design. The purpose of writing within a border shape is to get you to envision the content of an existing piece in a different way from the way you originally wrote it.

The vignette below was actually an advertisement. The border of a long, slim vertical rectangle dictates the short, factual statements, which result in a surprise ending.

THIS WILL MAKE YOU FEEL BETTER

If you sometimes get discouraged, consider this fellow: He dropped out of grade school. Ran a country store. Went broke. Took 15 years to pay off his bills. Took a wife. Unhappy marriage. Ran for House. Lost Twice. Ran for Senate. Lost twice. Delivered speech that became a classic. Audience indifferent. Attacked daily by the press and despised by half the country. Despite all this, imagine how many people all over the world have been inspired by this awkward, rumpled, brooding man who signed his name simply,

A. LINCOLN.

Here we have a highly compressed story of Abraham Lincoln, whose history fills many volumes. Borders ask us to choose our words carefully.

Directing Your Hand: Experiment with One of Two Things, or Both

1. In your Writer's Notebook, number and date a new page, and draw a long vertical rectangle on it. Select your vignette clustered from (PERSON) in chapter 2 and read it aloud. Quickly rewrite the vignette, guided by the borders of the rectangle, adding, subtracting, substituting without agonizing. Once the vignette is housed in the rectangle, re-vision thoughtfully.

2. OR If your (PERSON) vignette is exactly as you wanted it, pre-cluster (FAMOUS PERSON) and, as soon as a name waves and says, "Here I am!" re-cluster for specifics and quickly write your vignette in the vertical rectangle. When you come full circle, re-vision in a second rectangle.

After Writing

Try other borders—circle shapes, triangles, squares—to experiment with the paradoxically freeing constraints of borders. These activities are valuable for giving you concrete experience in disentangling essence from excess. If you would like to write more bordered vignettes, look at Robert Phillips's "vertical" poem, modeled on the shape of a Giacometti sculpture (Figure 13-2). Play a little and enjoy, clustering more (PERSONS) or doing your own version of Giacometti's Man or finding an image in a magazine that appeals to you. Riches for writing lie everywhere.

GIACOMETTI'S RACE

Bone-stack
beanstalk
broomstick
clothespole
gangleshanks;
they are
the thin
man inside
every fat
one
who
clamors
to climb out.
Every jaw
a lantern,
every face
a lean,
hungry
look.
Ancient
violence.
Violent
freshness.
Do not
trust them.
Do not trust
them.
But:
the beauty!

Tapers
flicker
in vertical
air!
Delicacy
of a hair!

Herring-gut
economy.
Studies
of the
minimal.
Learn to
love them.
Water,
not milk.
Rail against
fear of
paper
shadows.
Teach
survival on
slender
means.
Live off
the thin
of the land.

ROBERT PHILLIPS

Figure 13-2

Re-Designing: Thumb-Nail Sketches

A thumb-nail sketch is a brief verbal portrait. One way to re-member that less can be more is to write about someone by briefly naming those objects that define that person—and to use only nouns and adjectives, no verbs. Here is Mitsuye Yamada's thumb-nail sketch:

GREAT GRANDMA

great
grandmama's savings:
    dried seaweeds
    parched persimmons
    in boxed dividers:

bitter melon seeds
colored stones
powdery green tea leaves
   yellowed yarns
      pine cones
   fabric scraps in bags
   pressed brown dried seaweeds
life's allotment she'd say
When used up
       time to die.

Directing Your Hand

You can do one of two things: use one of your "people" vignettes from other chapters for this thumb-nail sketch or pre-cluster (WHOSE?) then re-cluster that person who says, "Pay attention to me" for detail, and write quickly with one limitation only: use only concrete objects that give a solid thumb-nail sketch of this person at a particular time; no verbs, only nouns and adjectives. Follow the sound pattern of Yamada's poem in writing your own. The coming-full-circle line can be a summarylike sentence or phrase, as in Mitsuye Yamada's poem: "When used up/time to die." It should be a general, clarifying, perhaps philosophical last line that pulls it all together. Re-shape as you wish.

BREVITIES: THE POWER OF THE SOUNDBITE

Some People Think

that poetry should be a-
dorned or complicated I'm
not so sure I think I'll
take the simple statement

in plain speech compress—
to brevity I think that

will do all I want to do.

JAMES LAUGHLIN

Becoming sensitive to word economy is as critical a strategy as filling up a page with detail. Brevity is the skill of expressing much in few words, whatever the task at hand: Some short stories are thirty pages; some, half a page. Some legal opinions run into hundreds of pages; some are three. In the realm of poetry, there are book-length poems and one-line poems. An example of brevity in nonfiction is a vignette culled from biologist Tyler Volk's book *Metapatterns*. One of his concluding passages reads:

> Where do we stand? Look literally beneath your feet. The sphere lives on concentrating all its profound power in a single image: Earth.
>
> Earth is our birth, our death, enveloping us within its component spheres of biosphere, atmosphere, hydrosphere, lithosphere, technosphere, and noosphere. Planet Earth becomes our god, inspiration, truth, perfection, equality, and source of power. Earth from space.

This is writing at its most essential and most compressed. If we place Volk's passage in an elongated diamond, we become even more aware of his elegantly simple compression; not one word is wasted:

Where
do we stand?
Look literally beneath your feet.
The sphere lives on, concentrating all its profound powers
in a single image: Earth: Earth is our birth, our death, enveloping us
within its component spheres of biosphere, atmosphere, hydrosphere, lithosphere,
technosphere, and noosphere. Planet Earth becomes our god,
inspiration, truth, perfection, equality,
and source of power.
Earth from
space.

I don't think Volk logically understood the meaning of this stirring passage when he was writing it. If his Sign mind had stopped to analyze or critique these particular sentences, he might have laughed; he might have been embarrassed, frustrated, or surprised that he, an academic, had written such "poetic" lines.

Had it not been for his Design mind's input, the scientist Volk might never have written this gracefully compressed passage, which encapsulates an entire book into a "Brevity."

I believe that our most important awarenesses—insights into ourselves, out-sights into others—do not come as a fifty-page brief, a fifteen-page article, or a thirty-page short story. Our most significant ideas and thoughts come about when we compress our insight into the fewest possible words.

Anything written, including short stories, novels, nonfiction, poetry, and memoir, can be compressed beyond anything we thought possible. In the past few years a new form, the "short, short," has appeared and become very popular. Let me give you an example with the short short story, "Cinderella." It reads as follows:

CINDERELLA

Cinderella, the soul, sits among the ashes. She is depressed, as usual. Look at her: dressed in rags, face smeared with grime, oily hair, barefoot. How will anyone ever see her for who she is? A sad state of affairs.

Winter afternoons, in a corner of the kitchen, she has long conversations with her fairy godmother, over a cup of tea. The fairy godmother has, accidentally on purpose, misplaced her magic wand. In any case, these transformations are only temporary. The beautiful spangled gown, the crystal slippers, the coach and footmen—all would have disappeared at the stroke of midnight. And then what?

It is like the man in the mirror, says the fairy godmother. No one can pull him out but himself.

STEPHEN MITCHELL

Directing Your Hand

Think of a particular children's story or fairy tale. Cluster words that signify the story's essence (such as (TRUTH/LIE) for Pinocchio or (FAIRY GODMOTHER) for Cinderella). Experiment with compressing the story to its bare essentials—putting your own spin on it as you write.

THE NUTSHELL

Like the haiku with its three lines, fifteen syllables, and no title, the "nutshell" is about as brief as you can get. In the nutshell, the title in effect becomes part of the poem. In the nutshell you express in very few words the essence of what you are feeling. In the nutshell, you say, "This is my stance. This is what I believe. This is what I stand for. This is IT." Nutshell are literally Sound Bites. Sappho, the Greek poet, writes six words in three little lines, the first of which is the title, for a truly stunning effect:

Pain Penetrates
　　me drop
　　by drop

SAPPHO (TR. MARY BARNARD)

Here is one of William Matthews's "nutshells":

The Past
　　Grief comes to eat without a mouth

And another:

Premature Ejaculation
　　I'm sorry this poem's already finished

WILLIAM MATTHEWS

And here is one by Kate Loeb:

Hush
Some secrets
   I keep
   even from
   myself.

Nutshells are the briefest moments of insight held in a filament of words. Notice that because the key concept (which is also the title) strikes sparks of recognition in us, it makes us think, makes us smile, makes us see the echo of several levels of meaning.

FEET

   There is a way
I hope you understand.
   My feet are lonely
without your hands.

MARINA PITA, AGE 9

Perhaps the ultimate nutshell is the tongue-in-cheek summing up of one man's life in fifteen words:

MY LIFE

zygote
in womb
on trike
in room
on bike
in school
on bus
in tomb.

PAUL WALKER

Getting the essence of a thought or feeling into as few words as possible is not new, as you saw with Sappho. Africans have an ancient form consisting of only two lines, called the Bantu; the first line is a concrete observation, the second line a generalization, such as

> The little hut falls down.
> Tomorrow come debts.

This form gives great pleasure, enabling us to join a specific moment in our lives with a general statement, which may be a cliché. In the juxtaposition of the particular and the clichéd, however, the whole brings new meaning. Enjoy these witty, trenchant, poignant student Bantu expressions:

- The bathroom hasn't been cleaned in two weeks.
  I wonder what's playing at the movies tonight.

- Everything is packed in boxes, and I can't find anything.
  Disorder breeds order breeds disorder.

- Baby's teething, I'm not getting any sleep.
  What goes around, comes around.

- My daughter's bed stands empty these nights;
  I am filled with memories.

- Closets are dark and musty.
  We all have skeletons.

- Writing poetry makes me nervous.
  I am afraid of my feelings.

- Parched plains slough off airborne coats of choking dust.
  Angry wind carries earth's soul.

Directing Your Hand

This is language play at its most pared down. Be curious to see what will turn up in the fewest number of words. Write as *many*

Bantus as you can, not just one: good, bad, indifferent. The idea is to produce many in order to get one that strikes you as ingenious. The key is to juxtapose a concrete event with a generalization, a title with what best describes it, a truism with a trenchant metaphor.

Begin by clustering one or more of the following:

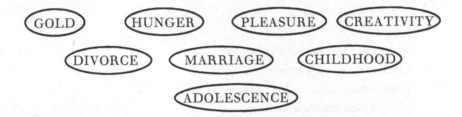

The key lies in the clustering, letting your mind associate, getting many ideas out on the same page until one feels right. Feel your way into it—for example, ADOLESCENCE is like . . . what? How do I show I'm HUNGRY? How does CREATIVITY feel?

Play with the other "nutshells," too: describe "The Future" in one line. Describe a part of your body in four lines, your life, in eight. What ideas would come up in your clusters? Which words would you select?

After Writing

We've reached the very nub of writing, the ultimate playfulness with language. I don't mean that nutshells or brevities are the best writing or the pinnacle of writing. But working to compress your writing lets you see the very bones of language, the most essential words stripped of all flesh. This paring down and revisioning can serve as a bridge to the fruitful expansion of your writing into larger, more cohesive patterns. Kate Evans achieves this cohesiveness in "Some Sleep." Notice her economy of language; all extraneous words weeded out so that we get almost a strobe-light rhythm of not one but two stories, juxtaposed:

Some Sleep
Quiet sheet, your chest my
     cheek white
breast, our hair
rest you there
    a week   while

In corridors somewhere, a sad street,
wrinkled women wheel to some
meal, others feed in bed.
     A tube stretches, shift on
         starched sheet. Tiny, weak
in white robe, damp chin,
she strokes cheek, asks again
         the day—
    Fine, fine they say.
I curve, sheet wrinkles
        knee touches
           wet
And in sleep
    we stretch, shift, forget.

KATE EVANS

When we can express ourselves so succinctly that every word evokes something essential, all our writing—regardless of length or genre or subject—will be more powerful.

Look at the wealth of information we are given in this little story in fourteen lines:

BOBBY MORRIS AND I

always ended up two partners
not chosen for the square dance.
Standing in our fifth-grade corners,
we'd eye each other shyly until the teacher

BREVITY AND RE-VISION: LESS IS MORE

told us to join our brown hands
and listen for the call.

Bobby would barely touch my fingers
and I his.
Feigning girl-boy loathing,
we never spoke,
but deep down
I knew he was as relieved as I
that we at least had our dark, Indian skin
in common
there in the middle of that polished, bright floor.

CATHY RUIZ

A Last Word and Heading On

This chapter has focused on brevity and redesign, turning the known, old forms, old words into new designs. All pruning is an attempt to let the heart of something show more clearly. You have played. You have worked. You have produced. Now you are ready to tackle a longer, more sustained work—an enormously satisfying design. Let's briefly look at how far you've come.

You have unlearned and relearned; you have cultivated your eye, ear, and hand; you have relearned to draw on your Design mind's sensitivity to patterns and wholeness through clustering; to improvise, with words, to discover a guiding vision through the trial-web shift; to listen for recurrences and language rhythms; to play with images; to know that voice has to do with empathy, with being able to put yourself into the shoes of another, into the thingness of things; to recognize and reconcile polarities; and finally, to re-design your ideas so that they accurately reflect your vision.

You are learning to compress language, to experiment and hone until your words become more evocative than explanatory. You are learning that what is "right" lies not outside you but within you.

From the brief to the extended, from brevity to constellation, may seem like a giant leap, but we will see that a longer piece of writing is merely a string of brief vignettes braided together into a cohesive whole. This process of braiding vignettes together is the subject of the final chapter.

FOURTEEN

DESIGNING CONSTELLATIONS: WORLDS WITHIN WORDS

A vignette is "a tendril-sized vine," containing all the attributes of the mature vine. Just as a molecule of DNA contains the genetic code for the entire human body, as a mini-whole, a vignette has structure and content that can stand by itself. In concentrating on vignettes rather than vines throughout this course, you have learned to shape a coherent whole again and again. Now you are ready for *constellations*. Constellation comes from the Latin *com*, meaning "with" plus *stellare*, "to shine." Constellation refers to any number of stars considered as a group; to any outstanding cluster or gathering of people; to any group of related thoughts, clustered around a central idea. For us, therefore, a constellation is any piece of writing that groups together as a pattern of meaning around an image, idea, phrase, object. It is any sustained piece of writing, long or short, that uses a cluster of vignettes to make a constellation of meaning.

A constellation is your crowning piece; it shines for you, through you, with you, because of you. It is a "stellar" piece, using many of the techniques you have explored throughout this book. It is made up of several or many or parts of vignettes, written over time, which evolve into a larger pattern of meaning as

Humans are animals suspended in webs of significance they themselves have spun.
CLIFFORD GEERTZ

If we cannot tell a story about what happened to us, nothing has happened to us.
J. P. CARSE

you discover the center around which they will cohere. If your poem or essay, magazine article or screenplay grows out of your vignettes, your constellation will shine.

When you constellate, you will not write what you think you *ought* to write; what wants to be written finds *you.* The constellation process will absorb you in the present moment, and only for very small segments of time, and what comes up is what comes up. The more you learn to trust the life force inside you, the more your natural creativity will flourish.

The secret of moving beyond the vignette is to realize that all vines originate from a vignette and that an entire vineyard is made up of vines, so that the process is simply one of following the natural growth that emerges, the trail that leads from vignette to vine, from star to constellation.

So, whether you are writing a poem or short story based on an incident in your life, or an essay, novel, play, or dissertation, the natural writing process begins in the same way: with a desire or a need to explore, with a word, an image, a phrase, a concept, an object that calls to you and inspires you. Through naming and clustering, a tentative trial vision swims into focus, which initiates the writing of your vignette.

All natural writing is generated from the inside out, not imposed from the outside in; it comes into being in this way whether we are aware of it or not. In an essay, a vignette might be a paragraph; in a novel, a chapter or episode; in a poem, a stanza; in a play, a scene or a snippet of dialogue.

In each case, the vignette is the initial step in what will become a series of steps. Those steps may be irregular, or they might seem to move backward at times—and at other times they may make a quantum leap, but writing happens one step at a time, one vignette at a time, one word at a time.

As we organize vignettes into a constellated whole, we achieve a sense of completion—which can then lay the groundwork for future ideas.

I just keep reviewing the elements I've been interested in. I heard Latin and gospel music along with rock when I was a kid. Those are the elements of my work. You go back and you recapitulate. And every time you reinvestigate, it goes deeper and you focus more clearly on what you respond to emotionally or musically.

PAUL SIMON

Every story is simply the name of a longer story. No one tells all the details of any story, so each story is shortened. . . . A story shortened so that it ceases to be understood is no longer a story.

ROGER SHANK

DESIGNING A CONSTELLATION WITH TWO-MINUTE AUTOBIOGRAPHIES

The whole is in the part. The many ways we can see our lives are infinite if we can open to them. If we do the activities in this book a second or a third time, each time with openness to nuance, we will never write the same thing twice. Like nature, human minds are playful, always unfolding in ways that surprise us. Each of our lives is "raw material" containing numerous creative possibilities. In each life we discover recurrences, images, metaphors, polarities. Each life can be designed and re-designed because our lives are not fixed. Each life is a malleable open-ended story made up of smaller stories.

Soon you'll get a chance to transform the untidy "stuff" of your experience into a nonlinear personal history by writing a series of two-minute "autobiographies" and then interconnecting them into a constellation. As you use the natural writing methods you've been learning throughout the book to write your compressed autobiography, you'll find yourself designing and re-designing your life experiences. The essential truths of your life will become distilled as you cluster events and feelings that group together to reveal who you are and what your story wants to say.

The best thing about a constellation is that, as the center shifts, so can the constellation. In this activity, you will be writing playful two-minute "autobiographies," which, when constellated later into patterns of meaning, allow you to experiment with multiple versions of your life story. We're not talking about a true version versus a false version, but about the different possible dimensions of your own personal story, which, depending on how you tell it, allow you creative choices in how you look at your life. This vision can and will change over time. How you saw your father at age six is not how you saw him when you were sixteen, or twenty-six. Memory, like history, is in an ongoing process of revision.

Natural writing is done in clusters, in chunks, in fractals, in holograms, so that the whole is evidenced in every part.

Hopefully I write what I don't know.
ROBERT CREELEY

The process of story creation, of condensing an experience into a story-size chunk that can be told [or read] in a reasonable amount of time is a process that makes the chunks smaller and smaller. Subsequent iterations of the same story tend to get smaller in the retelling as more details are forgotten.
ROGER SHANK

The confessional poem [poems of family relationships], is like a lens that magnifies and organizes particulars, a mirror that for an instant frames an identity. . . . It is an act of disclosure, in which experience is always richer than any ideas about it expressed in examples, conventions, or stereotypes.
DIANE MIDDLEBROOK

QUALITATIVE AUTOBIOGRAPHY

Human memory is a cluster of experiences, each labeled in complex ways. These labels (sound bites) allow for the retrieval of relevant experiences at the right time so that we have a story to tell.

ROGER SHANK

Our sense that there is meaning in something— in experience, in a poem, in a conversation—comes only when the elements that go to make up that thing take on a relation to one another, in other words, the meaning emerges only with our perception of a pattern. . . . We must connect one thing with another and finally assume the whole design of which the element is only a part.

JAMES OLNEY

A qualitative autobiography is not quantitative; it does not depend on retrieval of chronological details. It does not have to begin at the beginning and end at the end. It does not have to explain. In fact, it shouldn't. It must evoke. Your story is bigger, more complex, more fluid than a beginning, middle, and end. Your story is not fixed, but depends on an ongoing revision of memory. Your story, and the parts that make it up, are subject to ongoing redesign.

Creative acts most readily arise from the things that are most profoundly meaningful to us. The subject of "family," for example, triggers complex feelings—enriching or devastating—in all of us—and therefore has great potential for natural writing. "Family" is inherently compelling to writers. The practice of writing about one's family is as old as the Greek family tragedies, such as *Antigone, Oedipus Rex,* and *Electra.* In the twentieth century, great writers have used families as the basis for their most significant works: Thomas Mann in *Buddenbrooks,* Dostoevsky in *The Brothers Karamazov,* John Irving in *Hotel New Hampshire,* to mention a few.

By way of illustration, let's examine three quite different family histories, all triggered by the same set of instructions: (1) To write a series of two-minute autobiographies over a period of a month or so; (2) to cluster (FAMILY) to discern possible links; (3) to re-cluster key qualities from the (FAMILY) cluster to discover a "grappling hook"—a unifying metaphor, rhythm, or phrase that creates cohesiveness; (4) to write a two-minute autobiography to create the heart of an integral whole, based on the grappling hook in #3; (5) to expand this central vignette into a constellation by weaving together relevant segments of the previous vignettes— images, metaphors, or recursions that will act as a magnet to make the whole cohesive. Notice that none of these family histories is very long. Yet, each evokes in the reader's mind a constellation of people and events, making us feel *as if* we had read a long story. The shortest of the three focuses on an act: of doors slamming, which becomes the recurring element of the piece.

Figure 14-1

CLOSE FAMILY

And this is the way you relate to family
silently passing, not meeting eyes and
your door slamming becoming your only voice
screaming and silently hiding
in the confines of your room which is so
messy and inhospitable and
we wonder how anyone, especially this
unreadable outsider, could haunt such a place
and at the same time wonder if maybe
you are a mirage we somehow can't grasp, a ghostly miser
who only takes takes takes
never giving anything
especially not your precious self
even though that seems like all you have—
but we would not know for sure
because you just snap and slam
when we ask or try to slam get
close slam to you slam and
even in your selfishness we still
want to slam help slam you and
be there slam for you and slam
care for you and slam hear slam
you and we slam want to slam
love slam you slam

RHONDA SCOTT

By the time we finish reading this constellation, we see that the title is ironic, suggesting "Closed-Off Family" instead of "Close Family." We also see that the writer is illustrating a kind of emotional double bind between what the words say and how they say it. Finally, in its brevity there is ambiguity. Who is the "you"? And why is the "you" "screaming" silently? Do we know who to blame here?

The second constellation focuses on a strong emotion that is recursive throughout and that paradoxically binds a family together.

The germ of a design comes from real life. Never mind how the imagination will transform it into something rich and strange and, above all, unrecognizable. That happens later, if at all.

HOWARD NEMEROV

FEAR'S HOME

Fear knows the corners of our house, where to hide and wait. Fear stuffs the mattress of my bed; it wakes me often with creaks and moans. I reach out for comfort, but touch only the black-grey walls beyond, until I find my way out. I creep past the drowsy ghosts who guard my parents' bedroom door. Fear stands watch with me as I swallow breath after breath studying my mother's sleep-slack face, counting the steady rise and fall of my father's shoulders, listening for my brother's soft night noises from down the hall.

Fear filters through the wisps of my mother's cigarette smoke—weightless, acrid. She loses an hour in the black and white midday tragedies—poor Joann, poor Bert. The newspaper delivery man knocks at the door. My mother's laugh snaps like rubber bands, "I'm a little short this month, Harry, can you stop back?" Harry nods and my mother closes the door, slides the lock. Ashes sift from her cigarette as she soundlessly drifts back toward the TV and buries herself in a chair.

Fear curls and purrs beneath our kitchen table in the evening. It rises up in rage and pounds the kitchen walls at night; it matches in volume word for word my father's angry howls. He hates his boss, the bastard, his brother, the son-of-a-bitch, his father, his mother, his wife, his son, his daughter—anyone who will not affirm that he is right, he is good, he is worthy. His pain explodes with every dish that shatters against the wall, his dreams bleed night after night under his fist. In the morning fear crawls away to nurse the bruises. My father makes amends.

Fear stings my brother's skinny behind like swats from a thick paddle. He runs and doesn't look back. He runs from house to house along our street chasing trouble, ignoring the Chorus and their prophesy songs: he's an imp, he's stupid, what a temper, it's his fault. He runs intent across a summer afternoon to answer the ice cream man's taunting bell. I turn and look up from my popsicle, my mother turns from the television, my father turns the corner onto our street just in time to see my brother bounce back against the bumper of a slow-moving car, to heard the small thud as he drops to the pavement. Fear pulls us into a circle and whispers just below the ambulance wail, "This is what happens to people like you."

NAME WITHHELD

Notice that we are in the present tense, so we have a sense of simultaneity, a sense of the unending now, of nothing ever changing in this picture. Fear becomes the guiding metaphor; it "purrs" and "knows" the corners of the house; it "stands watch" and it "swats," insinuates itself everywhere. Fear personified is the anchoring principle, the grappling hook, for the whole, as this writer explores snapshots of ragged family bonds by transforming the climate of fear into words on a page.

The third constellation focuses on a kind of mantra, which has passed from mother to daughter. It threads its way through the whole story, which is told *to* a third person, the writer's new husband, who was not present at the events described:

> *There comes a time when one realizes that adventure is as humdrum as routine unless one assimilates it, unless one relates it to a central core which grows within and gives it contour and significance. Raw experience is empty . . . it is not what one does but what one realizes that keeps existence from being vain and trivial.*
>
> **LEWIS MUMFORD**
>
> *The events in our lives happen in a sequence in time, but in their significance to ourselves, they find their own order.*
>
> **EUDORA WELTY**

TO GREG

1. On our first date, I told you about the time
   when Eleanor and I were swimming in the Atlantic
   and she emerged from the waves with a fish flapping,
   struggling, trying to free itself from her bikini top.
   Judith and I had screamed with laughter
   as Eleanor shook the fish, and herself, free from the bathing suit.
   I told you how Daddy, who'd caught nothing all day from his perch on
       the pier,
   said he was going to send Eleanor down on his hook

instead of a worm. Mama had protested,
saying having no fish to clean was fine by her.
Judith and I squealed and teased,
threatening to tell everyone back home.
Eleanor screamed she would die of embarrassment,
and Mama took Judith and me aside, telling us,
"There are some things you should keep to yourself."

I told you how I played and hid
in the enormous boxwoods of my grandmother's yard,
how I skipped on the gravestones of Civil War soldiers,
sunken in the lush carpet of summer,
and how on those long summer evenings, I mushed my toes
in the soft, warm asphalt of the blacktop road.
I told you about running through the garden after the afternoon rain,
red clay oozing between my toes
as I sucked on strawberries I was supposed to be picking for ice cream.
I told you how Daddy never came home for ice cream,
how I peeked through the banister at 3 A.M. to see him
leaning on Mama, moaning it would be better if he went away,
the two of them staggering through the den
as Mama tried to support them both.
How I asked her the next day why he'd said what he said,
and how she told me it was nothing,
how she stroked my hair with her delicate hands,
"There are some things you should keep to yourself."

I told you about the Christmas morning in 1976,
when I was dazzled by the heart-shaped windows of the yellow elevator
in my bubble-gum pink dream house.
And how my father stumbled out from his room,
wearing the nappy argyle sweater he'd been wearing for days,
how he was reeking of whiskey and Winstons.
How he hovered, asking me how I liked my doll house,
and how I could not answer, but just sat there,
staring at Barbie smiling at us through the heart-shaped window,
how he was furious with my mother for answering for me,
and with the back of his hand scattered the home like a house of cards.

I told you how Mama had frantically pieced back the plastic poles and
    cardboard walls while I watched, gripping my doll.
I told you how I knew I could be different from them, given the chance,
how I wished he would kill himself,
not knowing five years later I would be begging to God to forgive me
for having wished for what came true,
wishing I'd listened to Mama,
"There are some things you should keep to yourself."

2. During that summer when we had forgotten
    that another world existed beyond ourselves,
    I told you about setting off for college to shape my new identity,
    shoving family aside, dismissing my past,
    arrogantly assured I was better than my own.
    I told you how I discovered how naive I had been.
    I told you about the fraternity parties,
    the drunken nights in bed with the man
    who beat me where it wouldn't show.
    I told you how I stayed with him,
    taking him home when he'd drunk too much,
    how I'd knelt in the bathroom, holding his head
    as I breathed the stench of Virginia Gentleman whiskey and vomit,
    and how it had felt so right, so comfortable,
    how I'd thought this was so good.
    I told you about the night I realized what I had done, was doing.
    I told you about the night six years ago,
    when I had decided that no longer having life
    was better than the life I had.
    I told you about staring, lifeless,
    at the lights on the ceiling of the emergency room,
    feeling nothing but the dull tugging of stitching
    weaving through my arms.
    I told you how Eleanor had wept at the scars,
    how Judith had bit her lip and cried,
    "How will we ever be able to hide them?"
    "What can we do to make them not show?"
    "How could you do this to us?"
    And nobody had asked,

"Tell us what happened."
"Tell us why."
I told you how that night, for the first time,
I had truly wept for the father I had let slip through my hands,
never asking him,
"Tell me why."
I told you how I started over,
about the doctor who helped me learn to live
for the first time in my life.
I told you how I had wept for the father,
wept for the mother, wept for the family
I slowly learned to love again.
And you took my arms, you caressed my scars,
and I did not wince at your touch.
The more you caressed them,
the more I forgot they had ever been there.
And you told me I should write it down,
that you wanted me to write it down to keep.
But I only smiled at you and said,
"There are some things you should keep to yourself."

3. The night before you and I were married,
　　we sat at the table with my mother-in-law to be.
　　She, wanting to know more
　　about the quiet girl her son was about to marry,
　　asked, "Tell me more about yourself.
　　Tell me about your life in Virginia."
　　All I could picture was the horror on her face,
　　how she would grieve for her son
　　if she knew he was about to slip a ring on the finger of one
　　who had once lain
　　on the bathroom floor
　　watching the blood from her wrists glisten
　　like garnets on the porcelain tiles.
　　Then you squeezed my hand.
　　So I told her about the time Eleanor and I were swimming in the Atlantic,
　　how the fish had flapped around in her bathing suit top.
　　And we laughed with delight,

and she said, "Please, tell me more!"
But I knew, for now,
there are some things you should keep to yourself.

NAME WITHHELD

This powerful story, told in the past tense without sentimentality, depends on the recurrence of "I told you" and "how I . . ." It unravels, little vignette by little vignette, and is constellated through the refrain, "there are some things you should keep to yourself." This constellation was not wrought out of Step A, Step B, Step C. It was wrought from irregular steps—a step back, a step forward, two steps back, three steps forward. It came about in steps we sometimes leap by twos, avoid by threes, or accept as long climbs—steps that echo how life stories are felt and remembered.

The author was not burdened by having to write hundreds of pages. Her autobiographical constellation derives its power from the exquisite compression of words. Its three short segments speak volumes, and the recurrent phrase "I told you . . ." reminds us that the author's story unfolded bit by bit because of an empathetic listener, who is woven into the story's very fabric.

RE-DESIGN INTO THE AESTHETIC WHOLE OF A CONSTELLATION

The autobiographical constellations above began as two-minute autobiographies. The two-minute autobiography is a vignette, improvisationally written from a cluster, then set aside. Then another is written at another time, then another. True to any living thing, these autobiographical vignettes will only tell a story over time, as a pattern forms naturally. This is a process of taking small steps, until an authentic path is cleared. Perhaps you will only have snatches of story that seem unrelated—until certain key metaphors or images or voices become the scaffolding for the whole. Whether images recur, voices ring true, or metaphors become suddenly luminous, the pattern will unfold to reveal itself. Each of us has the power to discover those patterns; they are not imposed on us. Even the eighty-year-old Oedipus at Colonnus,

To feel the intimacy of brothers is a marvelous thing in life. To feel the love of people whom we love is a fire that feeds our life. But to feel the affection that comes from those whom we do not know, from those unknown to us—that is something still greater and more beautiful because it widens out the boundaries of our being, and unites all living things.

PABLO NERUDA

To live, to err, to fall, to triumph, to create life out of life.

JAMES JOYCE, 1915

exiled and blind at the end of the play, utters those magnificent
words: "Even at my advanced age and even though I am a blind
wanderer, I must conclude that all is well." The pattern for your
autobiographical constellation—made up of pieces from all your
vignettes, as well as from fresh ideas inspired by those vignettes—will reveal itself, just as individual stars become part of
a distinctive pattern in the night sky.

The two-minute autobiography cannot be methodized any
more than clustering can. All we can do is name and frame
flashes of our experience, our thoughts, our feelings, into words on
a page. When we learn to do this without the irritable reaching
after a linear sequence, we can tap into riches, digging for gold
first in this spot, then in that spot, then in a spot way over there.

Achieving constellation is comprised of steps, but they are not
steps that move forward at an even pace; rather, they are the irregular steps of an infant learning to walk, some going sideways,
some going tentatively forward, some resulting in a fall, some
in a rush ahead. As we get used to these irregular movements
and stop expecting to move ahead in a precise manner, *then*
come some great leaps of discovery, insight, connection. Our two-
minute autobiographies, and their subsequent constellations, will
also come about in this way.

Here are a few student two-minute autobiographies, randomly selected to show different beginnings:

I could have died
     a long time ago.
My mother didn't hold
     her newborn child
she didn't know how to feed
     her baby:
A child having a child.
     How sad.
Running away from her mother
     she turned herself into another mother.
Are you finally going to kill me today?
     I don't mind,

if it makes you happy,
if it stops this madness.

STUDENT #1

I was tiny once.
Then something sprang from my chest—
two of 'em.
That a thought! Two blobs permanently attached.
I didn't like them.
They were the source of much amazement for many.
Not for me
My hips became a round viola shape
and my face had red carbuncles—
an early puberty.
I was only ten.
I felt like a weirdo,
awkward, large, robust.
Hormones ruled my life.

STUDENT #2

I remember walking away from my father. My mother took my sister's
hand and took my eight-year-old hand, and we walked along Imperial
Highway, heading toward McDonnell Douglas in the summer of 1968.
I think they argued about something important. I didn't know where
we were going. We had walked away before. The last time was from
my second father and before him, my first father. Now it was my third
father.

We must have dissolved into thin air because I don't remember
where we stopped. I can recall only two things clearly: I remember the
sinking pain, traveling downward, pulling me into silence as I clung
hard to my mother's right hand, and I remember wanting an ice
cream cone from the Foster Freeze as we passed it in the twilight of
that day.

STUDENT #3

When writing your two-minute autobiography, receptivity is
the key. Consider surrendering:

- the inflexible need for chronology

- the need for causal links

- the need for accuracy

Consider honoring:

- irregular movement among episodes, reflecting the associative patterning of human consciousness

- jarring elements and narrative lapses

- abrupt shifts in time and place

- shifting your gaze to the borders and breaks and gaps in your life

- unpredictability

- mingled voices

- openness to multiple versions of reality

Memory is retrieved as a soundbite. When you tell a story again, what you retrieve from memory is the gist of the story itself.
ROGER SHANK

What is written at this stage is unimportant. It may feel random, scatter-shot. But remember that you're not writing toward a single goal, a great memoir or the Great American Novel. Right now you are just tuning in to remembered, image, metaphor, recurrences, polarities, dialogue, wisdom, events, actions, clashes, insights, feelings. As you write your two-minute vignettes, your Design mind increasingly kicks in, engaging in the essentially Sign-mind process of getting something on a page.

The interesting thing is this: As you write these seemingly "throw-away" vignettes, the connections begin to appear. And in these connections lies the pattern, the essential truth of your story. Figure 14-2 shows the cluster that would result in "Fear's Home." When the "family" leads to the dominant impression, "fear," the beginnings of the constellation of the entire piece begin to surface. The clustering around "fear" shows four sections—which is how the final piece is structured, each section focusing on a family member. Yet, each one of these sections contains a myriad of memories, details, images, and events of a life-

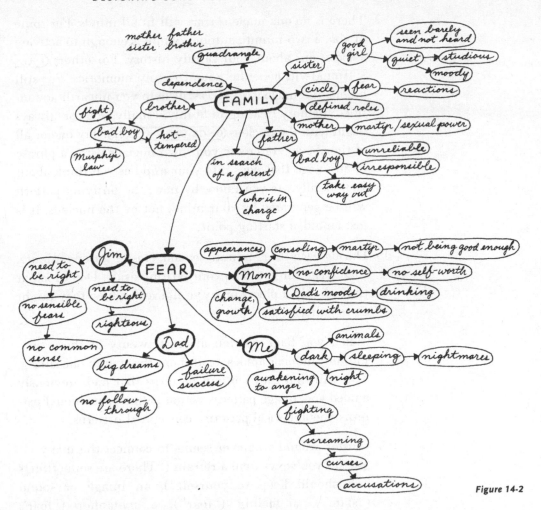

Figure 14-2

time of living together. The Design mind chooses those which come together around the dominant impression—and the constellation ultimately yields a strong piece of writing, which neither tells too little nor too much.

Directing Your Hand: From Vignette to Constellation

1. For the next month or two, set aside three minutes of your day to write one or more two-minute autobiographical vignettes. Use a new Writer's Notebook and begin with a cluster.

2. There is no one nucleus that will fit all minds. For some of you, a two-minute autobiography is enough to activate associations about your family history. For others, (I RE-MEMBER) will generate potent family memories. For still others, the nucleus (EVENT) will help you unearth action-filled memory relating to family. Finally, you can always begin with the nucleus (ONCE UPON A TIME). Try one or all of the above—or create your own nucleus using a phrase or an image that pops into your mind as you think about your family. As you know by now, the unifying pattern will be generated by your mind, not by the nucleus. It is just an aid, a starting point.

3. During each three-minute session, cluster for one minute, then write for two. Put your writing aside. Don't look at the individual pieces or try to figure out how they might fit together.

4. When you have written at least twenty of these two-minute autobiographies, read them through in one sitting. You will find they contain patterns that had previously eluded you: image patterns, sound patterns, emotional patterns, metaphorical patterns, conceptual patterns.

5. Cluster around whatever seems to connect the many vignettes you've written: a refrain ("There are some things you should keep to yourself"), an image or sound ("slam"), a feeling ("fear"), a metaphor ("fear's home")—any element that "constellates" the individual memories into a unified pattern.

6. One quality or object or act will speak to you more than the others and will help you to organize certain of these vignettes into a constellation. Constellating is a contextualizing process: a braiding or a swirling together of various parts.

7. As soon as you are able to name the organizing principle of your constellation, jot down three ways you might connect your vignettes. If you can, let these ideas simmer while you do something else for a while.

8. When you return to your two-minute autobiographies, try one interim step: From your constellation cluster, quickly write a three- to five-minute "movie script" like the one below. Don't stop to censor or think about what will fit or not fit. Just think about the key characters, the key objects, the key concepts, the key event, the recurrences. Simply wonder what will emerge. Read the "Movie Monosyllables" aloud. This is a playful interim stage, which may have little to do with your final product. By making a radical shift away from the many vignettes you have written, turning the constellation upside down, so to speak, you may well see the skeleton of your own evolving autobiography.

MOVIE MONOSYLLABLES

A man, a woman, an African moon.
The drums, the palms, the dictator.
A revolution in their embrace.
A man, a woman. Coming soon,

A man, a woman. One saw the crime.
An airplane ticket, a star-studded beach;
Doomed, imperial, collapsing waves.
A man, a woman. For the first time,

Locked together in the camera's iris,
a dark-haired stranger, a local wife
cling in closed circuits of a kiss—
Forbidden romance. Larger than life,

A girl, a soldier, a piano score.
One hour till dawn on his last leave
in a world blazing with war and war and war,
A man and a woman. As never before.

PATRICIA STORAGE

SHAPING THE CONSTELLATION

Creative work is done in interim stages involving interim decisions; we have to forego the wish to visualize precisely the final appearance of our work.

ANTON EHRENZWEIG

Give yourself permission to write fragments, as though your mind were the zooming-in and zooming-out lens of a camera, focusing on this and that object, this and that person. Let your writing be spare, choppy, brief. Don't try to make it deathless prose. This is an intermediate experiment to surprise your mind into a pattern that is you.

After Writing

Evaluate and see if any new angle presented itself through this step. While you are still in the constellating state, write:

- I was surprised . . .

- I discovered . . .

- I wonder . . .

If anything "constellating" came up in either of these two acts, hold any ideas by clustering or by writing them down in a place you can remember (I always put these in the back of my Writer's Notebook). Play with selecting those vignettes that seem to fit together. If handwritten in your Writer's Notebook, you might make copies, laying them end to end; you could also type your choices directly into the computer; if they are already there, begin to experiment with order by cutting and pasting directly into a new document.

COMING FULL CIRCLE

The Greek poet Sappho wrote about the power of words:

Although they are
Only breath, words
which I command
are immortal

Breath, life, aliveness. When the Inuit tells a story, she says, "let me breathe of it." As we breathe, so do we feel alive, so do we story, so do we write naturally. Let's come full circle to nutshell some of the essentials of writing naturally:

- **Passion in life:** It doesn't so much matter what you write about, but it must be something you are emotionally involved with. Passion fires up your neocortex and activates desire for making meaningful patterns.

- **Mind-leaping:** When we move out of the expected and connect with the unknown, our minds expand, and we learn and re-learn.

- **The Metaphoric habit of mind:** Through metaphor, simile, personification, and analogy, we reconnect the fragments of life, discovering bonds among dissimilar things, people, events. Metaphor pushes us to loosen the hold of practicality and logic. We make the strange familiar, the familiar strange.

- **Paradox:** We are bundles of contradictions. We are torn between head and heart, responsibility and spontaneity, mercy and justice. See this ability as a blessing, not a curse.

- **The Tension of doubt:** The early stages of any creative product are not accompanied by certainty. Passion maybe, compulsion maybe, momentary visions of enticing clarity maybe, but certainty—that we have come to the right forest and are following the right track—rarely.

When we create anything, the tension of not knowing how our imaginations will manage to fill in gaps and create coherence gradually becomes a challenge, not a burden. And so we keep a record through snippets of two-minute autobiographies until the constellation forms, as the student who wrote the following vignette realizes:

Keeping a Record
Darkness and light,
and the primal, instinctive motions of the hands
keep a record of the night,
a record of the light blooming in the tree of
forgetting and remembering.
Tools of writing don't tear up the world,
rather shape it to your vision,
the vision of the word,
the vision of the sun rising again.
Bloom, unknowing forms.
Write into the night.
Freedom,
freedom,
freedom to write.

STUDENT

Now that you have traversed the creative activities of this book, I invite you to cluster the nucleus (WRITE) so you can actually see how your experience with writing has changed.

Directing Your Hand

You write because everything dies, to save what dies.
You write because the world is an inarticulate mess, which you can't see
    until you map it in words.
Your eyes are dim and you write to put your glasses on.
No, you write because your mind is babble, you dig a track in the babble
    to find your way around yourself.
No, you write because you are shelled up inside your skull. You send out
    probes to other people in their skulls, and you wait for a reply.

AUSTIN WRIGHT, *Tony and Susan*

In preparation for the circle to a new beginning, cluster (YES, I WRITE . . .) And let that be your manifesto. Play and be serious. Let yourself know again and again why language counts. The best time to write is now.

BIBLIOGRAPHY

Alajouanine, Th. "Aphasia and Artistic Realization." *Brain* 71, 1948.

Allen, P. *Art Is a Way of Knowing.* Boston: Shambhala, 1995.

Arieti, Silvano. *Creativity: The Magic Synthesis.* New York: Basic Books, 1976.

Barron, Frank. *No Rootless Flower: Ecology of Creativity.* New York: Hampton Press, 1995.

Barrow, John. *The Artful Universe.* Oxford: Claredon Press, 1995.

Barzun, Jacques. *Simple and Direct.* New York: Harper & Row Publishers, 1976.

Behn, Robin, and Chase Twitchell, eds. *The Practice of Poetry.* New York: HarperCollins, 1992.

Bertelson, P., "The Nature of Hemispheric Specialization: Why Should There Be a Single Principle?" *The Behavioral and Brain Sciences,* 4:63–64, 1981.

Black, Max. *Models and Metaphors: Studies in Language and Philosophy.* Ithaca, N.Y.: Cornell University Press, 1962.

Bloomfield, Harold H., and Robert B. Kory. "Inner Joy," New York: *Playboy Paperbacks,* 1980.

Bogen, Joseph E. "Some Educational Aspects of Hemispheric Specialization." *UCLA Educator,* Spring 1975. Also in: *Dromenon,* February 1978; *The Human Brain,* Merle Wittrock, ed. (Englewood Cliffs, N.J.: Prentice-Hall), 1977; *Allos,* K. Gabino, ed. (La Jolla, Calif.: Lingua Press), 1980.

———. "Cerebral Duality and Hemispheric Specialization." *Behavioral and Brain Sciences* (in press).

———. "The Callosal Syndrome." *Clinical Neuropsychology,* K. Heilman and J. Valenstein, eds. London: Oxford University Press, 1978.

Bogen, Joseph E., and Glenda M. Bogen. "The Other Side of the Brain II: The Corpus Callosum and Creativity." In *The Nature of Human*

Consciousness. Robert Ornstein, ed., San Francisco: W. H. Freeman & Co., 1973.

———. "Split-Brains: Interhemispheric Exchange as a Source of Creativity." In M. A. Runco and S. Pritzker (eds). Encyclopedia of Creativity.

Brain/Mind Bulletin. Interface Press. P.O. Box 4211, Los Angeles, CA 90042.

Brande, Dorothea. *On Becoming a Writer.* Los Angeles: Tarcher, 1981.

Briggs, John. *Fire in the Crucible: An Alchemy of the Creative Genius.* New York: St. Martin's Press, 1988.

Britton, James. *Language and Learning.* Miami: University of Miami Press, 1970.

Broudy, Harry. "Impression and Expression in Artistic Development." In *The Arts, Human Development, and Education,* Elliot Eisner, ed. Berkeley, Calif.: McCutcheon, 1976.

Brown, Jason, and Joseph Jaffe. "Hypothesis on Cerebral Dominance." *Neuropsychologia* 13:1, 1975.

Bruner, Jerome S. *On Knowing: Essays for the Left Hand.* Cambridge, Mass.: Harvard University Press, 1962.

Burke, Carol, and Molly Best Tinsley. *The Creative Process.* New York: St. Martin's Press, 1993.

Buzan, Tony. *Use Both Sides of Your Brain.* New York: Dutton, 1976.

Carter, Jared. "Improvisation." *Poetry Magazine* 1994.

Chomsky, Noam. *Reflections on Language.* New York: Pantheon, 1975.

Chukovsky, Kornei. *From Two to Five.* Berkeley: University of California Press, 1963.

Corballis, M. C. "Toward an Evolutionary Perspective on Hemispheric Specialization." *The Behavioral and Brain Sciences,* 4:69–70, 1981.

Cornell, Judith. *Drawing the Light from Within.* New York: Simon and Schuster, 1990.

Creativity in Action. (Monthly newsletter giving theory and practice) (12 issues $50.00).

Creators on Creating. New York: Tarcher-Putnam, 1997.

Csikszentmihalyi, Mihaly. *Creativity: Flow and the Psychology of Discovery and Invention.* New York: HarperCollins, 1996.

———. *The Evolving Self.* New York: Harper Perennial, 1994.

Damasio, Antonio R. *Descartes' Error.* New York: Putnam, 1994.

Dewey, John. *Art As Experience.* New York: Capricorn Books, 1934.

Diaz, A. *Freeing the Creative Spirit: Drawing on the Power of Art.* San Francisco: Harper, 1992.

Didion, Joan. "On Keeping a Notebook." *Slouching Towards Bethlehem.* New York: Dell, 1968.

Donoghue, Denis. *The Sovereign Ghost: Studies in Imagination.* New York: Echo Press, 1990.

Dromenon: A Journal of New Wave of Being. G.P.O. Box 2244, New York, NY 10001.

Ealy, C. Diane. *The Woman's Book of Creativity.* Hillsboro, OR: Beyond Words, 1995.

Edwards, Betty. *Drawing on the Right Side of the Brain.* Los Angeles: Tarcher, 1979.

Ehrenzweig, Anton. *The Hidden Order of Art.* Berkeley: University of California Press, 1971.

Eisner, Elliot. *Educating Artistic Vision.* New York: Macmillan, 1972.

———. *Writing with Power.* London: Oxford University Press, 1981.

Elbow, Peter. *Writing Without Teachers.* London: Oxford University Press, 1973.

Els, Susan McBride. *Into the Deep: A Writer's Look at Creativity.* Portsmouth, N.H.: Heinemann, 1994.

Emig, Janet. "Children and Metaphor." *Research in the Teaching of English* 6:2, 1972.

Epel, Naomi. *Writers Dreaming.* New York: Carol Southern Books, 1993.

Ferguson, Marilyn. *The Aquarian Conspiracy.* Los Angeles: Jeremy P. Tarcher, 1980.

Field, Joanna. *An Experiment in Leisure.* New York: Jeremy P. Tarcher, 1987.

———. *On Not Being Able to Paint.* New York: Tarcher, 1983.

Foss, Martin. *Symbol and Metaphor in Human Experience.* Lincoln: University of Nebraska Press, 1949.

Frye, Northrop. *The Educated Imagination.* Bloomington: Indiana University Press, 1964.

Fuller, Renée. *In Search of the IQ Correlation.* Stony Brook, N.Y.: Ball-Stick-Bird Publications, 1977.

Galin, David. "Implications for Psychiatry of Left and Right Cerebral Specialization." *Archives of General Psychiatry* 31, 1974, pp. 572–583.

Gardner, Howard. *Artful Scribbles.* New York: Basic Books, 1980.

———. *Creating Minds.* New York: Basic Books, 1993.

———. *The Shattered Mind.* New York: Knopf, 1975.

Gardner, Howard, and Ellen Winner. "The Child Is Father to the Metaphor." *Psychology Today,* May 1979.

Gardner, John. From "Foreword." in Dorothea Brande, *On Becoming a Writer*. Los Angeles: Tarcher, 1934.

Gazzaniga, Michael, and G. E. LeDawe. *The Integrated Mind*. New York: Plenum Press, 1978.

Gendlin, Eugene. *Focusing*. New York: Everest House, 1978.

Gerard, R. W. "The Biology of the Imagination." In *The Creative Process*, Brewster Ghiselin, ed. New York: Mentor, 1952.

Ghiselin, Brewster. *The Creative Process*. Berkeley: University of California Press, 1952.

Gilbert, Judy. *Clear Speech*. Boston: Cambridge University Press, 1993.

Goldberg, Elkhonon, and Louis D. Costa. "Hemispheric Differences in the Acquisition and Use of Descriptive Systems." *Brain and Language* 14:144–173, 1981.

Goleman, Daniel. *Emotional Intelligence*. New York: Bantam Books, 1995.

Goleman, Daniel, Paul Kaufman, and Michael Ray. *The Creative Spirit*. New York: Plume, 1993.

Goleman, Daniel, et. al. *The Creative Spirit*. New York: Dutton, 1992. (Companion volume to the PBS series)

Gordon, W. J. J. *The Metaphorical Way of Knowing and Learning*. Mass.: Synectics Education Press, 1973.

Gray, James. "Understanding Creative Thought Processes: An Early Formulation of Emotional-Cognitive Structure Theory." *Man-Environment Systems* 9:1, 1980.

Grether, Tobias. *Homochronos: Evolution and Development of Consciousness* (unpublished ms.). Camarillo, CA.

Harnad, Stevan R. "Creativity, Lateral Saccades, and the Non-Dominant Hemisphere." *Perceptual and Motor Skills* 34, 1972.

Harrison, Jeffrey. *Signs of Arrival: Poems*. Port Townsend, WA: Copper Canyon Press, 1996.

Heard, Georgia. *Writing Toward Home: Tales and Lessons to Find Your Way*. Portsmouth, N.H.: Heinemann, 1994.

Henri, Robert. *The Art Spirit*. New York: Harper and Row, 1923.

Irmscher, William. *Teaching Expository Writing*. New York: Holt, Rinehart & Winston, 1979.

Jamison, Kay Redfield. *Touched with Fire: Manic-Depressive Illness*. New York: The Free Press, 1993.

Johnston, Charles M. *The Creative Imperative*. Berkeley: Celestial Arts, 1986.

Jones, Richard M. *Fantasy and Feeling in Education*. New York: Harper & Row, 1968.

Joseph, R. *The Right Brain and the Unconscious: Discovering the Stranger Within.* New York: Plenum Press, 1990.

The Journal of Creative Behavior. (For the serious general reader interested in creativity and problem solving) (V. 28, 1994, $36.00).

Keen, Sam. *Apology for Wonder.* New York: Harper & Row, 1969.

Kepes, Gyorgy, ed. *Sign, Image, Symbol.* New York: Braziller, 1966.

Kinsbourne, M. "The Neuropsychological Analysis of Cognitive Deficit." *Biological Foundations of Psychiatry,* R. G. Grenell and S. Gabay, eds. New York: Raven Press, 1976.

Koch, Kenneth. *Wishes, Lies, and Dreams.* New York: Vintage Books, 1970.

Koestenbaum, Peter. *The New Image of the Person.* Westport, Conn.: Greenwood Press, 1978.

Koestler, Arthur. *The Act of Creation.* New York: Macmillan, 1964.

Langer, Susanne. *Problems of Art.* New York: Scribner's, 1957.

La Violette, Paul. "The Thermodynamics of the "Aha" Experience." Presented at the 24th Annual North American Meeting of the Society for General Systems Research, San Francisco, California, January 1980.

————. "Thoughts about Thoughts about Thoughts: the Emotional-Perceptive Cycle Theory." *Man-Environment Systems* 9:1, 1980.

Lee, J. *Writing from the Body.* New York: St. Martin's Press, 1994.

Leondar, Barbara. "Metaphor and Infant Cognition." *Poetics* 4, 1975.

Levy, Jerry, Robert D. Nebes, and R. W. Sperry. "Expressive Language in the Surgically Separated Minor Hemisphere." *Cortex* 1:1, 1971.

Lewis, C. Day. *The Poetic Image.* London: Oxford University Press, 1948.

Lhermitte, François. "Mysteries of the Intelligence." *Réalités,* May 1976.

Lucas, F. L. *Style.* New York: Collier Books, 1955.

MacLean, Paul D. "On the Evolution of Three Mentalities." *New Dimensions in Psychiatry: A World View,* Vol. 2, Silvano Arieti and Gerard Chrzanowski, eds. New York: Wiley, 1977.

Macrorie, Kenneth. *Telling Writing.* Rochelle Park, N.J.: Hayden, 1966.

Maritain, Jacques. *Creative Intuition in Art and Poetry.* New York: New American Library, 1953.

McCluggage, Denise. *The Centered Skier.* Waltham, Mass.: Crossroads Press, 1978.

McGrayne, Sharon Bertsch. *Nobel Prize Women in Science.* New York: Carol Publishing Group, 1996.

Mearns, Hughes. *Creative Power.* New York: Dover, 1929.

Meinke, Peter. *Night Watch on the Chesapeake.* Pittsburgh: University of Pittsburgh Press, 1987.

———. *Scars.* Pittsburgh: University of Pittsburgh Press, 1996.

Merwin, W. S. *The Second Four Books of Poems: The Moving Target/the Life/the Carrier of Ladders/Writings to an Unfinished Accompaniment.* Port Townsend, WA: Cooper Canyon Press, 1993.

Middlebrook, Diane Wood. *Worlds into Words.* New York: W. W. Norton & Co., 1980.

Morris J. *Creative Breakthroughs: Tap the Power of Your Unconscious Mind.* New York: Warner, 1992.

Moss, Richard. *The I That Is We.* Millbrae: Celestial Arts, 1981.

Moustakas, Clark E. *Creative Life.* New York: Van Nostrand Reinhold Co., 1985.

Mueller, Lisel. *Alive Together.* Baton Rogue: LSU Press, 1996.

Nebes, R. D. "Direct Examination of Cognitive Function in the Right and Left Hemispheres." In *Asymmetrical Functions of the Brain,* M. Kinsbourne, ed. New York: Cambridge University Press, 1978.

———. "Man's So-Called 'Minor' Hemisphere." In *The Human Brain,* Merle Wittrock, ed. Englewood Cliffs, N.J.: Prentice-Hall, 1977.

Neihardt, John Gneisenau. *Black Elk Speaks.* New York: Fine Communications, 1997.

Nelson, V. *On Writer's Block: A New Approach to Creativity.* New York: Houghton Mifflin, 1993.

Nin, Anaïs. *The Diary of Anaïs Nin,* Vol. 5. New York: Harcourt Brace, 1964.

Olds, Sharon. *The Dead and the Living.* New York: Knopf, 1987.

Ortony, Andrew, ed. *Metaphor and Thought.* London: Cambridge University Press, 1979.

Paivio, Alan. *Imagery and Verbal Processes.* New York: Holt, Rinehart & Winston, 1971.

Pearce, Joseph C. *The Bond of Power.* New York: Dutton, 1981.

Peck, M. Scott. *The Road Less Traveled and Beyond: Spiritual Growth in an Age of Anxiety.* New York: Simon & Schuster, 1997.

Piaget, Jean. *The Construction of Reality in the Child.* New York: Basic Books, 1954.

———. *The Language and Thought of a Child.* New York: Meridian, 1955.

Pich, David R. "Beowulf to Beatles and Beyond." New York: Macmillan, 1981.

Pinker, Stephen. *How the Mind Works.* New York: Norton, 1997.

Polanyi, Michael. *The Tacit Dimension.* New York: Doubleday, 1966.

Ransom, John Crowe. *Poems and Essays.* New York: Vintage Books, 1955.

Restak, Richard. *The Brain.* New York: Bantam, 1984.

Richards, M. C. *Centering: Poetry, Pottery, and the Person.* New York: Columbia University Press, 1962.

———. *The Crossing-Point.* Middletown, Conn.: Wesleyan University Press, 1973.

Rico, Gabriele Lusser. *Metaphor and Knowing.* Unpublished doctoral dissertation. Stanford University, 1976.

———. "Reading for Non-Literal Meaning." In *Reading, the Arts, and the Creation of Meaning,* Elliot Eisner, ed. Reston, Va.: National Art Education Association NAEA, 1978.

Rico, Gabriele Lusser, and M. F. Claggett. *Balancing the Hemispheres: An Exploration of the Implications of Brain Research for the Teaching of Writing.* Berkeley: University of California Bay Area Writer's Project Monograph, 1980.

Rogers, Franklin R. *Painting and Poetry.* Lewisburg: Bucknell University Press, 1985.

Ross, Elliot. "Aprodosia." *The Sciences* 22:2, 1982.

Rothenberg, Albert. *The Emerging Goddess: The Creative Process in Art, Science, and Other Fields.* Chicago: University of Chicago Press, 1979.

Russ, Joanna. *How to Suppress Women's Writing.* Austin: University of Texas Press, 1983. (hilarious and brilliant book on why we get blocked)

Samuels, Mike, and Nancy Samuels. *Seeing with the Mind's Eye.* New York: Random House, 1975.

Sark, A. *A Creative Companion: How to Free Your Creative Spirit.* Berkeley: Celestial Arts, 1991.

Schank, Roger. *The Creative Attitude.* New York: Macmillan, 1988.

———. *Tell Me a Story: A New Look at Real and Artificial Memory.* New York: Scribner's, 1990.

Sewell, Elizabeth. *The Human Metaphor.* Notre Dame, Ind.: University of Notre Dame Press, 1964.

Schain, Leonard. *Art and Physics.* New York: Morrow, 1991.

———. *The Alphabet and the Goddess.* New York: Viking, 1998.

Sommer, Robert. *The Mind's Eye.* New York: Dell Publishing Co., 1978.

Sommers, Shula. *Journal of Personality and Social Psychology* 41:3, pp. 553–561. (Psychology Department, University of Massachusetts, Boston, MA 02125).

Spender, Stephen. "The Making of a Poem." In *The Creative Process,* Brewster Ghiselin, ed. New York: New American Library, 1952.

Sperry, R. W. "Hemisphere Disconnection and Unity in Conscious Awareness." *American Psychologist* 23 (2), 1968.

Stafford, William. "A Way of Writing." In *Writing the Australian Crawl.* Michigan: University of Michigan Press, 1977.

———. *My Name Is William Tell.* Lewistown, ID: Confluence Press, 1992.

———. *Passwords.* New York: Harper Perennial, 1991.

Sternberg, Robert. *Defying the Crowd: Cultivating Creativity in a Culture of Conformity.* New York: The Free Press, 1995.

Storr, Anthony. *The Dynamics of Creation.* New York: Ballantine Books, 1972.

Strunk, William, and E. B. White. *Elements of Style.* New York: Macmillan, 1979.

Thomas, Dylan. "Notes on the Art of Poetry." In *Modern Culture and the Arts,* James B. Hall and Barry Ulanov, eds. New York: McGraw-Hill Book Co., 1967.

Watts, Alan. *The Two Hands of God.* Canada: Macmillan, 1963.

Whitely, Opal. *Opal.* New York: Macmillan, 1976.

Whyte, David. *The Heart Aroused.* New York: Doubleday, 1994.

Wyke, M. A. "The Nature of Cerebral Hemispheric Specialization in Man: Quantitative vs. Qualitative Differences." *The Behavioral and Brain Sciences,* 4:78–79, 1981.

Zaidel, Eran. "The Elusive Right Hemisphere of the Brain." *Engineering Science,* September/October 1978.

Zangwill, O. L. "Aphasia and the Concept of Brain Centers." In *Psychology and Biology of Language and Thought: Essays in Honor of Eric Lenneberg,* George A. Miller and Elizabeth Lenneberg, eds. New York: Academic Press, 1978.

Index

About the Author

Dr. Rico, a professor of English and Creative Arts at San Jose State University, lectures widely on the application of brain research to writing, to learning, and to creative process—most recently on the roles of improvisation, play, and human time-consciousness in creativity. She developed *clustering* in her doctoral dissertation at Stanford. Honored as President's Scholar in 1986, she was selected Teacher/Scholar in 1993. In 1992 she held an Endowed Chair at Notre Dame in Belmont.

For information and/or ordering, please contact

- Gabriele Rico's web page: writingthenaturalway.com or gabrielerico.com

- *Creative Explorer*, a software program FAX (312) 222-9024

- Audiotape to accompany *Writing the Natural Way*, revised edition FAX (312) 222-9024